S0-AYI-786

COLONIAL EVANGELISM

Colonial Evangelism

A SOCIO-HISTORICAL STUDY OF AN EAST AFRICAN MISSION AT THE GRASSROOTS

T. O. Beidelman

INDIANA UNIVERSITY PRESS

BLOOMINGTON

Manufactured in the United States of America

Library of Congress Cataloging in Publication Data

Beidelman, T. O. (Thomas O.), 1931-
Colonial evangelism.

Bibliography: p.
Includes index.
1. Missions to Kaguru (African people) I.Title
BV3630.K32B44 306'.6 81-47771
ISBN 0-253-31386-4 AACR2
ISBN 0-253-20278-7 (pbk.)
1 2 3 4 5 86 85 84 83 82

To the memory of J. T. Last,
the first student of Ukaguru

Missions are natural social laboratories.

D. R. Heise

. . . being experimented upon by another is the most unsupportable of things.

Joseph Ernest Renan

Contents

Abbreviations used in the text:

I. R. M. = *The International Review of Missions*
C. M. G. = *Church Missionary Gleaner*
C. M. I. = *Church Missionary Intelligencer*
C. M. R. = *Church Missionary Review*
P. C. M. S. = *Proceedings of the Church Missionary Society*

Preface

In 1959, after I returned from my first fieldwork in Ukaguru (Kaguruland), Tanganyika (now Tanzania), East Africa (1957–58), I conceived the idea for this study and undertook supplementary research in the archives at the Church Missionary Society headquarters in London (1961).[1] Grants from the Ford Foundation (1961–63) and the National Science Foundation (1965, 1966) made possible further fieldwork in Ukaguru. I am especially grateful to the librarians and archivists at the Society for their help, and to the Wenner-Gren Foundation for financing two other periods of archival work (1975, 1976), as well as for aiding me in securing release time from my regular academic duties so that I might prepare this manuscript.

During my first stay in Ukaguru, I resided for over six months in the center of the only mission station now remaining in the Kaguru chiefdom of Kilosa District. The Church Missionary Society was kind in allowing me to rent housing at this station. I later moved to a market center about a twenty-minute walk from the mission center and about a five-minute walk from the mission secondary school for boys.

My presence at the mission station posed difficulties for both the missionaries and myself. I occupied housing later required for African nurses working at the mission hospital. Furthermore, it was clear after some months' stay that my presence was a source of strain and embarrassment to the missionaries themselves, as well as to myself. I was in Ukaguru to study the traditional Kaguru way of life, and this meant association with the sides of pagan life which the missionaries sought to eradicate. It was important to me that I was not too closely associated with either the European colonial administration or the missionaries whom many Kaguru considered merely another type of colonial. I found it essential and enjoyable to drink frequently and openly with Kaguru informants as well as to attend pagan dances in which I sometimes participated. I associated with a wide range of Kaguru, from sophisticated, English-speaking mission schoolteachers to pagan elders, beer brewers, and notorious women—publicans and sinners. My views and conduct regarding lifestyle, religion, politics, and, above all, the value of traditional Kaguru life clashed with those of the missionaries, who forbade drinking, dancing, and smoking and who frowned on many traditional Kaguru beliefs such as those associated with polygyny, widow inheritance, ancestral propitiation, rainmaking, exorcism, divorce, and the bush schools for the initiation of adolescents.

It is important to mention an uneasy relation with the mission since it helps explain the uneven nature of my data. I had opportunities to observe public occasions at the mission: church services, school classes, and the workings of the mission store. I counted some Kaguru employees of the mission among my friends and informants. I had less open relations with the European missionaries although I was always treated politely. The white missionary staff seemed to find me perplexing and difficult, and in my youthful intolerance and occasional maladroit behavior I may well have been. As a result, my data are not based on extensive and candid interviews with the missionaries themselves. I examined some local missionary records related to mission history, registration of marriages, and the organization of local church groups. I did not examine missionary records dealing with matters such as salaries, staffing, and the formulation of most policies. During my fieldstay I had no intention of studying the mission closely, and I doubtless lost many useful opportunities to secure data and gain insights. I saw my basic task as gathering conventional ethnographic data on the Kaguru. Supplementary data on the colonial administration and mission were collected only in so far as I had been taught to view a society within its broader social context and to appreciate the factors of social change and modernization. At that time I had not contemplated special study of these modern institutions. Because this study reflects a shift in my theoretical interest which occurred after I left the field, it is distorted by the lack of detailed contemporary material presented from the missionaries' viewpoint. It is weak in precisely those aspects of participation and conversation that are the essence of most anthropological fieldwork.

For all these reasons, this study combines two very different perspectives toward missionary life in Ukaguru. The earlier historical material is almost entirely from missionary accounts, published and archival, even in the case of information about the precolonial, pagan Kaguru.[2] In contrast, more recent material is based mainly on my own impressions as an outsider, as well as on information from local Kaguru both within and outside the mission. It is, therefore, weak in precisely those areas where the historical material is best, the perspective of the European missionaries. There appears to be considerable continuity from the earlier colonial period to the present in the attitudes of both Kaguru and missionaries; however, I have tried to be cautious in drawing conclusions where my data are thin, even though I believe that one can make some valid and useful conclusions based on immersion in both Kaguru ethnography and missionary writings.

Any study of groups which resemble one's own is in some respects far more difficult than research among alien, exotic societies. In residing with Kaguru, I was not disturbed by the kinds of exotic beliefs and behavior they presented. Nor was I dismayed when rebuffed or deceived by Kaguru. I experienced less difficulty than I anticipated in discussing sensitive topics such as witchcraft, adultery, and theft, perhaps because I was an outsider and therefore my opinion was already defined by Kaguru as not significant. Also they recognized that I could never, as a stranger, become deeply involved in local personal relations. Kaguru were quick to remind me that I would remain with them only a short time, and it was always made clear from our interactions that we were indeed operating out of profoundly different values and beliefs. Neither I nor the Kaguru were particularly sensitive to subtleties of speech and covert cues in mannerisms on either side since neither of us had really mastered the other's languages or styles of expression. In contrast, my relations with missionaries and colonial officials were far more complex precisely because we appeared to speak a common language and shared sufficiently common backgrounds to grasp many nuances of education, class, income, and personal character. Our mutual expectations were highly ambiguous. It was also clear that I had no commitment to colonialism and was agnostic in my beliefs. Though I later spent several years living in England, my American upbringing cut me off from much of the British, not to mention Australian, culture of the missionaries and colonial administrators.

More challenging than any cultural gap between me and my contemporaries in the field was the gulf which I later experienced in reading the early archives. To understand the past, I had to try to enter into the life and perceptions of Victorian Britain as well. Kitson Clark makes pertinent observations about the difficulty of writing the history of Victorian

England: despite deceptive similarities of language and place, it was a world apart from the England of today, especially in regard to religion (1973:100–101).

My relations with colonial Europeans were perhaps further complicated by my personal background. I began fieldwork at twenty-six, still rather immature, though having with some effort shed many earlier attributes of a middle-class, parochial, American Midwestern background with strong German Methodist religious teachings. I had earlier allowed myself to be drafted into a Korean conflict which I belatedly recognized as an occupation in support of a corrupt and repressive foreign government. In retrospect I can appreciate that my past was sufficiently similar to that of many of the colonialists and missionaries that I felt uncomfortable, even intolerant, regarding their views and conduct. Clearly, missionary thought and behavior were redolent of some of my own rejected past; and colonialism in Africa was not that different from some of the activities to which I had just lent myself. I hope that, with the years, my own perspective has widened and my sophistication increased to enable me to view the missionary way of life and colonialism in general more clearly and with less emotion toward either the missionaries or the missionized, the colonizer or the colonized. My experiences and subsequent analysis may even allow me to discern similar patterns in the new forms of ideological missionization and social coercion practiced by contemporary African elites upon their fellow citizens.

In my historical account up to the First World War I have been unable to avoid the citation of names since my archival references derive from personal correspondence, yet few if any of those involved can be alive today. In general, I have tried to maintain a sociological or anthropological perspective and have avoided psychologizing, but in any account of a small colonial enterprise such as a mission station or government post, the characters and personalities of particular individuals cannot always be ignored. In my treatment of the scene in 1957–58 I have tried to avoid specific mention of persons. The only exceptions to this involve a few references to the two most prominent African leaders at the mission, the Assistant Bishop and Archdeacon, who can hardly be avoided. Both of these men are now dead; and, in any case, my comments are based on common knowledge and in no way are defamatory, although they may be considered by some to be critical of certain policies. The very generality of much of my other data, however, has at least one virtue—I have betrayed no confidence and was privy to no secrets. I relied entirely on what was known to many Kaguru on the mission station or on what I or any other stranger could see. In no way did I falsely present myself to the missionaries or to others as a believing Christian or even as one who approved of many mission activities. In regard to colonial policies, I was forced by some of my Kaguru neighbors to make formal objections against certain local political abuses, such as forced labor, a gesture which caused me much difficulty with some local authorities.

In general, I was struck by the devotion, altruism, and fortitude of the missionaries, both in the past and during my fieldwork. If my descriptions of missionaries seem critical at times, this is in large part because I am viewing these men and women not only in their own terms but also in the terms of my Kaguru informants and from my own perspective both as an agnostic and as a social anthropologist. I have tried to be objective and show how and why the missionary system worked as it did, but it is neither possible nor desirable to efface personal values from useful social research.

Readers familiar with Christian literature will note that in my Introduction I have not attempted to place this study within the broader context of theology or church history. I have consulted a number of studies on these topics, far more than I cite; but while the published material is enormous, much seems poorly related to social theory as this is understood by social anthropologists and sociologists. This study concerns social anthropology and colonial history, and it is basically with reference to social theory related to those fields that I have cast my narrative and taken my references. In any case, where general literature involves policies about missionary training and methods, much of it would be misleading here since it does not necessarily reflect the views of Church Missionary Society members. On such topics I have confined myself to sources written either by members of the Church Missionary Society or by other Anglicans whose involvement or influence in Church Missionary circles was explicitly acknowledged.

To explain the working of the Church Missionary Society in one East African chiefdom, one must have some grasp of the wider setting, of colonial administrative policies, of the changing social attitudes of missionaries in the nineteenth and twentieth centuries, and of the general history of the Church Missionary Society and its relation to the broader Anglican tradition. One must even ask how this mission relates to others operating in this region. Of course, one must also have a clear picture of the social structure of the Kaguru, the African people missionized. I touch on all these issues, but each is a field in itself.

In citing various archival materials, all from the Church Missionary Society, I indicate the author, date of writing, and the persons to whom it was written. I have not indicated the archival file numbers since all items come from one set of files, devoted to the out-going and in-coming correspondence of the mission in Eastern Equatorial Africa, later termed the Usagara Mission, the Mission to German East Africa, and finally the Tanganyika Territory Mission. Unless indicated otherwise, letters from missionaries in the field were sent to the Secretary for the African section of the Headquarters of the Church Missionary Society in London. In a few cases, where the date of writing is not available, I have indicated a date on which the material was received. Some archival material consists of published pamphlets and circulars put out by and for the mission.

Initially a researcher may despair at much of this correspondence, sometimes written in a crabbed hand on both sides of onion-skin paper. Occasionally some words in the correspondence are undecipherable.[3] Yet, as one reads about the difficulties of early communications between up-country East Africa and the coast, with messengers robbed or murdered, packets stained by rain, and letters sometimes smuggled out sewn within garments, one's frustration gives way to surprise and pleasure that so much has survived.

Missionary writing, even the archival material meant for confidential use within the mission, has its own bias. Missionaries seek to confirm the purpose and sincerity of their efforts, yet need to present a sufficiently grim picture of heathen conditions and the struggle of evangelization to promote more support from home—but always with enough glimmers of success to encourage enthusiasm. A reader is sometimes hard put to keep some balance in evaluating such accounts (cf. Kingsley 1887:3). The language, too, is peculiar: "every occupation has its jargon. But none can be quite as nauseous as the dialect used in missionary circles" (Leys 1926:262).[4]

Some readers may view this study as a harsh and unbalanced criticism of Christian missions and colonialism; it is not intended as such. Both were important in the history of Africa and must be described for us to understand what Africa is today. Yet it is difficult to write about any social institution without a mixture of admiration and criticism, for all social life exhibits a profoundly ambiguous moral tone, a pathos well appreciated by such masters as Durkheim, Simmel, and Weber. To know is to love; yet it is also true that sometimes when one knows someone or something very well, one no longer admires or cares as ardently as before. I hope this study will make missionaries more understandable, especially to my colleagues in the social sciences. Whether missionaries are then more valued or liked is another matter.

One of the main arguments in this study is that nearly all studies of colonial societies concentrate upon the broader picture and rarely provide material on how a grassroots system worked, especially from the perspective of the local European protagonists. For that reason, I should have liked to present extensive quotations of how local missionaries and their superiors viewed Islam, Roman Catholicism, women, and other topics, even though we already have accounts of how Evangelicals and C.M.S. in general viewed these issues. Unfortunately, to do so would have increased this monograph's length in a way that would have given disproportionate weight to these issues and driven costs beyond reason. I therefore hope to publish supplementary essays elsewhere to add to our grasp of the personalities and characters of these particular missionaries. The first of these has already appeared (1981).

All English quotations from the Bible come from the King James version; this is the version utilized by the Church Missionary Society during the period studied.

I am grateful to Dr. Jon Anderson, Miss Sandra Cohn, Ms. Mary Huber, Prof. John Middleton, Prof. Rodney Needham, and Prof. Edward Tiryakian for reading various drafts of this manuscript.

COLONIAL EVANGELISM

1 Anthropology, Culture, and Colonialism: Mission Theory and Analysis*

Anthropology and Colonial Societies

IN THE PAST, ANTHROPOLOGISTS devoted themselves mainly to exotic societies, often preliterate. As such societies disappeared, many anthropologists turned to studying modernization in new states of the Third World while others sought the exotic at home, especially in ethnic minorities and deviant groups. Most anthropologists continue to ignore the mainstream of their own society, the organizations and beliefs associated with governments, churches, business, and education. These core areas are left chiefly to sociologists, political scientists, historians, and social psychologists, who have written much of value but who tend to operate within our cultural viewpoint. Anthropologists might offer a supplementary perspective through their abilities both to empathize with what is alien and to question what we take for granted. Of course, all great social scientists possess the ability of finding novelty in the commonplace—Durkheim on religion and suicide, Simmel on money and strangers, Huizinga on play—but this attitude has been particularly encouraged within anthropological tradition.

Before anthropologists begin exploring familiar culture, they might gain considerable insight by considering a sector which falls between the exotic and everyday, the past and present, not only because this might allow them to develop methods of analysis but because this might clarify some of the processes by which modernization has taken place. Colonial life is a topic neglected by anthropology even though only two generations ago it involved nearly half the world and was witnessed by most anthropologists as part of their fieldwork.[1] At best, anthropologists stud-

*This chapter expands material first presented elsewhere (Beidelman 1974). For a useful response see Wyllie 1976.

ied "culture contact," the impact of colonial forces upon native societies among which they were doing fieldwork. They wrote little about the profound changes which Europeans underwent as well. Confining our examples to Africa, we have studies of Native Authorities and local government in Busoga (Uganda), Ngoni (Malawi), and the northern emirates of Nigeria, but no comparable ethnographies of the British administrations which headed these systems. We have studies of Christianized Africans among Tswana (Botswana) and Ngoni (Malawi) but no examination of the Europeans who ran the missions. We have studies of migrant labor in Zambia and Tanzania but no accounts of plantation managers and labor officers who directed activities. It is as though anthropological curiosity stopped at the color bar and that European colonialists were just like us.[2] There are no anthropological or sociological studies of European officials, planters, traders, or missionaries anywhere in Africa. There are useful general historical accounts, biographies, and reminiscences by retired colonialists, but little comparable to what competent anthropologists or sociologists would undertake.[3] Past anthropological research often leads one to imagine the societies described as existing outside any immediate colonial experience, which is ironic since anthropology's best practitioners have advocated the study of a society in its totality.

Furthermore, colonialism is not dead in Africa if, by colonialism, we mean cultural domination with enforced social change. I refer not only to continued economic and political influence by former colonial powers but also to domination of the poor and uneducated masses by a privileged and powerful native elite fiercely determined to make change for whatever reasons. Such native elites resent being studied but welcome examination of their European predecessors and consequently may in part be understood indirectly by retrospective analysis.

Anthropology, Colonialism, and Complex Social Organization

Today we are preoccupied with various plans for social control and change, from far-reaching programs of underdeveloped nations to policies of Western governments bent on accommodating our lives to increasing technology, expanding population, and changing expectations of what the good life should be. In the colonial past we find grandiose attempts by a small group of innovators such as missionaries and administrators to implement radical changes upon a massive and often unwilling or uncomprehending population. Colonial life presents cases of planned social control and change almost unrivaled in their scale and radical nature.

Weberian theory has proved particularly valuable in facilitating understanding of the complex organizations by which such changes are imposed. Such organizations are rationalized, routinized manipulators of highly technical, standardized information, objects, and procedures. Is it then true that there may be only one optimal form of organization and procedure for a given task? For example, would a certain size electrical factory, police agency, or bank be "rationally" organized and run in the same manner in Japan, Russia, America, and Tanzania? It is unlikely. Many practices and beliefs that earlier passed among sociologists as "rational" are in reality fixed within a particular Western cultural purview. The issue hinges on the importance of culture, values, and modes of thought both beneath and beyond supposed rationality and technology. Writers such as Bayley, Bendix, Crozier, Dahrendorf, Dore, Nakane, and Rohlen recognize that ostensibly similar complex organizations exhibit profound cultural diversity.[4] As a consequence, anthropology, the study of culture, occupies a strategic position in formulating these sociological theories.

Questions about social relativism and universalism are well-worn issues among anthropologists, yet examination of colonial organizations may renew interest in the problems. For example, a seemingly homogeneous group, such as a mission society, may be examined as it functions in different cultures within one colony or even in different colonies. Two contrasting societies, such as Protestant and Catholic missions, may be examined as they function within one culture. Two different types of institutions, such as a mission and a civil administration, may be contrasted in one cultural area. Anthropologists have long compared exotic, separate cultures; the vast social, cultural, and geographic variety within colonies and empires provides equally wide prospects.

The Nature of Colonialism

Colonial societies established by Europeans in sub-Saharan Africa have an imperialistic bent in that they require subjected natives; in contrast, colonial societies in the strictest sense of the phrase, such as those established by the British in North America and Australia, eradicated indigenous peoples as part of their success.[5] Imperialistic colonialism involves a sense of mission, of spreading a nation's vision of society and culture to an alien, subjected people. Writers as different as Maunier and Brookfield agree that colonialism exhibits "an expansionist and proselytizing ethos" (Brookfield 1972:3) based on a sense of both "duty and domination" and manifested in a policy of "paternal guardianship" (Maunier 1949 I:168, 249). This involves an attempt to transform a subject people who are judged inferior yet capable of conversion to a "higher" level, albeit one judged unequal to that of their masters and teachers. While such notions are intensified in a religious mission, they appear in all such colonialistic endeavors.[6]

The adjective *colonial* should not lead us to confine our examination to formal colonial and imperial systems that have now nearly vanished. Similar features appear in the relations between great powers and underdeveloped nations, and even within complex structures in advanced metropolitan states. A basic feature of what is usually termed colonial activity is simply the interaction between disproportionate social groups which possess in different degrees the power to dominate.[7] To appreciate this apparent overgeneralization, we must reexamine our conventional notions about what defines social or cultural units. The cultures of American coal miners, sales clerks, policemen, and university professors involve differences nearly as great as those between colonialists and their subjects. Differences can be demonstrated even within occupations, through variations between ethnic groups. In anthropology the concept of subculture has been employed to deal with this; yet differences within culture or society also involve differences within single complex organizations regardless of how homogeneous their makeup may be by ethnicity, age, or sex. Consider the differences in roles, status, knowledge, beliefs, and values among directors, physicians, nurses, orderlies, technicians, clerks, custodians, and patients in one large hospital, or the differences among hospitals attached to research, governmental, and religious agencies. One could similarly consider prisons, factories, universities, governmental agencies, or retail stores. All have pyramidal organizations; policy is determined apically and implemented through tiers of lower functionaries. Those at the apex have less control of the lower echelons than they claim or believe. The flow of information is crucial in accounting for how matters actually work, yet actors at different points secure different information and opportunities, forming subworlds to the system. Each is used and uses others according to knowledge and goals, though within limits set by the organization and broader culture.

In these features, modern complex organizations display qualities resembling those reported for colonial or imperialistic societies. Their large scale and technological demands require hierarchical, bureaucratic organization in which elites, privileged in education and income, administer a subordinate multitude. In both colonial societies and modern complex organizations, staff serve as buffers and manipulators between decision-makers and an administered populace. These have more need of uniforms and formal procedures than have their masters, whose greater power and distance require fewer manifest signs to define and protect them. Differences in education, skills, activities, style, and rewards assume such dimensions as to form subcultures between ranks of the organization.

Similarly, in African colonial society the European minority administered a vast native population through native staff who stood educationally, economically, and culturally betwixt-and-between modern European and traditional native cultures. The semievolved state of these staffs was essential to their usefulness; representing neither European nor native life, they interpreted each to the other.

The preceding points raise opposing questions as to whether subcultures may be the outcome of complex social organizations or whether they feature modified structures assumed wrongly to be determined by rational, objective, universal principles. Complex organizations in the West are not, of course, the same as in colonial states, but there are sufficient similarities for us to transfer understanding of each into the other.[8]

Missions as Examples of Colonial Organization

The preceding issues could be investigated in many situations. I have chosen a Christian mission in Africa mainly because this colonial form relates to my past research.[9] Some might maintain that if a social scientist aims to study colonialism, he would be better advised to concentrate on either economic affairs or political administration. Yet there are good reasons to begin with missions because of what Brown terms their "cultural arrogance" (1944:217).[10] Christian missions represent the most naive and ethnocentric, and therefore the most thorough-going, facet of colonial life. Administrators and planters aimed at limited ends such as order, taxation, profits, cheap labor, and advantages against competing Europeans; and in that quest they sometimes attempted psychic domination as well. Missionaries invariably aimed at overall changes in the beliefs and actions of native peoples, at colonization of heart and mind as well as body. Pursuing this sustained policy of change, missionaries demonstrated a more radical and morally intense commitment to rule than political administrators or business men. While missionaries deliberated about the results of their policies, in their repeated protestations that they pursued only sacred ends they underrated the impact of their deeds.

The study of missions reveals that Europeans responded to alien cultures in ways which were callously ethnocentric and mindlessly romantic, at times poignantly altruistic and confusedly well-meaning. Here was not only conflict between Western and African cultures but tensions and contradictions within Western aims which were not as consistent as many studying culture contact would have us believe. As Baudet puts it: "The complex of motives involved in European man's relation to non-European man and his world is intricate. The dichotomy of the European soul is an essential part of that complex" (1965:54).

The Study of Missions in Africa: A Survey

Given the social significance of missions, and the vast amount that has been written about them, it is ironic that no extended sociological or anthropological study of a particular mission at the grassroots exists.[11] The nearest to this are several studies by missionaries themselves, prepared as histories and analyses to facilitate mission work.[12] These are hardly objective, though some (Welbourn, Tippett) are perceptive and subtle. Other missionaries have written surveys of mission work which display considerable insight, though not in any consistent and sustained manner with meaningful reference to social theory outside the missionary context.[13] A few African novelists have written wittily and powerfully about the impact of missions upon African life, always from a negative viewpoint.[14] Norman Leys is one of the few colonial administrators to write critically about missionaries (1926, Chapter 9).

Since this monograph deals with a mission in Africa, I limit subsequent discussion to African material. Research on missions and Christianity in

Africa appears to be more detailed and sophisticated than that in other parts of the missionized world. In confining myself to Africa, I have not distorted our understanding of the state of mission studies, unless it be in conveying a more optimistic picture than is actually the case. I have cited a few studies outside Africa when they seem significant. There is, however, one aspect by which missions in sub-Saharan Africa (excluding Ethiopia) differed radically from those in the Near East and Orient; they were better able to dominate a politically subject people.

The best recent social research on Christian missions in Africa has been conducted by historians, cf. a survey by Strayer (1975). Historical interest is generally credited to the British historian Roland Oliver, although a strong case can be made for the Swedish missionary Bengt Sundkler.[15] Though rarely cited today, Edwin Smith also influenced some.

Many British-trained historians, sociologists, and missionaries cite Oliver's works as inspiration for their own or write in a manner deriving from him.[16] Such studies concentrate on a particular nation or region, but the social and historical perspective is broadly conceived. None deals with the grassroots level, how a mission works at a particular station and on a day-to-day basis. Some of the best (Ekechi, Linden, Welbourn) are useful, yet there is the tendency for many to become scissors-and-paste accounts of events rather than convincing pictures of social activities and beliefs. Nor is it always easier for historians than for missionaries to maintain neutrality. Oliver writes as a seemingly devoted Anglican, for the basic premises held by missionaries are never questioned; Murphree writes as a former missionary turned historical anthropologist; Taylor, as a practicing missionary later to become a bishop. Temu writes with such antimissionary vehemence that he descends to diatribe.[17] Gray observes that the historical perspective, even when critical, usually lies within a broader Christian tradition (1969); and once an author's allegiance to Christianity is conceded, we may wonder if a writer agrees with the doyen of mission historians, who writes that "what [effects] from the stand point of the Christian faith are the most important escape the historian's art" (Latourette 1945:489). Herskovits, not a Christian, has rightly remarked that "there is perhaps no aspect of the African experience that has been analyzed with less objectivity than the Christian missionary effort" (1962:204).

A number of missionaries have published studies which have merit as history and social analyses, although they were written from a Christian perspective and understandably concentrate on application to mission work.[18]

Of course, missionaries have always compiled official histories of their groups,[19] of particular missionary movements, and of missions in general.[20] Biographies also provide rich data but are devoid of social analysis.[21]

A few missionaries such as Junod, Guttmann, Raum, Huffman, Huber, Cagnalo, Crazzolara, Bernardi, and Smith and Dale distinguished themselves as ethnographers in Africa. Since the International Conference on the Christian Mission in Africa, held at LaZoute, Belgium, in 1926, many writers have prepared analyses of African thought and culture in order to facilitate missionary work, e.g., Willoughby (1929), Smith (1930, 1936), Heterwick (1932), Tempels (1959), Parrinder (1969), Dickson and Ellingsworth (1969), Mbiti (1969), Shorter (1974, 1975), and Bhebe (1979). These works are of considerable interest as insights into missionary thinking but make sense only if fitted within the missionary subculture of the writer and the culture of these people he seeks to interpret.

Beginning with Sundkler's classic work (1948), many missionaries, historians, and sociologists have considered separatist groups: Schlosser (1949, 1958), Parrinder (1953), Shepperson and Price (1958), Andersson (1958), Pauw (1960, 1975), Welbourn (1961), Baëta (1962), Hayward (1963), Webster (1964), Sangree (1966), Welbourn and Ogot (1966), Peel (1967, 1968), Turner (1967), Barrett (1969), Murphree (1969), Daneel (1970a, 1970b, 1971, 1974), Halliburton (1971), Fabian (1971), Jassy (1973), Greschat (1974), *African Studies* (1974), Wyllie (1974), Martin (1975), Jules-Rosette (1975), West (1975), Sundkler (1976), Barrett (1977), Turner (1977), Dillon-Malone (1978), Wipper (1977), deWolf (1977), DeCraemer (1977), Hastings (1979), Bond, Johnson, and Walker (1979), and Fasholé-Luke (1978). It is ironic that separatist groups have received greater scholarly attention than the missionary bodies from which they derive.

Theoretical Issues

This section is organized according to six broad, analytical principles or themes, each allowing for the organization of data pertinent to the study of missions and to basic sociological theories. For each theme, I suggest the data required to sustain inquiry and I indicate broader theoretical issues which these data suggest. Where possible I provide examples from missionary research in Africa that make sense sociologically.

Secular Attributes of Missionaries

Christianity is framed in universal terms which ideally should override ethnicity, nationality, class, and income. Theoretically, missionary activities might be expected to reflect similarities regardless of these variables. Yet missions, even within the same religious order or denomination, act in terms not defined entirely by formal religious beliefs and organization.[22] Notions of comfort, style, security, self-esteem, honor, privacy, sexuality, age, and status vary with national culture and class, education and income. Yet most studies of missionaries ignore these features and tend to consider all missionaries essentially the same.

It is essential to consider any missionary group in terms of the ethnicity, class, and economic background of its members. The cultural background of missionaries influences their behavior in ways not necessarily determined by their Christian beliefs and work, and it also relates to the broader colonial milieu in which these missionaries function. This may seem obvious, but such distinctions are not well made by researchers. Thus, Ajayi tends to lump all missionaries together (1965:xiv), and Ekechi notes denominational differences but makes relatively little of other distinguishing features such as nationality and class (1971a, 1971b, 1972). In fact, it is important that Catholic missionaries in Nigeria tended to be non-British while Protestants often were. In an essay on missionaries in the Far East, Beaver contends that nationalism has little importance for missionaries (1957:23); Delavignette takes a similar view for Africa (1950:97). Even Heise (1967), one of the few sociologists to write about missions, fails to grasp this although Carlton (1967), a missionary, criticizes the omission. In contrast, Reardon (née Slade)(1968:83–96) and Markowitz (1970) emphasize the important relations between Belgian colonial politics and the Roman Catholic Church, in contrast to non-Belgian Protestant missions. Guenther contrasts African and Afrikaans missionaries in one station in Botswana but is too brief to be useful (1977). The only writers keenly aware of the importance of cultural differences seem to be Brown (1944:214) and Welbourn (1971:311), who also recognizes that missionaries form special subcultures in colonial life: "There is, in fact, no single missionary culture . . . a detailed study of these differences should yield important results (Welbourn 1961:196).

The C.M.S. in Ukaguru illustrates how ethnicity must be considered within a larger and shifting context. During the earliest period of missionary contact, the British exerted political influence at Zanzibar and Mombasa. Without British connections, the C.M.S. could not have meddled in Arab and African affairs. During the subsequent period of German rule, the C.M.S. was critical of colonial rule and defended African interests. In contrast, after the British received the Tanganyikan mandate, the missionaries warmly supported local colonial doctrine and were hostile to African criticisms of the status quo.[23]

As a second illustration of ethnic variables, contrast the Belgian Congo with Tanganyika. In the Congo, Belgian Catholic orders were integrated into the colonial power structure and until shortly before independence were uncritical of the regime, whereas Protestants, mainly from English-speaking nations, were less sympathetic (Slade 1959; Markowitz 1973).[24] In Tanzania, Catholics were rarely of British background and were unsympathetic to British rule. Shortly before African independence, Catholics covertly backed nationalist activities, while Protestants, mainly British, remained conservative and uncritical.

So far I have considered how ethnicity relates to patriotism and imperialistic sentiments. Attitudes about drink, dress, personality, diet, and etiquette are also related to ethnicity, and to class and education.[25] For example, there are important class differences among members of the Anglican church. Members of the Church Missionary Society are for the most part of humbler social background, and somewhat "lower church" theologically, than the Universities Mission of Central Africa which they term "high church." This is reflected in attitudes toward drink, diet, smoking, dress, and comportment. Similarly, in the field I was repeatedly struck by differences in the lifestyles of American, Italian, and Irish Roman Catholic missionaries; the variables were complex since the factors of class, education, and ethnicity relate to the different religious orders involved.

Mission finances involve more than support for evangelism. Missions with broad international backing, such as some Roman Catholic orders, or with rich funding, such as some American or German groups, provide lavish equipment, buildings, salaries, and charities both in their training establishments and in the field. This encourages attitudes and manners different from those of poorer missions, presents models of modernization to converts, and encourages the association of material well-being with moral worth.

Other aspects of mission life appear theologically based, yet do not derive from the Bible. Missionaries demand that converts reject cultural forms in no way opposed to Christian tenets: traditional dress, grooming, music, diet, and naming (Ekechi 1967:679; Berkhofer 1972:35). Phillips describes how American Protestants forced a Muslim convert to break dietary prohibitions (against pork) in public to prove his faith (1975:13). Missionaries disagree as to whether drinking, dancing, and smoking contradict Christianity. This may relate to theological issues, but such differences are found even within the Anglican Church.[26] At one extreme, some Africans and Europeans even contend that mission attitudes about sex and the family, especially polygyny, are Western and lower middle-class rather than essentially Christian (Welbourn 1971:336; Ajayi and Ayandele 1969:84; Ekechi 1976; Sithole 1972).

Religious Beliefs and Missionary Activities

Many writers on African life and history consider all missionaries in one category. Others select a particular missionary group for study and narrate events and anecdotes devoid of theoretical implications. These researchers never undertake a systematic review of the relations between particular religious beliefs and the organization and character of mission life. A few missionaries attempt to evaluate the methods of missiology, though in such cases we cannot expect objective, systematic exposition of Christian beliefs.

Historical accounts describe intense conflict between competing Christian missions (Smith 1966:150–51; Ekechi 1971b:70–87, Chapter 9; 1972; Berkhofer 1972:92–93; Wrigley 1959:44; Low n.d.; 1971:34–37; Ingham 1958:36–78; Murphree 1969:11). This animosity was (and is) particularly intense between Evangelical Protestants and Catholics. Delavignette typifies colonial administrators who complained about recurrent problems in moderating between antagonistic missionaries. This was embarrassing to missionaries and administrators alike since colonialists sought to present Africans with the illusion that Europeans formed a solid front toward the indigenous population (Delavignette 1950:103). All over the Third World zones of missionary comity were established. Granting each denomination exclusive rights to certain regions prevented competition for converts and reduplication of expenditures.

The most striking contrast in missionary beliefs affecting policies and activities involves Protestant and Catholic conceptions of a religious leader as a priest or pastor.[27] All priests must have the equivalent of a college degree. Therefore, a priest has a greater educational and social commitment than most pastors. European Protestant pastors attend some college, but African pastors often have only primary schooling and can neither read nor speak a European language. Even African priests have college educations and know one or more modern European languages, Latin, and some Greek.[28] Although this contrast is extreme, it indicates that while Protestant groups embrace a wide range of standards, sometimes with a double standard for European and native clergy, the sacerdotal power of the Catholic priesthood has led that church to require higher and more consistent clerical standards.[29]

The issues involved are more than theological since African religious leaders are role models for Africans and represent native interests to secular agencies. African pastors and priests gain prestige and powers of leadership from secular skills and qualities such as familiarity with European languages, ease in relating to Europeans and Europeanized African elite, and familiarity with modern technology. Their abilities are symbolized by European lifestyle in dress, mannerisms, transportation, and furnishings. When clergy are poorly educated, they are not entitled to the same pay as more educated Europeans.[30] Therefore, African Protestant pastors are poorly paid and must cultivate the soil to make ends meet (Johnson 1977:19, 64; Strayer 1978:24–78). They lack modern furnishings, everyday shoes, and stylish clothing. This contributes a note of Christian simplicity consistent with deeply engrained Protestant visions of self-abnegating, pietistic Christians; but for most Africans conversion to Christianity is associated with securing access to modern skills and superior social status, rather than with developing homely virtues defined by dour, atavistic missionaries. Finally, the investment in time, psychological commitment, and effort required to attain the Catholic priesthood is far greater than for a Protestant pastor, and this leads to stronger incorporation into the religious structure.

The celibacy of priests makes recruitment difficult in African societies, which view an unmarried, celibate adult as abnormal and antisocial.[31] In this sense, a married Protestant pastor presents the ordinary African with a more human and appealing model for emulation. Yet a married European missionary, especially one with children, requires more funds to be maintained, though wives missionize when they have time. The married European missionary also presents disturbing implications for Black-White relations at mission stations. George Orwell somewhere remarks that *mem-sahibs* soured the romantic paternalism of colonial life, much as Leslie Fiedler argues that women threatened American men's enchantment with the early frontier. European wives and children at mission stations created a new and less flexible domestic colonialism exhibiting overconcern with the sexual accessibility or vulnerability of wives, with corresponding notions about the need for spatial and social segregation. Families created a demand for a larger staff of servants involved in secular rather than religious tasks. Cohen remarks how the arrival of white women and the automobile drastically reduced informal contact between European colonialists and Africans (1971:122–23). No such domestic enclave developed to distract work at a Catholic mission, so Catholic stations may enjoy more stability and continuity of staff than Protestant ones. With wives and children, missionaries submitted more requests for leave with consequent disruptions in routine. Rotberg maintains that Protestant missionaries succumbed far more to the problems and distractions of station life than did Catholic priests (1965:53).

Religious beliefs influence the ease with which Africans convert, just as they affect the recruitment and training of clergy. Protestants tend to emphasize individual, personal enthusiasm rather than more formal ritual, beliefs, and group life. Commentators differ as to whether these traits favor conversion to Roman Catholicism or Protestantism, or even how well missionaries themselves know their theology. Neill, himself an Anglican bishop, remarks on the theological crudity of Anglicans as compared to Continental churchmen (1965:128) and readily concedes that Evangelical Anglicans, the group from which British missionaries were most readily recruited (especially the C.M.S.), were vague in their theology (1965:242–43), and preferred to emphasize zeal and sincerity, demonstrated through a puritanical code of personal conduct.

It is difficult to separate theological and organizational from economic factors when contrasting Protestants and Catholics. Some observers maintain that the Roman Catholics tend to form more concentrated missionary colonies whereas Protestants favor more diffuse groups scattered over the countryside. This may be because Catholics enjoy a centralized autonomy, or it may be because richer Catholic orders more easily support the higher costs of a larger station (Heise 1967:51; cf. Mylne 1908:88–107, whose innovative analysis inspired Heise's model). Linden suggests that tighter control by a Catholic hierarchy reduces internal conflicts within a mission (1974:52). Brown contrasts Protestants and Catholics in Samoa and claims that success in conversion rests on correspondence between the forms of church organization and the indigenous forms of native societies (1957:13–14). Ekechi (1971b:192–93) suggests that Catholics more readily accommodate themselves both to government policies and to local cultures, presumably because of their more international perspective. Leys credits Catholic conformism to their attitudes about education; he presumes Protestants to be more inquiring and free-thinking (Cell 1976:108). Barrett claims that their tendency toward accommodation leads the "higher" churches to present Christianity without radical changes in the indigenous society while "the evangelical societies . . . were determined to introduce the benefits of Western civilization with the revolutionizing of society that this implied" (1968:141–42). Latourette (1945:22) maintains that Catholics are more involved in secular services than Protestants. Maunier opposes Protestant preoccupation with political emancipation to Roman Catholic contentment with humanizing or dominating power (1929 I:252). In contradiction, Axelson provides an extreme contrast within the Roman Catholic clergy itself. In the seventeenth-century Congo, the contemplative and retiring Capuchins were trusted and liked by natives for their good services and political neutrality. Other priests lent themselves to the worst excesses of traders and administrators, even involving themselves in the slave trade (1970:132).[32]

Protestants and Roman Catholics have sharply different views on the religious significance of literacy. Protestants place deep importance on individual reading and inspiration from scriptures and therefore give priority to translating the Bible into indigenous languages. They remain in the forefront of linguistic research in many parts of the Third World.

Roman Catholics discourage unsupervised study of the Bible and attach more religious significance to the liturgy and priestly instruction. They do not see education tied to enabling natives to read mainly for religious purposes. These differences may also relate to the more universalistic character of Roman Catholics. The congregational bias in Protestantism is consistent with the encouragement of local dialects. Lee (1968) describes how African Catholic priests and nuns are forbidden to use their native dialects rather than the *lingua franca.* Different attitudes toward language may also relate to different views toward accommodation and secularism. Ekechi observes that in southeast Nigeria, the C.M.S. emphasized vernacular education as a path to reading Scripture translated into local languages but also associated *lingua franca* and English with higher education and consequently with distrusted secular skills and attitudes. Roman Catholics had no such reservations and accommodated themselves to the colonial government's needs and support for more secular education in English (1971b:183–86).

Various writers have thus contrasted Protestants and Catholics over a wide range of issues; this leads to useful insights, but can oversimplify to the point of contradiction and confusion.

Religious beliefs may be associated with more deeply personal attitudes. For example, commitment to missionary work is sometimes rooted in attitudes about expiation (Delavignette 1950:98–99; Bavinck 1960:303) and even escapism and romanticism (Warren 1967:51). Missionaries may hold ambiguous views, combining sublimated feelings of guilt and unworthiness with notions of moral superiority stemming from their sense of self-sacrifice (Welbourn 1971:315–17). This is related to ideas about the comparative virtues of receiving and giving: while the missionary may feel pleasantly altruistic abroad, his position *vis-a-vis* his home is, uncomfortably, one of receiving charitable support. He sometimes experiences anxiety and guilt, especially if he is enmeshed in a tradition of rigorous self-inspection. This sometimes leads to increased tensions within the mission station (Loewen and Loewen 1967:194–95).

Introspective tendencies are particularly associated with the Evangelical revival in Britain which led to the founding and expansion of the C.M.S. Such beliefs may have been reactions against the supposed insufficiency of reason to provide coherence in the face of the turmoil of the Industrial Revolution and against the apparent subordination of the individual to demands of complex organizations and impersonality of modern life (Altholz 1969; Warren 1967:37). Evangelical Protestants in particular emphasize individual sincerity demonstrated by strict conformity to a stringent moral code (Harries 1953:342–43). This sometimes leads to isolated missionary settlements free from supposed contamination by unconverted heathens and worldly Europeans. Preoccupation with individual conduct, plus distrust of society at large, leads some missionaries to take little interest in understanding, much less accommodating, the

Europeans whom they encounter abroad, just as they reject those they left at home.

Although the revivalism of the Victorian age led to increased missionary activity in Britain and America, this was confined to Protestants and, more particularly, to lower Evangelical groups, such as the C.M.S. It may be that the social and economic changes of that period most disturbed the middle and lower class, the main groups to whom "low" church doctrines appealed (Warren 1967:37, 54–55). When such groups took root in Africa, further cycles of revival occurred. As Barrett notes (1968:141): "Within the Anglican communion in Africa far more schisms have occurred from evangelical missions such as the Church Missionary Society than from such Catholic missions as the Society for the Propagation of the Gospel, or the Universities Mission to Central Africa."

I noted striking differences between Roman Catholics and Protestants, yet the differences within Protestant or Catholic groups seem nearly as great. With closer study other variations may appear which may prove more complex and significant than those cited here.

Theories of Conversion and Associated Beliefs

Conversion has prompted considerable theorizing. Missionaries write to determine the means which best sustain their religious aims. Religious historians consider the reasons behind conversion among various peoples. Social anthropologists and psychologists consider conversion as social change and alteration of personality. These approaches overlap and complement one another. It is remarkable that anthropologists have provided so few analyses of various theories of conversion.[33] Just as we study a cosmology to understand the ways members of a society act, so we must comprehend a missionary's theories about conversion before we can determine why he proceeds along a certain course in his attempt to convert others. Missionary views about the process of conversion ultimately amount to a theory of social change. It is, therefore, odd that despite the profusion of theories and descriptive writings on social change, related missionary beliefs and activities remain outside the scrutiny of most social scientists.

Missionizing makes sense only if one has a negative evolutionary view of a culture one is trying to change. Allen observes that mission work is a kind of education and in that respect resembles the conduct of parents toward children (1919).[34] Missionaries also encourage certain stereotypes about themselves and their work in order to secure recruits and funds; their tone is modeled after the New Testament accounts of the apostles' struggles. The tone and content of such literature today may relate to the fact that the aged are said to be typical mission supporters (Exley 1973:167).

In general, missionaries promote a picture of benighted misery, ignorance, and cruelty in traditional African life which will strike home to supporters. The dramatic tone of missionary accounts of African misery, while not wholly inaccurate, is often related to periodic financial crises. McGavran, a missionary himself, recognizes that such propagandistic aims distort many missionary accounts, even those sent to missionary home offices (1970:77–78; cf. also Ajavi 1965:261–62 and Jarrett-Kerr 1972:7). Missionaries, unlike colonial politicians and economists, tend to proclaim the equal humanity of Africans and Europeans, at least in God's eyes and in terms of the hereafter. Yet this does not ensure any lack of ethnocentrism or color bar in missionary affairs. The darker ethnic groups may be described as human but childlike, emotional or unable to grasp rational, objective thought, and different from (and by implication subtly inferior to) Whites.[35]

Such thinking insidiously dominated many earlier colonial educators involved in mission school policies. Some early anthropologists such as Westermann, long associated with mission groups, encouraged an ethnocentric disdain of African culture when writing for missions (1937:vii): "The pagan African is more easily convinced to adopt a new faith, because in his own religion he has less to lose than people adhering to a higher religion, and the adoption of Christianity includes for him membership in a higher social class."[36] Westermann recommended that "the missionary is—and must be—inexorable in trying to exterminate everything connected with the old religion, because his experience has taught him that any form of syncretism is the death of genuine Christian life" (*ibid.*:134–35). Even at this date missionaries such as Smith and Dale, Junod, and Gutmann were writing sympathetic anthropological accounts of African culture. Much depended upon the missionaries' period of residence and linguistic commitment. Smally (1958:191–94) observed that those who master a local language tend to appreciate the totality of the indigenous social system but those who work in a broken, pidgin idiom relate only to individuals peripheral to the system.

Markowitz (1973:13–14) has observed that some missionaries view Africa romantically; they contrast its underdeveloped rural areas favorably to the disruptions and conflicts of modern Western society. Missionaries who have fled modern Western life, which they rejected as contradictory to their own values, seek to reconstruct in Africa a new Christian society which is clearly impracticable in Europe and America. In this sense, missionaries sometimes demand a level of Christian conduct beyond what they have ever experienced among ordinary people at home (Allen 1919:56).

Kuper has written tellingly of the interracial, intercultural confrontation between Europeans and Africans (1971:291). This conforms to Mitchell's concept of "categorical relations" between races or ethnic groups (1966:53).

The primary impetus for mission work lies in the Scriptural quotations of Jesus and St. Paul; the latter is often seen as a model for a mission career.[37] McGavran (1959:67–71) surveys various aims of missionaries. Saving souls is only one such aim. Missionary work may also be an act of service and love in helping the poor and suffering. Good acts contribute to God's glory; even though no one is converted, the act of evangelism shows faith, serves as penance, and confirms that all is being fulfilled toward the Last Judgment. If no one is converted, the missionary should simply accept that as God's will (e.g., see Bavinck 1960:303).[38]

Ideals about conversion are closely related to the degree to which missionaries accommodate Christian belief and practice to the traditions of those they evangelize. The Catholic missionary theorist Luzbetak (1970:341) defines accommodation as "the respectful, prudent, scientifically and theoretically sound adjustment of the Church to the native culture in attitude, outward behavior, and practical apostolic approach." Apologists for a flexible approach sometimes cite St.Paul: "To the weak become I as weak: I am made all things to all men, that I might by all means save some" (1 Cor. 9.22).[39] Such views about conversion amount to a theory of applied social change.

Some writers associate Roman Catholics with tolerant accommodation and Protestants with more repressive hostility toward African beliefs and institutions (Kuper 1947:116–17; Welbourn 1975:405; Harries 1953:342–43). Several factors are cited, the most common being that Catholics view conversion as a gradual affair while Protestants demand dramatic, radical change in conduct. It is also maintained that Roman Catholics view their work in terms of a broader community while Protestants tend to emphasize the individual.[40] Protestants have been less able to contain various divergencies than have Catholics; African separatist churches mainly derive from Protestant bodies. Yet Linden observes that there is a wide range in criteria for conversion and conduct set by different Catholic orders (1974:54).[41] These are merely tendencies; generalizations are dangerous where we are considering, in the case of Catholics, a huge international institution and, in the case of Protestants, hundreds of different systems of belief and conduct. To illustrate the dangers in such stereotypes, we may contrast Placide Tempels and Bruno Gutmann. Tempels, a Catholic priest, advocated sensitive philosophical consideration of indigenous African beliefs in order to make Christian doctrine meaningful to Africans. Ironically, some of his teachings led to a charismatic religious movement outside the Church (Tempels 1959; Fabian 1971; DeCraemer 1977). Gutmann, a Protestant pastor, was harshly criticized by his colleague, Raum (1936:501), for his tolerance of African customs and his desire that traditions such as circumcision, religious use of drink and dance, and female initiation be incorporated into Christian activities.[42] Yet no schism occurred in the church at Kilimanjaro where Gutmann and Raum worked.

Even a liberal apologist for missionary work such as Sundkler remarks on the persistent disparagement of African culture by both missionaries and their converts (1960:90). Missionary attitudes toward African culture have softened, however, especially since the great international conference of missionaries at La Zoute, Belgium, in 1926 (Harries 1953:372). In Protestant circles such as the C.M.S., a term often used for accommodation is *identification,* meaning *empathy,* an "adventurous meeting" between two cultures (Warren 1961:229–38). Muldrow (1971) surveys recent uses of this term. Yet, for all the terminology, the missionary maintains that his beliefs are true and those traditionally held by his converts are not. The missionary's "aim is active aggression upon Heathenism, wherever and whenever it can be reached" (Mylne 1908:88). This means an attack on traditional life since African beliefs about the supernatural relate in diffuse and complex ways with beliefs about other aspects of their society. In this sense, mission work involves what some theologians term elenctics, denigration of traditional non-Western beliefs and practices. This was the anthropologist Westermann's advice to missionaries (1937:134–35) and the basis for Leenhardt's warning (1930:229):

"The missionary who devotes his energies to digging channels for paganism runs the risk of being swamped by the flood." Of course, those most likely to be converted are those already alienated from the traditional system (Peel 1967:292–306).

The interior mental states of converts are not easily accessible by verbal means where no common language has been mastered. This, in turn, creates a religion of formal rules of behavior, what Weber associates with sects and what the missionary Allen associates with Old Testament legalism rather than truly Christian spirit (1919:56). In this sense missionaries sometimes demand such seemingly irrelevant behavior as abandoning traditional dress to show transition out of traditional beliefs (Rotberg 1965:40); or, odder still, they forbid African school children to wear European dress because this would signify secular, materialistic ambitions inconsistent with Christian modesty and pietism (Ekechi 1971:182; Sundkler 1980:69–71).[43]

While churchmen have always written about missionizing, there were no coherent analyses of conversion or missionary tactics before the twentieth century (Harries 1953:371). In one of the few sociological papers on missions, Heise (1967) develops a model of two contrasting types of missions, based on the writings of Mylne (1908:93), a British missionary who worked in India. A similar model is used by McGavran, a well-known missionary theorist critical of current practices. Heise, Mylne, and McGavran contrast diffuse and concentrated missions, relating their attributes to theories of conversion, theology, finance, and size. Of course, all missions develop out of some nucleus, but in one case this produces a concentrated ghetto of converts segregated from the unconverted population while in the other, it produces converts sprinkled throughout the population. Heise maintains that richer missions, such as those of the Roman Catholics, favor concentration while poorer ones prefer diffusion (1967:51). The concentrated mission does not aim to disrupt all institutions of a society but to isolate and protect converts from backsliding. Proponents of concentration see their work as slow but sure and related to the establishment of a coherent Christian community (1967:51–52). McGavran criticizes concentration, maintaining that these missions produce static, overstaffed stations which confuse social services, such as teaching and medical aid, with the proper missionary task of evangelism (1955:56–58). If, however, one associates religious change with economic influence, then larger stations seem likely to have more impact (Cole

1961). Protestants emphasize internal states and dramatic conversion, thereby perhaps discouraging group conversion (Harries 1953:342–43).[44] Both Protestant and Roman Catholic missionaries sought to establish exclusive settlements where they could more easily control morality and expel backsliders (Rotberg 1964:201–202; 1965:58–59; Mobley 1970:75). Sometimes these were composed of refugees from diverse ethnic groups who had little outside the mission to hold them together (Etherington 1976)[45] Mission stations were among the few theocratic communities remaining in the twentieth century (Sundkler 1960:98–99).

All missions might be described as "greedy institutions" demanding total control rather than compartmentalized conduct (Coser 1974:67–88). Coser's perceptive analysis of the demands put upon Victorian servants could be applied to converts living at a mission station—and to most African servants employed even a century after the Victorian era. Missionary stations often were islands of Christian conformity within larger, variegated colonial societies; Africans assumed one set of behavior within the station and another outside (Fountain 1971:205). In their attempt to establish isolated Christian groups immune to and militant against the outside world, missions have resembled sects much as Weber defined them (Berger 1971; Weber 1948).

The large, highly organized missionary station was the result of the belief that conversion could be facilitated by social services, especially schools and hospitals (Warren 1967:113–14). This is decried by McGavran (1956:8) and by Allen and Cochrane (1920), who attack acceptance of government subsidies for social services. To mission purists, the only proper aim is evangelism; although educational and medical services earn secular praise, they dilute the energy and funds for evangelism and make missions vulnerable to government control (Allen and Cochrane 1920:2–3, 10–11): "An earthly organization does not become the Church: it corrupts her" (Brannen 1977:179). This view, however, is not typical of most contemporary missionaries, who emphasize such services (Luzbetak 1961; Exley 1973).

Just as Europeans presented colonialism as a caretaking operation which would last only until Africans had sufficient experience for self-government, so missionaries described themselves as serving only until an African church would be strong enough to run itself. Yet Europeans were reluctant to give up their roles as pastors after evangelism bore fruit (Ajayi 1965:178–79). Standards for judging African responsibility sometimes seem far higher than those applied at home (McGavran 1959:117, 118; Allen and Cochrane 1920:130–31).

In many areas missionaries were hostile to teaching English. They preferred education and biblical study in the vernacular so that Africans would not gain disturbing ideas and entertain dangerous ambitions (Temu 1972:85–86; Strayer 1978:20–24). The C.M.S. in West Africa opposed industrial education for such reasons. Repressive measures, including the notorious mistreatment of Bishop Samuel Ajayi Crowther, the first C.M.S. African bishop, demoralized Africans seeking to run their own affairs (Ekechi 1971:179–92; July 1967:177–95; Ilogu 1974:83–85; Neill 1965:259–60; Beyerhaus 1969:46–49).

Today European missionaries feel self-conscious about the neocolonial implications of missionary activities and, in the Church Missionary Society, for example, sometimes speak of a missionary as "a gift of one Church to another" and as a "fraternal worker." By the time independent Africans questioned mission procedures and presence, missionaries were serving as specialists and technicians; they were more like other highly paid foreign advisers than evangelists or pastors (Beyerhaus 1969:48–50).[46]

Careers in Mission Work

Careers within missionary organizations resemble careers in other colonial institutions. They exhibit an initial phase of adventure and romanticism as staff operate single-handedly on a shoestring, mingle with natives, and learn local languages and customs. With success in conversion, staff spend more time at headquarters supervising an ever-expanding body of subordinates. European colonialists envisioned a transformation, after a traditional society was imbued with new values and techniques, to a local structure that might eventually stand on its own. Administrators spoke vaguely of eventual local political autonomy and a church to be headed by African pastors and supported by local funds. Difficulties arose, however, both as to who would determine when Africans were fit for self-government and as to how services would be continued without European skills and funding. In both government and missions some questioned whether many services and certain standards were essential at all or whether their supposed necessity was simply another way to perpetuate neocolonial dependence.

Duties of missionaries changed radically with success. Initially a single missionary was involved in a wide range of tasks from evangelism and teaching to research on language and customs, road-building, house-building, and trading; Stock has termed this the "period of individualism" (1899 II:412). As converts and staff increased and governments subsidized mission work, missionaries specialized and increasingly occupied themselves with administrative paperwork. Africans were employed not only as servants and menials but also as teachers, bookkeepers, nurses, and junior administrators, taking up work earlier done by missionaries. Eventually most evangelism was conducted by Africans rather than Europeans (Murphree 1969:63; Cohen 1971:123; Slade 1959:205–206).

A mission station has a developmental pattern: an initial stage of enthusiasm and loose organization with a few supervisors; a stage of success with growing routinization and understaffing in relation to the rapidly growing number of converts; and a final stage when increase in converts and scope of enterprise leads to further routinization and lower standards in staff (Sundkler 1966:70; Pauw 1960:69). At that point, "the mission station organization encourages the view of evangelization as a work rather than a life. The jobs that need to be done easily become more important than relationships with people" (Fountain 1971:201). The station forms a "cultural security nest," a "fathered colony," insulated from the indigenous culture (*ibid.*:202; McGavran 1955:45–47). This parallels broader developments of other colonial organizations (Welbourn 1961:211).

Missionaries form a subculture sharing common attributes wherever they serve. Each station forms a microcosm apart from nearby traders, administrators, and planters. Furthermore, missionaries (at least Protestants) produce other missionaries. For example, in his recent autobiography, Max A. C. Warren, the retired General Secretary of the C.M.S., recounts a life imbued with Bible study and evangelism at home and at school, play, and work. Kin, teachers, and friends were "church people" and missionaries (1974; cf. a similar C.M.S. autobiography, White 1977). Missionaries are often apart even from home church people; their children often attend schools for mission children; and even when exposed to cosmopolitan institutions such as Cambridge University, they confine themselves to other religious people. Practicing missionaries continue their routines even on leave, conferring with other missionaries, taking brush-up courses, teaching future missionaries, and touring to seek funds and recruits. An early C.M.S. theorist wrote self-critically on missionary insularity (Cust 1889 II:x).

Insulation both strengthens and weakens missionaries. It sustains intensive lives undistracted by the economic and political turmoil that has shaken most colonies; yet it so shelters them that they sometimes lose touch with the wider world. Station life, inward and single-minded in its demands, suffers from interpersonal tensions. Missionaries sometimes feel guilt or disappointment when the high demands they set themselves and others are not continually met. At times they lose themselves in routine in order to compensate for failure to convert (Hardin 1971:223; Exley 1973:129, 140–41; Luzbetak 1970:122–29; Loewen and Loewen 1967:175; McGavran 1955:50–53, 79–80). Delavignette considers such a hectic purview typical of all colonialists, not just missionaries: "The fact is that colonial life is burdensome and busy. It teaches one not to entertain curiosity about the wide world" (1950:19).

Although European personnel are better trained than most Africans, European missionaries are not equally educated. In the C.M.S., for example, few missionaries were trained pastors. True to their evangelical tradition, the C.M.S. recruited many who demonstrated religious enthusiasm but little theological training. Until recent decades, men with university education were exempt from mission training, while women and less educated men had to have it (Warren 1974:136–37). Now the C.M.S. requires all to undergo training, though the mission is committed as never before to recruiting workers with secular skills, such as teachers, doctors, nurses, and administrators.

Once a mission gained a large body of converts, important internal distinctions in prestige and lifestyle developed among native Christians. Whereas initially Africans were employed as catechists, evangelists, translators, and servants, many were later needed as teachers, clerks, artisans, and drivers and had to be recompensed competitively with secular employees. No such competition benefited African catechists and pastors. With Protestants such as the C.M.S., the vernacular was preferred for evangelism; therefore African clergy did not need English. Those who sought it did so to become teachers and clerks, struggling for better wages to climb the "ladder to influence and power" (Sundkler 1960:116–17). An ambitious family man could not afford to become a pastor when he could receive several times more salary as a government-subsidized teacher (*Ibid.*:39; Oliver 1952:282). As differences in education and salaries grew between African clergy and service personnel, the African religious staff lost prestige. Protestant writers lament this, noting that the success of missionary education led to fewer and less qualified African recruits for purely religious work (Sundkler 1960:39–41, 155–58; 1966:118; Taylor 1957:9–10; 1958a:89, 134; Andersson 1958:69–70).

Although Africans residing on mission land and employed by a mission conformed to mission rules, increasingly secular criteria determined the style of life of the African staff. If European religious leaders retained prestige, it was more on account of secular than religious criteria (Welbourn 1961:191; McGavran 1933).

Compartmentalization of Sacred and Secular Affairs

In the nineteenth century when missionary efforts expanded in Africa, European and North American societies underwent profound secularization; religious beliefs were questioned or segregated from the rest of social life. In contrast, in traditional African societies religion remained an essential part of everyday affairs. Ironically, missionaries, grieving over the loss of religious pervasiveness at home, arrived in Africa to destroy such beliefs among natives (Welbourn 1976). The most poignant and destructive aspect of evangelism in Africa was the missionaries' failure either to appreciate fully the integrated quality of traditional African life or to appraise realistically the discordant bases of their own societies. Yet missionaries thought they could introduce modern life and beliefs into Africa according to their own ideal Christian terms, devoid of disruptions by the secular forces present at home (Markowitz 1975:13–14). It was never clear whether missionaries wished to convert Africans into Black Europeans or to create a new type of Christian, innocent about material goods and politics. Yet what first impressed Africans and encouraged them to imitate Europeans were military power, material goods, and technical skills (Welbourn 1961:177). Here, mission work and conversion in recent centuries differed sharply from what took place during earlier periods when missionaries held little cultural superiority over the missionized—indeed where the opposite was sometimes the case (Scott 1968:269–76).[47]

Missionary work in Africa involves preaching the written word to illiterates. Yet the relation between conversion and literacy assumes greater importance because of the relation between literacy and wider, secular aspects of European life. Mission education underwent further secularization after the First World War when diminished economic support led missions to seek government subsidies. Although conservative missionaries objected that this would confuse the Gospel with Western civilization,[48] few missions rejected the course, and most had always coupled scientific medical services with their work (Dougall 1946) because of the Christian association of physical with moral healing.

The conference at La Zoute marked an important change in mission attitudes about secular services (Allen 1927:5–9). Missions had always sought some economic support from governments; but after La Zoute, missions and colonial administrators became more aware of their common problems and interests. By this time, both missions and colonial governments had expanded beyond their current resources; missions needed funds, and administrations needed staff and educational facilities.[49]

Missionaries had little choice between subsidization and giving up schools altogether. Without government support they could not absorb modern standards and techniques; and where governmental schools competed with inadequate mission schools, the latter suffered (Smith 1966:169; Oliver 1952:267). So the uneasy relation between Christianity and modern society in Europe and America drifted to Africa as well, often transmitted by mission education until it bred "the new nationalism which desired to be both African and technological at the same time and had at least the suspicion that Christianity was an enemy of both" (Welbourn 1975:422). One uneasy coupling replaced another.

Education has a broader meaning than classroom instruction. Missionaries demonstrated the use of firearms, matches, and kerosene; the efficacy of their medicines; the merits of cotton cloth over leather and bark; and the wonders of sewing machines and bicycles. It was often a mission that first dominated a local economy, distributing foreign goods, supplying food during famines, and introducing cash. Missionaries may not have seen road-building or trading as more than incidental to their work, but natives viewed these as integral parts of what a missionary was and promised for the future (Ajayi and Ayandele 1969:98; Cole 1961; Fountain 1966; Oliver 1952:69). To a missionary the construction of the first European-type house was hardly remarkable and only meant smoothing the way toward saving souls; for Africans such a house prompted amazement and emulation (Andersson 1958:83).

Missionaries failed to appreciate the full implications of their actions. They presented Christianity as somehow integrally connected with literacy, Western medicine, and such technological wonders as guns and textiles;[50] a C.M.S. Committee Secretary asserted that modern thought is essentially a Christian product (Manley 1908). Others combated modernism, however vainly (Ellison and Walpole 1907:39; cf. Leys quoted in Cell 1976:277).

In their attitudes toward Western modernism and African tradition, missionaries appeared confused and contradictory. Natives were criticized for traditional dress (or undress), yet blamed for materialism when they purchased European clothing, shoes, and ornaments. European medical practices were vaunted as superior to supposedly irrational, heathen notions of Africans, but missionaries claimed miracles in healing and decried applying scientific skepticism to Christianity (cf. Miller 1973).

Missionaries encouraged Africans to avoid tribalistic politics yet were startled when natives took up modern nationalism—even though themes of nationalism and anti-imperialism fill the Old Testament, and the New preaches egalitarianism at odds with colonialism and racism. Reading the Bible for themselves "meant that the taught could discover for themselves what the teachers had failed to find" (Leys quoted in Cell 1976:285).

Missions encouraged an independence from tradition which eventually led to confrontation between paternalistic missionaries and converts. African traditional societies emphasize conformity. While this is a generalization, it is true enough when such societies are contrasted with urban, industrialized states. Initially missionaries capitalized upon deviant and independent-minded elements within traditional societies. Protestants particularly emphasized individual conscience, maintaining that this could sustain one against the community—when the deviant was Christian and the majority pagan. Such evangelistic attitudes facilitated conversion of those with individualistic, critical attitudes corresponding to those of the alien missionaries and thus subverted the local social order. Missionaries introduced disruptive attitudes characteristic of the supposedly materialistic and corrupt societies they left behind, even as they attempted to stamp out traditions which actually supported the communal cohesion they admired. Assertive and critical attitudes, once awakened, did not subside with the decline of traditional communities; instead, such attitudes were directed toward promoting egalitarianism and material well-being.

Parallels in Colonial Structure

In many respects all colonial structures are similar, though some separate missionaries from administrators and traders (Ayandele 1967:59–60; Carlton 1967; Etherington 1977). Beyerhaus (1969:39) describes missionary life as "an adventurous and sacrificial act," a phrase similar to the terms mouthed by officials seeking cadets for colonial service. Although we may consider colonial life exotic and challenging, Delavignette seems justified in considering it monotonous and parochial. It was isolated because of difficulties in communication with the outside world, but also insulated in other ways: colonialists formed an ethnic bloc separate from the indigenous masses. While colonialists spoke nostalgically about their homeland, they developed a perception and way of life which alienated them from home. If and when they returned, they found it difficult to adjust (Delavignette 1950:20; Exley 1973:138). Regardless of their class, colonialists developed peculiar attitudes about manual labor. It was rare to find them without servants, though this became increasingly rare at home. Colonial life created diffuse authoritarianism, especially where stations were isolated. Europeans assumed a range of competence and authority greater than anything allowed at home. Government administrators combined functions of executive, legislator, and judge, as well as builder, military leader, ceremonial head, and savant. Missionaries served as pastors, evangelists, teachers, builders, administrators, judges, and doctors. With the wide range of tasks went an intensity of activity that absorbed most waking hours so that colonialists developed few diversions.

The station exemplified this life, whether centered around government offices, churches, or plantations. One missionary even compares a mission station to an authoritarian plantation (Fountain 1971:201–202). Within this world, the colonialist became the undisputed ruler, sometimes benevolent, sometimes harsh, but insulated from effective criticism and unaware of changes outside his narrow realm (Taylor 1957:11).

Europeans were transformed by this experience of dominance, even as natives were altered. Setting out to transmit their culture to aliens, colonialists viewed themselves as immutable embodiments of European tradition. Colonialists had to change to be effective; yet to believe in their mission, they could admit to no such change.

The religious colonialist saw his task as never-ending. He saw an autonomous African church as unattained, much as colonial administrators doubted the imminence of self-government (Allen and Cochrane 1920:116). Yet the task of colonial rule required a native staff, which gained skills and aspirations which colonialists later could not control (Warren 1967:147–48). Like other imperialists, missionaries saw themselves as means of change; but they could not accept that change when it occurred since it would end a way of life which they had absorbed.[51]

Conclusion

Anthropologists and sociologists have been remiss in studying colonial institutions even though they give lip service to considering the total social context of societies they investigate. Colonial institutions should be studied not only because they provide invaluable insights into the development of the Third World but also because they reveal striking similarities to our own complex social organizations. The immense variety of colonial situations provides a matchless social laboratory for relating cultural, historical, and geographical factors to possible universal principles of rational organization inherent in complex, hierarchical institutions. Although all colonial organizations display similar characteristics, missions are the quintessential example; they aim at the most far-reaching domination, attacking the most deeply held traditional beliefs and values as well as economic and political forms. Despite the obvious value of such research, few studies have been made and those that have are of a broad nature describing activities for an entire administration, missionary order, country, or region. What is lacking are grassroots, intensive studies of how particular groups actually functioned on the ground, the kinds of studies which are commonly associated with anthropologists and which we do best. Through such studies we may best gain insights into how cultural and ideological factors actually mold these groups. Such studies would examine the day-to-day workings of beliefs and values by which colonialists picture themselves and their activities, as well as the stereotypes they hold about those they seek to dominate and change. Ideally, those who study missionaries and other colonialists should already be familiar with the native societies where these operate. All colonialists possess certain common traits, determined by hierarchical, elitist structures, by policies of domination and social change, and by the developmental cycle of newly founded institutions. Yet these vary in ethnicity, class, income, education, and, in the case of missionaries, such key issues as the difference between Protestants and Catholics regarding celibacy and education of clergy, commitment to literacy and to use of native versus alien languages, and secular versus religious activities and ends. Clearly, generalizations and contrasts have often been rashly formulated, and in some respects we cannot characterize a simple colonial type and certainly cannot generalize about missionaries as a single group. It even seems doubtful that we can easily do so regarding ethnic type or religious denomination, for English Catholics differ in important ways from Germans and Italians, and low-church Evangelicals are not the same as high-church Anglicans. Only after intensive, detailed studies of particular groups, such as that provided here, can we begin to tease out useful issues for comparison, definition, and generalization. For these reasons, this monograph is concerned with prosaic, everyday activities, views, and reactions of individual missionaries and the native peoples with whom they worked. While I try to provide a wide range of material, the nature of the data governs the emphasis of my report. Historical data comprising the first two-thirds of the monograph stress the views of missionaries reporting home on their experiences and, less clearly and then by inference, views of the illiterate natives subjected to evangelism. The last third comprises views of local Africans and the impressions of an outsider, a bystander-anthropologist; it is weak regarding a frank and detailed perspective of the colonialists themselves. The two broad sections of the work are, then, mirror-images methodologically, contrasting and complementing one another. This is the inevitable outcome of studying a mission, first using historical material and then utilizing first-hand observation of people unwilling to be studied. These are limitations, but defensible as outcomes of an ethical approach to fieldwork and an exercise in contrasting methods of collecting and analyzing data. Similar problems are posed to anyone first approaching this field historically and then seeking to study those sensitive and defensive to outside scrutiny.

2 Before the Missionaries Arrived: Traditional Ukaguru at European Contact

BEFORE DISCUSSING THE ARRIVAL OF the Europeans in Ukaguru, I briefly describe the world they encountered.[1] For this work to make sense, the reader requires a general picture of what traditional Kaguru society was like. While I portray the past Kaguru world as a whole, I will stress those features that bear directly on points raised in subsequent chapters. I emphasize those Kaguru beliefs and customs which disturbed or perplexed missionaries or whose significance they misjudged. For this study, we should be as interested in understanding the stereotypes which colonialists held about Kaguru as in understanding what Kaguru were actually like.

I also indicate significant alien influences that were rapidly altering life in Ukaguru even before Europeans arrived. Early missionaries pictured African society as traditionally timeless and Africans as ignorant of an outside world. Although Kaguru were alarmed and baffled by the Arabs and Europeans who began descending upon them in ever-increasing numbers during the middle of the nineteenth century, theirs was long an area of ethnic diversity. Natives were aware of alternate modes of living, even though most regarded these with fear or contempt. For Kaguru, Arabs were another alien and dangerous tribe. Their problem was to find ways by which Arab presence could be adjusted to traditional Kaguru aims; ambitious Kaguru leaders tried to fit them into a new system of political alliances (Beidelman 1978).

Had the C.M.S. missionaries better understood the fluid state of economic and political affairs in Ukaguru at the time they arrived, they might have been better able to take advantage of this unstable situation. They failed to appreciate the economic and political importance of the Arabs and consequently did not understand how or why European traders, soldiers, and diplomats perceived the Arabs differently.

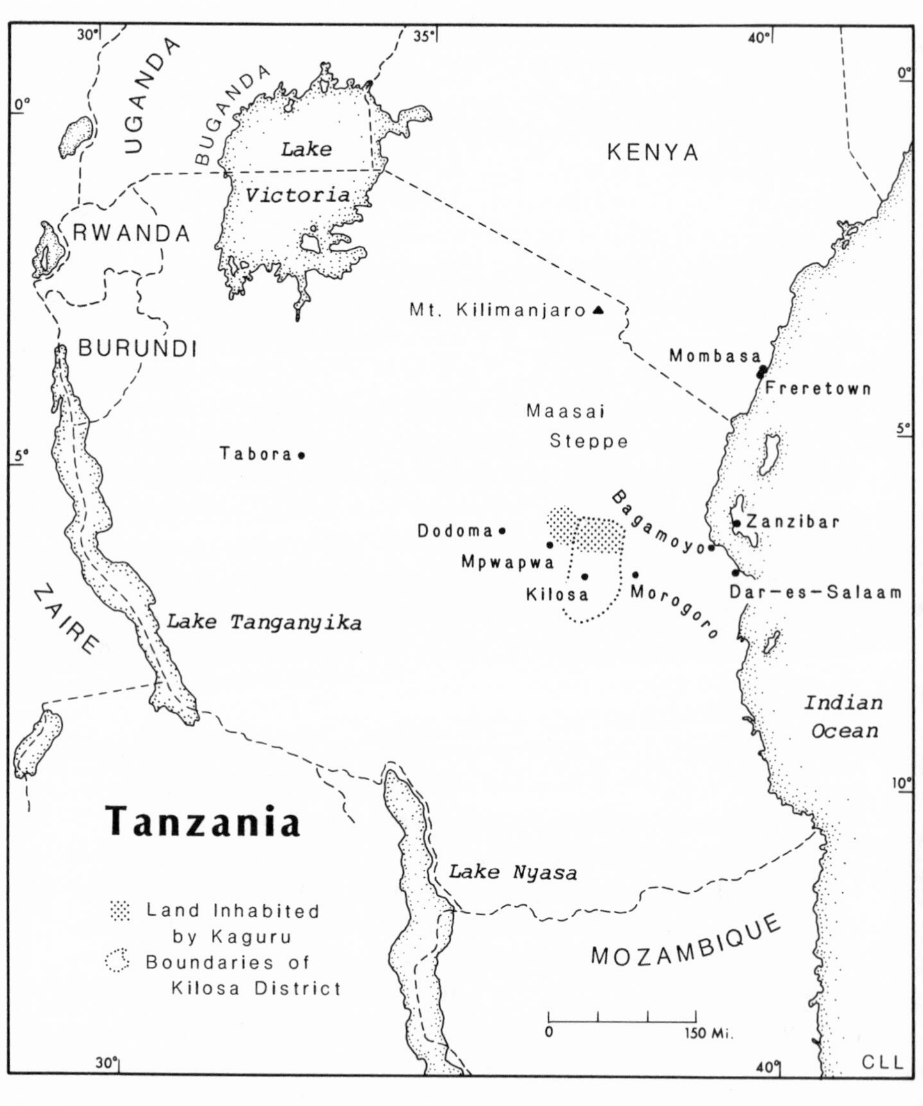
30°
35°
40°
0°
5°
10°
UGANDA
BUGANDA
Lake
Victoria
KENYA
RWANDA
BURUNDI
Mt. Kilimanjaro
Mombasa
Freretown
Maasai
Steppe
Tabora
Bagamoyo
Zanzibar
Dodoma
Mpwapwa
Kilosa
Morogoro
Dar-es-Salaam
ZAIRE
Lake Tanganyika
Indian
Ocean
Tanzania
Lake Nyasa
Land Inhabited
by Kaguru
Boundaries of
Kilosa District
MOZAMBIQUE
0
150 Mi.
CLL

General Area

The area known as Ukaguru occupies approximately 3,600 square miles about 160 miles inland from the Indian Ocean, due west from what is now Tanzania's capital and major port, Dar es Salaam. Ukaguru's location, terrain, and climate established it as a corridor of trade and refuge for wandering peoples even before the caravan trade began in the nineteenth century. As one leaves the coast, with its relatively comfortable life of fishing and agriculture, one encounters gently rolling hills covered by savannah and scattered forest, a country subject to sharp contrasts between rainy and dry seasons and unable to support much population. About one hundred miles inland, the land levels into a broad plain. At the height of the rainy season, much becomes a morass of water and mud divided by dangerously flooded rivers. Spectacular clusters of mountains and hills rise westward of this plain, separating the coastal lowlands from a broad, dry central plateau which stretches several hundred miles from the sea. These rugged highlands, which run north and south across Tanzania, are cut by mountain passes and separated from one another by stretches of thirty to fifty miles of rolling lowlands. The highlands which the traveler from the coast first encounters are the Luguru Mountains. Southwest of these are the Sagara and Vidunda. To the north are the Ngulu, and to the west the Itumba, which form the core of Ukaguru. These highlands are inhabited by culturally similar peoples. They provide the last ready supplies of food and water for travelers crossing the central plateau, notorious for famines, droughts, harsh and desolate countryside, and bellicose inhabitants. Early travelers and traders, from Arab caravaners to Christian missionaries, considered these highlands the last sojourn before a harrowing trek west or as a place of recovery before a march to the coast.

Native Africans regarded these areas as havens from the harsher surrounding countryside. Although hardly immune from famine, the highlands suffered less from drought or disease than neighboring areas, especially Ugogo and Maasailand to the west and north. Furthermore, the mountains provided defence against Maasai, Baraguyu, and Hehe, warlike peoples who raided their weaker neighbors, especially during hard times when their own herds were depleted. The peoples who inhabited the highlands displayed contradictory traditions: they grudgingly accepted and absorbed refugee bands to augment their defence forces and were willing to trade tobacco, beer, handicrafts, and grain for needed livestock; yet they suspected and feared outsiders who could be enemies. On the eve of European contact, the highlanders underwent considerable disturbance on account of periodic droughts that plagued their lowland neighbors (and to a lesser extent themselves) and led to raiding, and because of increasing strategic imbalances among local groups as caravans seized supplies, raided for slaves, and introduced tools and firearms. Turmoil also stemmed from a series of catastrophic epidemics of human and livestock diseases carried by the caravans.[2] Although important changes occurred with the arrival of the first Europeans, these were, thus, only the last of decades of shocks which altered native life and perhaps made it susceptible to new beliefs and forms of organization.

The Area of Ukaguru

Ukaguru may be divided into three types of terrain: lowlands, plateau, and mountains. The southwestern fifth of Ukaguru is lowland under 2,000 feet. This is fairly level country cut by rivers which flow from hills and mountains to the north and receive about 30 inches of rain annually. This would be more than sufficient for local crops were it not that rains do not always arrive or end predictably, nor do they always fall regularly: flash floods may wash out plantings or a few dry weeks shrivel crops in the fields. The lowlands are unhealthy during the rain; water stands in the fields; mosquitoes, ticks, worms, and other parasites abound. In the past, the level terrain made it difficult to defend lowland settlements against raiders seeking women and livestock and against pilfering caravans. Today the area retains an air of unsettled confusion, because sections are now covered with sisal estates which employ a large, ethnically mixed, and unstable population of migrant laborers.

The Itumba Mountains form the west-central third of Ukaguru. This is a precipitous area over 4,500 feet in height; many peaks are over 6,000 and some over 7,000 feet. The mountainsides receive as much as 100 inches in rainfall. Water abounds so that rudimentary irrigation allows cultivation of two crops a year. The land is cool and damp with morning ground-fog and, rarely, even frost. Temperatures average 10 to 20 degrees F. cooler than those of the lowlands and plateau. Because there is too much rain to allow reliable cultivation of sorghum and millet, maize, bananas, and some rice are preferred, as well as tobacco, vegetables, sugarcane, and fruits. Many mountainsides have been denuded and provide pasture, but some dense forests survive. The precipitous terrain is easy to defend since approaching strangers are visible for miles. Kaguru were adept at bow-and-arrow warfare as well as hurling boulders down on advancing raiders. In unsettled times Kaguru fortified settlements atop ridges and daily trekked to the valleys to cultivate and draw water. Yet Kaguru dislike the damp and cold, so when conditions became more peaceful under colonial rule, many moved to the plateau. Today (1963) these mountains are isolated, especially during the rains, and remain the most sparsely populated part of Ukaguru with less than a tenth of the total population.

The remaining half of Ukaguru is plateau between 2,000 and 4,500 feet high; there about two-thirds of all Kaguru now reside. Low, rolling hills are covered with thin scrub, dotted with taller trees, and occasionally marked by parklike woods in higher areas not worth cultivating. Prominent peaks and eruptions of rock are scattered across the plateau at five- to ten-mile intervals. These rise as high as 6,000 feet, and streams fan out from their bases throughout the year. There is no serious water shortage in most of the plateau although there is marked decrease in rainfall as one moves westward. In good years the Kaguru enjoy 30 inches of rain, although droughts occur every few years. The plateau is crossed by many streams which form arable valleys leading to the lowlands. These valleys are wide and flat; they are also relatively fertile because they are replenished annually by alluvial deposits during floods. They form a nearly continuous patchwork of cultivation while the lands are covered by light scrub scarred by scattered slash-and-burn agriculture.

The Seasons, Economy, and Technology

As in most of Tanzania, life in Ukaguru is governed by two contrasting seasons. The rains commence in late November or early December, peak in February or March, and slacken until the dry season which begins in June. The rainy season opens with spectacular downpours and several weeks of heavy, regular rain nearly every day. As the season progresses, it rains less predictably. If the rains are too irregular, come too late, continue too long, or fall heavily over the wrong periods, this can spell disaster. It is not simply a question of how much total rain falls but also when and how much at what times. As a result, every third or fourth year may be lean for Kaguru and about every seventh or eighth brings famine. In such years conditions are far worse for the Kaguru's neighbors to the north and west (Brooke 1967).

The rainy season brings hectic and continual activity: first clearing, laborious hoeing, planting, and periodic weeding; later planting of supplementary crops such as peanuts, beans, and potatoes which require deeper, more intensive cultivation; and finally, harvest. The rainy season means intense work for men, women, and children from dawn to dusk. Failure to maintain work schedules corresponding with the rains can mean hunger. There is little time for socializing, and most Kaguru fall bone-tired into bed each night. After the rains cease in June, weeding ends and there is little to do in the fields except drive off pests (children are employed to do this).

There is no such pressure in the dry season. No rain falls from late June to October, and the earth becomes hard as concrete. Some use the time to repair houses, make and mend tools, and weave mats and baskets. For women the chores of fetching water and firewood, tending children, and preparing meals provide routine throughout the year, yet even they now have more leisure. In the dry season men have less to do and spend much time drinking beer if the harvest was good. A few travel for trading.

It is in the dry season when Kaguru socialize, when kin and neighbors visit, and when youths are circumcized. Initiation of girls takes place whenever they commence menstruation and many factors determine the time for weddings, but Kaguru prefer celebrations in the dry season if possible. Then they have more time and ampler supplies of food and beer for entertaining. Group tasks such as path clearing and house building are also undertaken when beer for workers encourages cooperation.

Kaguru have always practiced a mixed economy of cultivation and herding. Like most East Africans, they take pride in livestock as a sign of prestige. These are grudgingly slaughtered and maintained with little notion of careful culling or breeding. Before colonial rule, Kaguru found it difficult to defend livestock from their warlike neighbors. Most cattle were (and still are) held in the mountains and western plateau, but people in all areas have many sheep and goats. Every household also has its flock of chickens. In most of Ukaguru the staple is maize, though in the drier western areas this is replaced by millet and sorghum. Kaguru also grow yams, potatoes, legumes, peanuts, sugarcane, and tobacco. The last requires considerable care in cultivation and curing but repays the extra labor since it is easily traded for other goods. In the past, Kaguru smelted iron ore from the mountains, in order to fashion hoes, spears, and arrow points for items of trade. Metal and livestock were the only assets, besides women and children, that men could amass over the years. Foodstuffs could not be stored for long periods, and in any case one harvest barely stretched until the next. While Kaguru were and are hostile to other groups around them, they trade tobacco, gourds, baskets, mats, stools, beer, and metal goods with them (the Maasai and Baraguyu refuse to break the soil and thus produce no such goods themselves).

Traditionally, Kaguru wore hides; they also shredded fiber for grass kilts or pressed it into barkcloth. Women wore only skirts, men a kind of toga that exposed their bodies when they moved. Boys often went naked while girls wore only a pubic apron. On ceremonial occasions, both sexes decorated themselves with red ochre mixed with animal fat or castor oil. They smeared their hair with fat and ochre and twined it into ornate braids. Metal and shell jewelry was greatly prized as were trade beads later. The favorite weapon was poisoned arrows, although short prodding spears, clubs, knives, and matchets were also used. Material culture was relatively simple, even by East African standards.

Social Organization

It is not clear whether Kaguru thought much about themselves as a united and separate people before colonial conquest. They speak a Bantu language similar to those of their neighbors. At the time Europeans arrived, differences in dialects within Ukaguru, such as between the lowlands and mountains, were so great that some missionaries thought these were different languages. Before schooling by Europeans, almost no Kaguru spoke Swahili.

Kaguru had no traditional chiefs or centralized political organization. Big men, or leaders, held transitory influence over neighborhoods, but this was through force of character, intelligence, age, and carefully engineered ties of marriage. A few who were especially ambitious made alliances with leaders from other ethnic groups, including Arabs, both to dominate their neighbors and to gain economic advantages through trade. Settlements were fairly large (not scattered as today) with anywhere from six to forty houses, usually within a palisade so that livestock and granaries were defended from attack. Kaguru stuck together for better defense from one another and outsiders. With such pressure gone, today there are few large villages and many live in lone homesteads.

Unlike most peoples of Tanzania (but like their neighbors to the east and south), Kaguru are organized into matrilineal clans and lineages (Beidelman 1971c). One belongs to the lineage of one's mother, not one's father, and ideally access to land and control of certain ritual activities and rights over others, as in bridewealth or bloodwealth, pass from a man to his sister's son. This is not to say that there are no important ties between men and their children, including some rights to marriage and blood payments, but traditionally these should be subordinated to matrilineal affiliations. In the past, settlements tended to be formed around a man, his sisters, some of their children, and perhaps some of their grandchildren; but at the same time men sought to dominate their own wives and children as well. While matriliny was the purported ideal, many sought to promote father-right when they could get away with it. This meant that wealthier and politically influential men got the best of both matrilineal and paternal principles, but others lost control of their own wives and children, either through divorce or through wives refusing to leave their natal villages. A father and a mother's brother struggled for one's obedience; a woman's brothers and her husband struggled for her loyalty since this eventually related to control of her children. Some men permanently resided with their mothers and sisters and only visited their wives in other villages.

Kaguru kinship was an affront to what ordinary Europeans saw as rational and proper domestic life. Marriage was somewhat unstable; divorce was allowed and sometimes even encouraged. Since a child born without a legal father was still a member of his mother's lineage, fatherless children were accepted with little distress; extramarital relations, although not encouraged, were not harshly condemned. Adulterous men paid fines to the wronged husband or father, and the erring woman was sometimes beaten but paid no fines. Adultery by itself was not considered strong grounds for divorce. Widows were inherited by the matrilineal kinsmen of the deceased, and the sororate was often observed.

Legal access to women and their children (what we call marriage) was primarily determined by payment of bridewealth reckoned in metal goods, livestock, and, usually, brideservice. The intended husband often spent some years visiting the girl's kin (the Kaguru word for a junior affine means "he who cultivates"); this period of service was especially long and difficult when a youth could muster little bridewealth.

Kaguru youths, primary concern after initiation was securing bridewealth. Fathers and mothers' brothers competed to control young men seeking help in such payments and to secure the lion's share of payments received from young women's marriages. Young people could be compelled to marry against their wills in order to fulfil their elders' obligations over sororate or widow inheritance. Polygyny was valued, but obviously only the elderly and prosperous could practice it because of the cost. Payments were usually larger also if a woman was expected to leave her kin and reside permanently with her husband in his village. In such a system, one's claim to rights in women and children could be sustained best through complex supporting ties of kinship and marriage; hence, residence was crucial. Social controls existed only so far as networks of kin extended, since kinship and politics were closely related. While blood brotherhood covenants could be made between people without bonds of blood or matrimony, consanguineal or affinal connections were more dependable.

Beliefs and Values

Kaguru defined the good life as sufficient food, health, and numerous children for support in their old age and remembrance after death. Religion was expressed through rites and ceremonies which sustained human fertility and health, warded off natural disasters and illness, and ensured good harvests. Kaguru were concerned with maintaining their view of order in both society and nature and saw these two spheres as inextricably connected. To achieve social and cosmological harmony it was important that the two sexes be carefully defined in their conduct and duties. Kaguru women remained perpetual minors, forever subordinate to men, first to their fathers and maternal uncles, then to their husbands. Kaguru observed (and still observe) prolonged and complex ceremonies at a girl's first menstruation. These aim at teaching proper sexual and moral conduct. They are held indoors at the girl's settlement and end with a dance and feast where her availability is proclaimed to suitors. No radical change is experienced by or expected of girls whose supposedly inherent instability is an attribute which Kaguru cite to rationalize their subordinate position. Girls continue to reside at home and work with the women of their family; the great changes in their lives come with marriage and motherhood.

Kaguru boys are considered moral and legal minors until circumcision at puberty. This operation is performed on a number at once and is followed by several weeks of moral and sexual instruction at initiation camps in the bush. Dancing and feasting mark youths' recovery and return as warriors and potentially marriageable men. Circumcision and marriage mark profound changes in boys' social states. A youth is made clean, both physically and morally, and the instruction and ritual accompanying his operation should mold him into a responsible social being. After initiation, a youth can speak for himself in disputes, fight on his own, court girls, and claim his share from labor. Both boys and girls are excluded from most ritual and ceremonies until after initiation. Since initiation provides the first occasion when a young Kaguru is confronted by formal and sustained explication of what society is about, initiation is considered the very heart of Kaguru culture.

Kaguru believe that improper moral conduct or even unvolitional deviancy may lead to illness, infertility, and misfortune for oneself and one's kin. Certain heinous acts can even jeopardize the fertility of the land or hold back rain. Twins, breech deliveries, and children who cut upper teeth first were slain in the past. The true cause for unusual events, including misfortunes, can only be determined through divination. This requires a visit to a native doctor who attempts by supernatural means to discern the cause. One could have neglected propitiating certain ancestral ghosts; once these are identified, proper sacrifice and invocation should placate them (Beidelman 1960). One might have behaved unjustly in one's obligations toward kin or neighbors or even broken certain prohibitions regarding sex or diet. In this case one must acknowledge one's faults publicly, make redress to the wronged parties, and offer sacrifices to the ancestral ghosts who have been disturbed. Finally, one might be guilty of neither neglect of the dead nor improper conduct but instead be the victim of the malevolence and jealousy of some neighbor or even kinsman. Such a person's sorcery or witchcraft can harm, even bringing death; one can purchase countersorcery medicine or even denounce an enemy as a witch and demand that he or she submit to ordeals to determine guilt or innocence. This was risky for false accusation led to heavy fines or even death, if the person denounced was socially powerful. The punishment for witchcraft was death; but usually only the socially weak, lonely, and commonly disliked were successfully accused and convicted. Of course, many Kaguru secretly suspected others of witchcraft and sorcery but dared not openly voice their views.

There is social sense in these past beliefs and practices; and though modern Europeans would reject them, similar beliefs characterized everyday European thought as late as the seventeenth century. For Kaguru there is a correlation between physical health and well-being and moral worth. Misfortune leads a Kaguru to seek help by taking stock of his or her social relations and trying to remedy an unresolved misunderstanding or abuse. If the sufferer feels convinced of his own upstanding character and has propitiated the ancestors, he might blame those about him. One does not suspect randomly but blames those with whom one already has strained relations. Beliefs thus serve to secure conformity among kin and neighbors and legitimate dislike of those who fail to meet social obligations (Beidelman 1963c). Finally, as with the ancient Greeks and Jews, sin or pollution could spread by contagion so that neighbors and kin could be harmed if one did wrong.

Kaguru offer sacrifices to ancestral ghosts at births, initiations, marriages, and funerals. On these occasions the Kaguru involved undergo important alterations in their social relations, requiring new definitions and expectations in status and behavior. Such *rites de passage* are important in providing means by which Kaguru express common beliefs and values and actually see assembled before them the people who comprise their moral world. At these rituals God is not usually addressed directly. Instead, Kaguru address ancestral spirits, the supernatural counterparts to the Kaguru local kin system. Kaguru communicate even with these only during times of difficulty. Some sophisticated Kaguru compare their beliefs toward ancestors to Catholic beliefs toward saints—both are intermediaries with the vaguer and more powerful supernatural force of God. To make contact with ancestors, sacrificial blood of animals or fowl must be shed and the bodies eaten; beer is also libated and consumed. Without this communion, *rites de passage* are meaningless. The eldest members of lineages and households stand nearest the ghosts; therefore, only they should make sacrifices or take charge of important supernatural inquiries. Even older men should not do so while their fathers and uncles are able-bodied.

Another aspect of Kaguru religious behavior extends beyond domestic affairs to the political realm. Most Kaguru clans are associated mystically with particular areas. Although people from many different clans reside in any given area, only one clan is dominant, considering itself the traditional "owner" and validating its claims through legends. This clan usually has more members in that area than has any other, though not as many as all the others combined. The dominance of a local clan is expressed in several ways. The prominant leader in that area is of that clan or at least connected to it in some way; he might be a son of a man of that clan or, very rarely, married to one of its women. Newcomers who want to settle in an area should ask permission from the local clan leader. Finally, and most important, each year before the rains, elders of the "owner" clan arrange ritual by which they are purified and the land cleansed and made fertile. This ensures regular rains and the general fertility of the resident people and livestock. In case of drought the "owners" are expected to collect contributions from local residents for payment to a rainmaker, rain being a divine sign of moral well-being. The supernatural state of the "owners" thus relates to the well-being of all inhabitants of the area. In their common interest in the land, all residents are united.

Traditionally Kaguru were organized in fairly small groups, mainly around local "owner" clans which maintained their positions through continued alliances with other groups and repeatedly validated their dominance through communal ritual (Beidelman 1971c). Clearly in such a system no clan or leader could afford to alienate local people, since all members of a group had to stand together against outsiders, not only neighboring ethnic groups but other Kaguru living several valleys away. A leader courted a following and could not afford to exploit neighbors unduly since what power he had depended upon approval and support of kin who themselves were diffusely linked to others. Few succeeded without such support, and what exploitation or dominance existed was in terms of elders trying to maintain control over juniors and men seeking control of women. No leader or clan exerted pervasive influence over others although occasionally a rainmaker, doctor, noted warrior, or witch finder might gain temporary prominence. Tenuous social ties existed beyond local neighborhoods. especially for trade. Men did not give or take women beyond the range of effective social relations for fear of being unable to retrieve them, their offspring, or bridewealth.

In this system, the major figures of authority were traditionally older men. Although personality, intelligence, and bravery facilitated leadership, these were useless without a following of junior kin and affines. To command obedience and support took time, so only elders gained extensive influence. Ritual knowledge was valued, but this was taught to men slowly, as they aged. A wide range of modern factors (access to firearms, literacy, wage labor) undermined Kaguru gerontocracy.

So far I have been mainly concerned with traditional Ukaguru, as it appears to have existed prior to the arrival of European explorers such as Burton and Speke (1857) and Stanley (1871). Yet by the time these men and the C.M.S. missionaries (1876) reached Ukaguru and wrote their accounts, they were not describing a stable, traditional society insulated from outside influences. Whether or not they realized it, they encountered a society in the turmoil of violent and rapid change. What were sometimes described as time-honored and accepted customs were actually often contested and poorly defined, either innovations imposed in recent decades or traditional practices which had come to be rejected by some. Furthermore, the ethnic heterogeneity of Ukaguru had never been so pronounced as at that time. In the past, outsiders had been gradually absorbed, eventually taking on clan names and kinship ties consistent with the Kaguru majority; but such absorption had involved smaller numbers so that such infiltration created little disturbance.

By the 1850s Ukaguru had become a thoroughfare to caravans which traveled throughout the year, though mainly in the dry season. Many were small, a few hundred porters and guards; but some involved over a thousand porters alone. The large ones were led by Arab traders and financed by Indian merchants. The Arab caravans were for ivory and slaves; the European, more often for political ends, though the stated purpose might be scientific or humanistic. Formed in Zanzibar or in the coastal dhow ports such as Bagamoyo and Saadani, caravans pressed ever more deeply inland toward the populous regions around the great central lakes. Since Ukaguru lies directly between Zanzibar with its coastal ports and the inland kingdoms rich in ivory and potential slaves, virtually all caravans passed either directly through the center of Ukaguru (Magubike, Mamboya, Geiro) or along its southern and western borders (Kilosa, Mukondokwa Valley, Mpwapwa).

Any people would be alarmed at being confronted repeatedly by hundreds or even thousands of travelers, frequently armed and often in frantic search of supplies. Although some caravans purchased produce, others simply seized what they could. Consequently, Kaguru often abandoned areas along trade routes in favor of less accessible, more defensible hills. Sometimes a friendly caravan would go out of its way to visit a settlement, only to find that it had been suddenly abandoned by frightened natives. Reliable figures are unobtainable, but it is conservatively estimated that at the height of the caravan trade somewhere between 50,000 and 100,000 people passed through Ukaguru annually. This may have exceeded the local population of Ukaguru at that time (Beidelman 1962).

The flood of strangers unsettled the population for hundreds of miles around. Cotton cloth, beads, and metal work which flowed outward from the route disrupted trade patterns and stimulated new demands. Because caravans brought diseases, some camping sites were shunned as sources of infection. Much of East Africa suffered from epidemics of cholera, sleeping sickness, smallpox, and livestock diseases such rinderpest and East Coast fever. These sometimes spread far from the infecting caravan track and led to periodic conflicts. For example, the pastoral Maasai and Baraguyu lost large numbers of livestock which they sought to replace by raiding their sedentary, less warlike neighbors such as the Kaguru. By the time the first Europeans arrived, local cattle keepers had long been terrorized. By then, too, a newly arrived colony of warlike Kamba (still present) had trekked southward from Kenya to hunt ivory and raid travelers. The most adventurous and enterprising African caravaners and traders, the Nyamwezi, whose homeland lies three or four hundred miles west, established small settlements along the route and made their living by trading with and catering to those passing by. A large Nyamwezi settlement, nearly autonomous, was situated in the very center of Ukaguru at Mamboya. Today in Ukaguru one is still struck by various pockets of alien groups that impart a sense of diversity, even sophistication, to what at first might appear an ethnically insulated area.

In terms of local affairs in Ukaguru, the most dramatic aspect of the new trade involved the introduction of firearms. The Ngulu and Zigula, who acquired arms before the Kaguru did, raided their neighbors for slaves, women, and livestock. Even where arms were few, the mere presence of a few alien, armed men, such as Nyamwezi traders or mercenaries, meant that local politics would never be the same. Even before the Europeans arrived, African and Arab caravaners supported opportunistic Kaguru, offering to help them suppress dissidents. If an ambitious Kaguru leader could ensure that his area provided a peaceful sojurn for caravans, with supplies at fair prices, he might gain wealth for himself and his followers, perhaps arms, and certainly assurances that he would be supported in attempts to extend control (Beidelman 1978). By the 1870s caravaners had long given up taking slaves or ivory from Ukaguru. There were few herds of elephants left along the eastern half of the trade route, and the local population was too sparse and the land too precipitous to make slaving easy. It was more practical to encourage hunting and raids in the interlacustrine kingdoms and then collect the loot produced, exchanging it for arms, ammunition, and trade goods. The caravaners were interested in developing way stations along their routes where they could be sure of supplies and peaceful conditions, and Ukaguru was affected (Meyer 1909:195).

By the 1890s several Kaguru leaders had gained influence over areas far greater than any united in the past, although their influence still rested on the support of followers (who provided goods for caravans). Their power was based on Arab arms and ammunition, and upon distribution of trade goods supplied by Arabs or extracted from petty traders and travelers. Some such Kaguru even had understandings with their traditional enemies; one leader cooperated with Baraguyu in raiding. By the time the first missionaries arrived, most outsiders, Arabs and Europeans alike, spoke of Kaguru "chiefs" or "sultans" as though they traditionally had leaders of this sort; in fact, many Kaguru actually resented these upstarts and disliked the trend toward centralization. Leaders established through the support of Arabs, Nyamwezi, and other similar forces later became "chiefs" recognized by the successive German and British colonial governments. The most prominent chief, at Mamboya, was a descendant of the leader established at the main Arab station garrisoned by the Sultan in Zanzibar.

The caravans, led by Arabs and manned by coastal Africans, encouraged association between modern developments and aspects of coastal Islamic life. Kaguru were (and are) intensely hostile to Islam since they associated it with the slave trade, but Kaguru do imitate any group with power. Thus, features of coastal life—such as dress, the Swahili language, food, spirit possession cults, and emphasis upon rights of fathers and husbands, rather than maternal uncles or brothers—emerged among those dealing with the caravans. This eventually led to local differences and disputes as to what constituted proper custom and behavior, a situation which doubtless aided mission work.

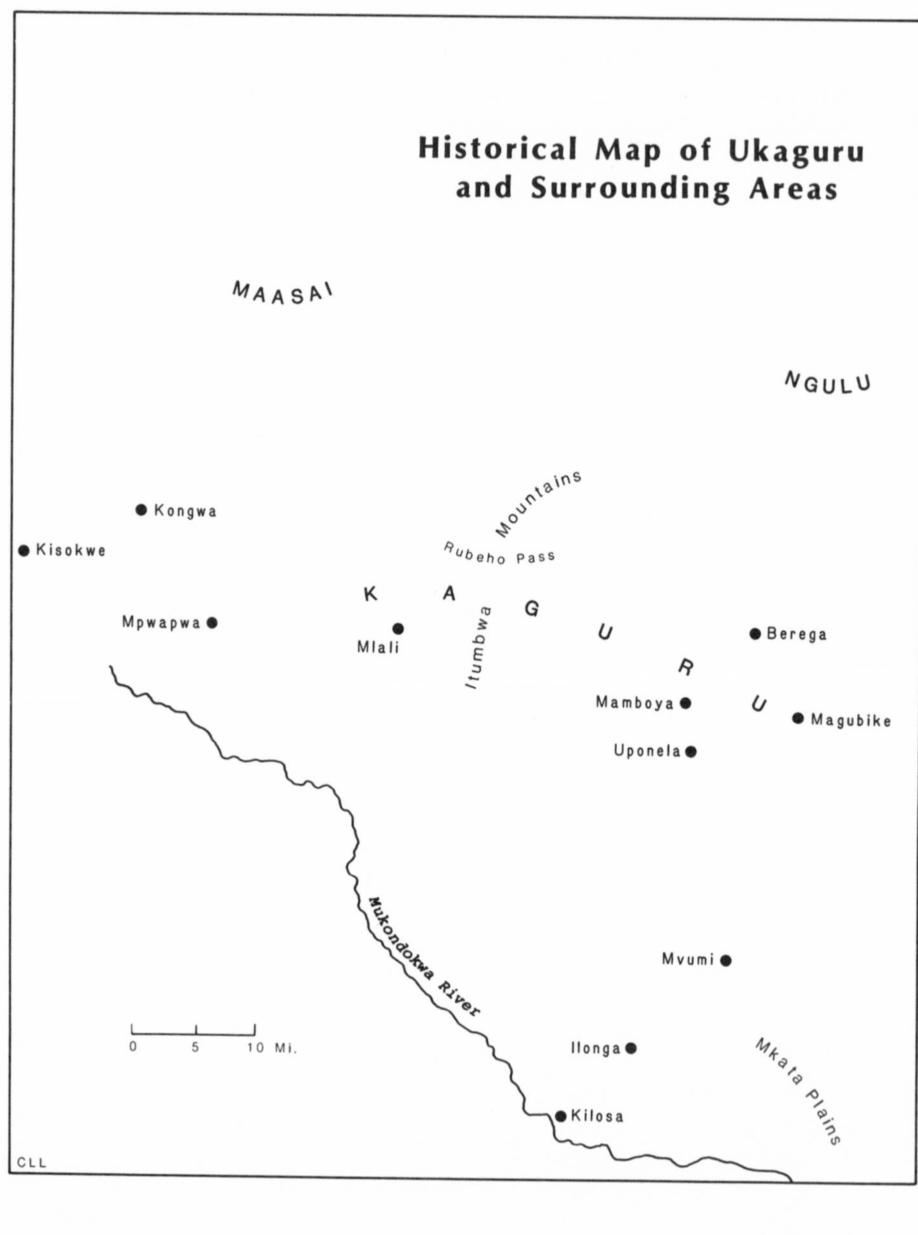
Historical Map of Ukaguru and Surrounding Areas
MAASAI
NGULU
Mountains
Kongwa
Kisokwe
Rubeho Pass
K A G U R U
Mpwapwa
Mlali
Itumbwa
Berega
Mamboya
Magubike
Uponela
Mukondokwa River
Mvumi
0 5 10 Mi.
Ilonga
Mkata Plains
Kilosa
CLL

Ironically, although Europeans eventually brought about even greater breakdown in traditional life, initially Kaguru saw these strangers as possible guarantors of a return to order and peace after decades of increasing and unregulated conflict. The C.M.S. disclaimed secular influence, and it would have appalled them that many Kaguru first regarded the C.M.S. as "white Arabs," new allies with influence on the coast. In this Kaguru were right and the missionaries unmindful of the full impact of their activities. The Arabs themselves realized the similarity, seeing the C.M.S. as both political and economic competitors.

Ukaguru is a deceptively beautiful mountain area in contrast to the surrounding countryside. Africans long saw it as a refuge, and the explorer Stanley compared it to the Alleghenies. First appearances led early missionaries to overestimate its fertility and healthfulness, so they were unprepared for occasional years of famine or for radical alterations in social life between the rainy and dry seasons. Mission work could come to a standstill during famine or when inhabitants were putting in a crop or harvesting. Conversion, usually of women and younger men, tended to subvert the moral authority of the Kaguru kin group. Mission views on polygyny, divination, protective magic, prevention and detection of witchcraft, reverence for the dead, and use of alcohol also led to complex disruption of Kaguru order. None of this should prove surprising, though the nature of Kaguru matrilineal social organization, the poverty of the countryside, the irregularity of the economy, and the character of C.M.S. evangelical Christianity all lend a particular cast to mission experience in Ukaguru.

3 C.M.S. Background and Early History in Ukaguru, 1876-91

THIS CHAPTER PROVIDES TWO SETS of information essential to understanding the analyses in the rest of the book. First, before I embark on an account of the C.M.S. in Ukaguru during the late nineteenth and early twentieth century, it is necessary that the reader have some idea of the social and ideological background of the mission society as it existed in the late Victorian era when operations began in that area of Africa. Since I am writing for anthropologists and sociologists as well as for historians and theologians, the background I provide may seem obvious and simple to some, but it would be rash of me to assume such knowledge on the part of all or even most of my readers. Second, although most chapters of this monograph are organized around social anthropological problems, some sense of historical sequence is essential if the reader is to appreciate the ways in which the myriad factors analyzed fit into a broader framework. For that reason, I provide two descriptive historical accounts, one here of the events involving the C.M.S. in Ukaguru up to the declaration of formal colonial rule in 1891 and one later of events from 1891 until the 1920s. These are the only two sections of this book devoid of extended analysis. Such an arrangement seemed the best way to provide a coherent historical picture without muddling chapters constructed not around events but around themes determined by theoretical issues.

The C.M.S. and Victorian Evangelicalism

The C.M.S. was founded in 1799 by John Venn and Thomas Scott. From the first it placed more stress on spirit and right motivation than on formal clerical training; laymen and clergy alike were workers for Christ. The direction of the C.M.S. was never monopolized by clergy, and it showed flexibility in the kinds of missionaries it sponsored.[1] The C.M.S. sent missionaries to West Africa, and later to India, Canada, the Pacific, and the Far East. Its annual reports conjure up an international panorama which some have likened to field reports from a worldwide spiritual battlefield.

That the C.M.S. was highly innovative in some of its methods partly accounted for its becoming a great worldwide mission. It established a missionary training college at Islington as early as 1825 and pioneered in mission propaganda at home (Bradley 1976:78). Its members saw work overseas as related to strengthening faith at home and sent frequent deputations to tour parishes.[2]

The C.M.S. is one party of the Church of England, but not in the sense that Holy Ghost Fathers are components of the Roman Catholic Church.[3] All Roman Catholic missionaries are closely incorporated into the church hierarchy; no such integration or homogeneity applies within the Church of England, which, by comparison, is vaguely defined (Neill 1965). English frequently refer to a "high" and a "low" church. In these terms the C.M.S. represents a "low" or Evangelical party in contrast with the U.M.C.A., which is associated with the "high" or Anglo-Catholic group. There are distinctions over ritual, church organization, revival, evangelization, and the activities and lifestyles which measure Christian life.[4]

The C.M.S. considers emphasis on ritual, vestments, and other aspects of formalism as tending toward Romanism. The Holy Eucharist is valued, but as communion rather than as mystical repetition of Christ's sacrifice. Formal theology is underplayed in favor of Bible reading and prayer; they are thought to cultivate individual spiritual states, signified by good works and asceticism. Good works may be signs of true Christian life but are no insurance of salvation. Stress is on heartfelt grace. These qualities lead "low" churchmen into anti-intellectualism; and their puritanical sense of self-discipline makes them, to use Kitson Clark's phrase, "suspicious of pleasure." The C.M.S. sees itself possessing "more Scriptural and truly Primitive teaching" (Stock I:220) than Catholics and as being free of materialistic concerns; their publications reveal persistent and intense Anti-Catholicism and distrust of *rapprochement* with secular authorities.[5] Bradley states that Evangelicals such as the C.M.S. emphasize censoriousness (Bradley 1976:27). Some "low" church members are not as spontaneous or individualistic as the most extreme nonconformists yet are nearer to them than to conservative, "high" church members within the same Anglican community.

The C.M.S. emphasized the Holy Ghost, which was manifest through an individual's constant struggle toward a rectitudinous life and through zeal and skill in preaching God's message. "The doctrine of conversion stood at the heart of Evangelical theology" (Bradley 1976:21). Missionaries abroad had already preached often at home. The C.M.S. defined true religiosity in terms of self-denial, abstinence from drink, smoking, dancing, gambling, and many forms of play. The Sabbath was strictly kept. The body and one's leisure were not to be wasted outside God's services (Bradley 1976:28) since this might give some opening to the "total depravity of man" (*ibid.*:20). The C.M.S. emphasized useful and constant work, self-examination, and continuous personal improvement, but gave little scope for cultural flexibility, ideological or affectual ambiguity, fun, aesthetics, or intellectualism. Kitson Clark, a balanced and generous-minded historian, describes Victorian Evangelicals as making "the fewest concessions to the intellectual currents of the nineteenth century" and showing "a mixture of dynamic benevolence, spiritual integrity, and oppressive and intrusive intolerance" (1973:71, 73).

The C.M.S. saw disasters as means for facilitating the ordained end; they believed in the "power of Providence" (Bradley 1976:22). Revelations about the horrors of the slave trade suggested a divine opportunity by which Europeans might end a social evil and thereby use Africans' subsequent gratitude and needs for rehabilitation to convert them. Likewise, the poverty and illness of Africans signaled rich grounds where European medicine, technology, and education might be linked to evangelism.

The missionary movement in Britain cannot be separated from the Industrial Revolution and rise of the lower middle classes. This led to revival not only of evangelism but also of fundamentalistic religious beliefs in general. The lower middle class and some of the working class viewed their surroundings and themselves ambivalently. They felt revulsion and uneasiness over widespread urban poverty and exploitation of workers, and they questioned earlier values framed in terms of a nonindustrialized, less urban world. New ideas in science, in technology, and even in biblical criticism unsettled many; in their uneasiness some reverted to more primitive religion, stronger in enthusiasm and service than in theology or organization. The Evangelicals sought to ameliorate the conditions of the lower orders in a paternalistic manner, yet consistently supported harsh measures against radicalism (Bradley 1976:113–16).[6] As Leys observes: "To them Christianity was not a solution of all the problems of life so much as a means of escape from them. . . ." (Cell 1976:284). Bradley describes this in terms of Dickens's phrase, "telescope philanthropy," and quotes *Punch* on the Evangelicals:

> Just as connoisseurs take a backward step to consider the beauties of a picture, so do many of these good folks require distance to see the miseries of human nature through an attractive medium. They have no taste for the destitution of the alley that abuts upon their dwelling-place, but how they glow—how they kindle at the misery somewhere in Africa. [1976:79]

There was also cultural pride and conviction that English culture was immensely superior to and more desirable than the benighted misery reported abroad. Africans' weakness in the face of European guns was considered proof of their inferiority and their need for supervision and instruction:

> the Evangelicals had very largely been responsible for implanting in the Victorians. . . . their curiously ambivalent view of the native peoples of the Empire as, in Kipling's famous phrase, "half-devil and half-child." Evangelical missionary propaganda portrayed the natives as depraved and corrupted, yet with immortal souls which were not beyond salvation. [Bradley 1976:89]

Elliott-Binns writes as late as 1936 of "new lands and child races," of "these weak peoples, for whom He has died, [who] needed protecting" (1936:375). Missionaries were an essential part of empire (see Clarke 1915:1814). Cust, an influential C.M.S. propagandist, told students at Balliol College, Oxford:

> Why are the ends of the world, Regions which Caesar never knew, of which the Prophets and Evangelists never dreamed, laid open to us? We go out and come in like Kings and Rulers. . . . Our Merchants have a sweep far exceeding that of Tyre: wherever our cottons can go, our Bibles must go also. Each ship and each camel must have its due proportion of clothing for the body and clothing for the soul, wherever our soldiers and sailors

> can go, our Missionaries *must* go also; it is not a question of policy or possibility, but of Duty....

He characterizes the missionary as "the highest type of human excellence in the Nineteenth Century" (1895:103–104).

C.M.S. Entry into East Africa

In the first half of the nineteenth century, the C.M.S. concentrated its attention in West Africa. Then, in 1894, they sent a German missionary, Johann Krapf, to evangelize Ethiopia. When he was refused entry, he went on to Zanzibar and obtained leave to work on the Kenya coast (see Stock 1882). These early labors brought few converts since

> the missionaries were directed distinctly not to follow the ordinary methods of conducting a Mission, not to settle down at one place, establish schools, and collect a nucleus of adherents round them, but branch out far and wide, witnessing to the Truth in successive tribes and countries, assured that if the Spirit of God blessed their word by an awakening in any particular point, the Providence of God would provide for the sustaining of such fruits. [Stock 1916 IV:131]

When Krapf and his follower, Rebmann, made spectacular geographical discoveries of mounts Kilimanjaro and Kenya, the C.M.S. did not capitalize upon them: "The true friends of the Society exercise a holy jealousy of much that is attractive in the eyes of the world, lest it compromise the Christian simplicity and divine character of the work" (*ibid.*:131). The C.M.S. compared themselves to the peripatetic Paul or Christ, scorning the allegedly more methodical, less spiritual Catholics as well as secular colonialists.

Explorers kept the opening of East Africa in the news: Burton and Speke (1857–58), Speke and Grant (1860–63), Stanley (1871–72), and Cameron (1873). (Cameron met Livingstone's servants carrying his body to the coast.) It was Livingstone above all who appealed to the public, especially to missionaries; he provided the model for Evangelicals who were keen to bring Christ and Victorian culture into Black Africa.[7]

Also stemming from Livingstone's work was the enormous pressure which both church and secular groups put upon government to end the East African slave trade. As a result, in 1872 the British signed a treaty with Zanzibar which restricted the slave trade and established a consul in Zanzibar who was to force the sultan to adhere to this new policy. In the same year, a U.M.C.A. mission was established at Zanzibar, a Catholic Holy Ghost mission came to Bagamoyo on the mainland, and the C.M.S. renewed activities near Mombasa. The consul, Sir Bartle Frere, encouraged mission expansion, Roman Catholic as well as Protestant, French and German as well as British. Indeed, he tended to prefer Roman Catholic methods because they emphasized material services and community life rather than the individualistic antisecularism promoted by Evangelicals such as the C.M.S. His attitude made the C.M.S. uneasy, and they were persuaded to modify their more rigid policies. Then Frere helped them to secure land near Mombasa on which to establish Freretown, a settlement for freed slaves (1875) to be trained in practical skills. With this means of increasing their influence, the C.M.S. approached the missionizing tactics of Roman Catholics which they continued to condemn when carried to more consistent ends by their competitors. (cf. Oliver 1952: 39–41; 51–56).

These years saw another wave of enthusiasm among British Evangelicals at home. The American evangelists Dwight L. Moody and Ira Sankey toured Britain in the 1870s and 1880s. Stock's description of Moody's deep impact upon the C.M.S. reminds me of my first months in Ukaguru when I encountered Swahili newssheets and posters of Billy Graham (Stock III 1899:26).

There was ever-increasing secular pressure upon the C.M.S. to expand and intensify their efforts in East Africa. Yet until 1875 this was viewed in terms of building up stations along the coast from which Europeans could agitate against the slave trade and where converts could be protected and trained to carry the work inland. Then, in 1875, Stanley, while touring Buganda, sent a message which was published in *The Daily Telegraph* (November 15) of London. In the message he pled that missionaries be sent up-country, claiming that the rich interlacustrine kingdoms such as Buganda were ripe for conversion. Three days later, the General Secretary of the C.M.S. received an anonymous gift of the then large sum of £5,000 for the specified purpose of founding Nyanza Mission, that is, one in the region of the Victoria Nyanza (Lake Victoria) 600 miles inland and, at best, four months' journey from the coast. Further funds were offered until the total reached over £13,000. The C.M.S. advertised for volunteers, and by 1876 a party had been formed to survey the route and establish an outpost in Buganda and a way station *en route* at Mpwapwa on the western borders of Ukaguru.[8] In the following century, the main interest of the C.M.S. in East Africa remained Uganda; but as a by-product of that concern, way stations in Ukaguru and westward continued to be maintained.[9]

The Founding Years in Ukaguru

The preliminary expedition of 1876 consisted of seven men led by Lt. G. Shergold Smith (age 30), who had served fourteen years in the British navy and had led 200 African mercenaries in the Ashanti Wars: G. J. Clarke (age 28), a mechanical engineer; W. R. Robertson, a blacksmith; J. Robertson, a carpenter; Dr. J. Smith, a physician; and the Rev. C. T. Wilson. Most were not even members of the Church of England. All were selected for their youthful hardiness, experience in leading men, and practical experience.[10] The Home Committee instructed them not to travel on Sundays, to worship regularly, and to restrain their "natural love of sport" by hunting only for food. The travelers managed about seven miles a day and required forty-two days from the coast to Mpwapwa (they lost six in rest on the Sabbath). Their reports home underestimated the difficulty of the trip for future travelers since they made the journey in the dry season.[11]

The group reached Mpwapwa on 24 August 1876, and all but Clarke passed further inland. Clarke, a lay missionary, remained behind to set up a way station. For a companion he had a coastal sailor named Hartnoll, who, although not properly part of the expedition, had tagged along. The two found it difficult to erect a small house, secure supplies, and cope with natives. After a few months they abandoned their station; Clarke had become seriously ill because they had failed to make proper arrangements for supplies.[12] The missionaries in Uganda fared worse: Mackay became ill and was sent back to Zanzibar, Dr. Smith died of dysentery, and Lt. Smith and O'Neill were murdered in Ukerewe. Yet by early 1879 seven more C.M.S. missionaries were in Buganda.

In the spring of 1878, a new group reestablished the Mpwapwa station in more realistic numbers: Dr. E. J. Baxter, a physician (age 24), in charge; J. T. Last (age 28), a builder; Alfred Copplestone, a carpenter; and J. Henry, an accountant and storekeeper.[13] None was a clergyman, though

Last had trained briefly in the Church Missionary College at Islington. They were joined by forty-nine freed slaves from Freretown who agreed to work in return for food and pay, though their number dwindled quickly as they missed the easier coastal life. The mission found it easier to employ pagans recruited from caravans.[14] By the end of 1878, the station had twenty-five acres in maize, sorghum, beans, groundnuts, cassava, and sweet potatoes; a small herd of livestock; and a flock of chickens.[15] Six small huts for married coastal people had been built as well as houses for missionaries. By then Copplestone and Henry had gone and Baxter was on the coast. Last was for a time the only missionary overseeing farm and construction work, supervising the coastal people, studying language, and organizing shipment of supplies. Baxter and Last were joined in the fall of 1879 by the Rev. J. C. Price (age 24), who had been trained at the Church Missionary College, and Henry Cole (age 30), a lay missionary and agriculturalist (*P.C.M.S.* 1878–79:39). Cole had been sent to relieve Baxter of farm work so that he might devote more time to medicine. It would have been easier to buy food locally since most missionaries were ignorant about farming and livestock.[16] Price was the first clergyman at the station, and the others were expected to assume a larger share in secular chores to free him for evangelism.[17]

This small group, under enormous pressure at work and very different in temperament and backgrounds, quarreled. Last, the most restless, sought errands elsewhere and persuaded his fellows and those at home that imminent danger of "Jesuit aggression" necessitated founding a second station at Mamboya, fifty miles (then five days) eastward in the heart of Ukaguru. Last set out with an entourage of coastal people who preferred his leadership since he was adept at languages and food supplies were better eastward. Mamboya was nearly as important a caravan stop as Mpwapwa and had as residents many Nyamwezi and coastal people. Last stayed with the Nyamwezi's leader until he built accommodations for himself and his staff. Like many missionaries, he wanted to found a Christian village which he could govern alone.[18]

By 1880, Cole increased the Mpwapwa gardens to fifty acres, but poor weather frustrated his exhausting efforts. Last fared better and made such a good case for the Mamboya site that he secured permission to marry. His wife, Annie Jackson, arrived in November 1880; the first white woman in Ukaguru (and probably Tanzania), she taught women and traveled extensively with her husband (*P.C.M.S.* 1880–81:38).

Cole was married in 1881 to H. Millington and set up a third mission station at Kisokwe, over the hill from Mpwapwa. At this time the Mpwapwa mission took on Charles Stokes (age 32), an Irish lay evangelist who had been serving the C.M.S. in Uganda since 1878. Stokes was an able leader who got on well with Africans. He organized caravans and large teams of workers. Stokes married Ellen Sharratt, a U.M.C.A. missionary in 1883, against the objections of both missions. Thus, in January 1883, there were three missionary wives, one at each station. Mrs. Last died in March, Mrs. Cole in July, and Mrs. Stokes the following spring shortly after she bore a daughter, apparently the first European born in Tanzania. The following year Stokes married (civilly) a pagan African. This appalled his colleagues. The mission severed official ties though it still employed him for caravans.[19] Cole was sent home to study at the Church Missionary College and did not return until 1885 (as a deacon). Baxter went to England to marry. The Rev. J. Roscoe and his wife joined Last at Mamboya. Some months later Last began sleeping with African women and was sent home. This left Kisokwe abandoned and the remaining two stations each with one man.[20] In the 1880s stations were so short of staff that there was no continuity in the work (Briggs 1918:31). By 1885, the Mpwapwa-Mamboya area was being termed the Mission in Ussagara, though this was a misnomer since the Sagara reside south of the Kaguru in an area dominated by Roman Catholics.

In 1886 the first C.M.S. Bishop of East Africa, James Hannington, was murdered in Busoga, before he reached Buganda. He was replaced by Bishop Henry Parker, who toured the area. Setting out from Zanzibar, he passed through Mamboya and Mpwapwa *en route* to Buganda. Before reaching Buganda he died of fever in early 1889. In the same year the Rev. Cole returned to Ukaguru with a second wife, Alice Mary Baxter, his colleague's sister. The Coles managed alone at Mpwapwa much of the time. When Roscoe became ill, the Rev. A. N. Wood, originally bound for Buganda, remained to replace him, serving single-handed at Mamboya for eighteen months. Wood, because he was new, had no knowledge of local languages and work suffered, though this was the year the church building was completed. During this same period Dr. S. T. Pruen (age 27) and his wife and Stuart Watt and his wife were temporarily stationed at Mpwapwa and Mamboya. Neither couple belonged to the C.M.S. and both eventually left; the Pruens returned to England because of poor health, and the Watts missionized in Kenya (Watt n.d.; Pruen 1891).

In December 1886, ten years after the first missionaries arrived, the first Africans were baptized; they were not locals but escaped and abandoned slaves. By 1889, at Mamboya there were one African teacher and four baptized Africans. Though many sporadically came for instruction, there were no regular students preparing for conversion (*P.C.M.S.* 1889–90:55). Although the missionaries saw their first few conversions as the major event of the decade, the arrival of the first Germans, members of Carl Peters's German Colonization Society, was of greater objective importance.[21] At the year's end Dr. Baxter returned to East Africa (but not Ukaguru), bringing his new wife from England, Clara E. Worsley. Baxter was replaced by the Rev. John Beverley (age 26) who earlier had served elsewhere in East Africa.

On 28 April 1888, the Sultan of Zanzibar signed an agreement yielding control of the mainland to the German trading company. This disturbed many Arabs, who in any case had never been well controlled by the Sultan. Scattered violence broke out on the coast and culminated in a revolt led by an Arab, Bushiri. Many missionaries on the coast fled and a few were murdered, though the astute and assiduously neutral Holy Ghost Fathers at Bagamoyo (whom the C.M.S. viewed as their chief local rivals) remained on good terms with the Arabs. In 1889 Roscoe and his wife were advised by secret messenger from the British in Zanzibar to flee. By then regular communication with the coast had been cut off for over four months. After a harrowing sixteen-day journey, which the pregnant Mrs. Roscoe undertook in a carrying chair, the couple were imprisoned by Bushiri and held for ransom. The British paid it, and Mrs. Roscoe gave birth the day they reached safety. After recuperation in England, they returned to East Africa, but not to Ukaguru. Despite repeated remonstrances from superiors, Wood refused to leave Mamboya, and Price and Cole stayed in Mpwapwa. The Kaguru kept them aware of Bushiri's movements; and when he approached with 600 men, they warned Wood, who fled to the bush. Kaguru also warned the missionaries at Mpwapwa. The two missionaries and a dozen African converts with their families fled by night, hiding in the bush at Kisokwe. Bushiri burned the mission at Mpwapwa and the German fort as well. He killed one of the Europeans there while the other fled. Some buildings at Mamboya survived, though all were damaged and supplies stolen. When the German trading company could not subdue the rebellion, the German Imperial Government intervened by sending Hermann von Wissmann to restore order. With the help of Sudanese and Zulu mercenaries, Von Wissmann quickly and ruthlessly ended the revolt. He established a garrison of a hundred men at Mpwapwa and rebuilt the fort. Three uncooperative Arabs at Mpwapwa were shot and their bodies hung publicly to impress local Africans. Bushiri was executed in 1889.[22]

In 1890 the C.M.S. named Alfred R. Tucker as its third bishop to East Africa.[23] Tucker set out from Zanzibar in a caravan led by Stokes and reached the mainland in July; just before his arrival, the Germans and British had signed a treaty recognizing German interests in southern East Africa and British interests in Zanzibar, Kenya, and Uganda. The time seemed excellent for renewed C.M.S. effort in Uganda. Tucker spent a few days in Mamboya and Mpwapwa and reached Buganda in December. His impact was considerable during his two-month stay. He returned by the same route, reaching Zanzibar in April. Tucker's vigorous campaign for funds in England saved the East African effort; it raised £15,000 in two weeks. The difference between these years and the earlier decades was that now the British government officially recognized interests in East Africa. This had indirect implications for the German sphere as well since the C.M.S. still saw the way-station missions as essential to the greater Uganda effort. Tucker returned to East Africa in 1891 to spend many years securing the mission. On 1 April 1891, the area formerly controlled by the German trading company became the Imperial Colony of German East Africa and the mission became the C.M.S. Mission of German East Africa (Tucker 1911:18–69; *P.C.M.S.* 1889–90:51–54).

The missionaries had been reluctant to flee the area during Bushiri's uprising because local Africans were showing interest in conversion. The Rev. Price claimed he could not abandon Mpwapwa, whatever the dangers, when over two hundred local Africans had submitted to instructions and as many as four hundred attended a service in 1891. Once political stability was confirmed, conversion increased remarkably. The Rev. Wood writes after his fifth year at Mamboya that twenty-five Christians had been baptized and another thirty were catechumens. Seventy-three others (30 boys, 43 girls) attended classes in reading; the girls were also taught sewing.[24] These were Kaguru, not outsiders. In this sense, 1891 marks a double turning point in missionary attitudes. With secular government, the C.M.S. had to consider how it would come to terms with secular forces it hitherto thought it could ignore (if only because Arabs, as heathens, lacked what they considered legitimate institutions). The age of heroic individuals who ignored secular pressures had ended; and although the arrival of European government encouraged African interest in education and hence conversion, the C.M.S. viewed this with misgivings since these stations in German East Africa were now the only C.M.S. posts in Africa not under British rule.

4 Contradictions in the Sacred and Secular Life: The C.M.S. Work in Ukaguru, 1876-91*

THIS CHAPTER CONSIDERS SOME OF THE beliefs and activities of the C.M.S. during the early period of heroic individuals in Ukaguru before the establishment of colonial rule. I hope to show how missionaries built up a stereotype of their lives as ascetic and profoundly committed to their Evangelical ideals. I also hope to show how, despite the sacrifices and suffering, missionary success required skill and commitment of a nature at odds with denial of secular life.

The Victorian Evangelicals saw themselves as "serious," by which they meant they were undistracted by worldly society. Not only were leisurely pastimes considered dangerous distractions from God's work, but material comfort, intellectualism, and much that we term "culture" were also not for them:

> Missionary service should be regarded, not as a profession, but as a vocation. It is to be the one thing of life. Everything else is subsidiary. Rest, change, exercise, and relaxation are, of course, necessary for bodily and mental health, but the faithful missionary will employ these solely as recreation, the better to fit him for his Master's service. He will watch lest they ever usurp a place to which they have no right. Even the study of nature or art, the love of exploration, the society of fellow countrymen have been to some a very real cause of danger.[1]

The C.M.S. exhibited profound ambivalence, at times reaching contradiction, in that they saw themselves bringing to benighted pagans a higher view of life, yet a life free of the materialism of modern industrial society.

*A more detailed version of this chapter, containing extensive quotations from archival and other sources, appears elsewhere (Beidelman 1981).

> It cannot be too often or too strongly insisted upon that the first work of a Christian Mission is to Christianize, not simply civilize. Christianity can never be evolved out of civilization. Civilization, in its best sense, follows in the wake of Christianity. [Tucker 1911:47]

Yet the missionaries marked themselves apart from and superior to Africans through such "secular" means as these: widespread literacy, modern hygiene, firearms, shoes, clothing, canned goods, bicycles, compasses, and lamps. The C.M.S. interpreted external materialistic superiority as only an outside sign of deeper differences, but Africans and many secular Europeans recognized no such distinction.

In this sense, the C.M.S. saw themselves apart from other Europeans, even other missionaries. Mere civilized comportment, some piety, and good will were not enough; the "true" missionary had to be a born-again Christian who had himself experienced a second conversion through revival or some other profound inward experience which was marked by a radical and dramatic change in behavior (cf. Watt n.d.:22). Like other Evangelicals, the C.M.S. were fond of such terms as "truly religious," "acceptable," and "serious" to convey their difference from others who also claimed to be Christians (Bradley 1976:30). In this, the C.M.S. in Ukaguru set themselves apart from and superior to the greater body of Europeans. They disparaged the other Europeans, yet had to deal with them. This posed few problems during the earlier period; it became a major difficulty after formal German colonial status in 1891.

Missionizing

During the first fifteen years the C.M.S. were in Ukaguru (1876–91), missionary life corresponded to their idealized notions of their calling. As we shall see, even during German rule, the C.M.S., because of their alien nationality, continued to view themselves as divorced from the secular sectors of colonial life. Dissociation from government was important to the C.M.S. for two reasons: first, it allowed them to pursue activities unassociated with the secular needs which they considered inimical to spiritual life; and, second, that missionaries could struggle in the wilderness unprotected and unencouraged (even thwarted) by government was a sign of divine protection. Such views perhaps explain why the very first C.M.S. in East Africa were encouraged not to follow a methodical program of conversion and even held services and preached in English to natives who could not possibly understand them; they trusted to the "Providence of God" for support.[2]

Stereotypes of adventure and sacrifice inspired mission recruits and contributions even after conditions became safer. Where the C.M.S. adhered strictly to an idealistic, sacred vision, their welfare was jeopardized and their work suffered; where they developed more practical, secular skills, they compromised their self-image and found less time and energy for evangelism, but they did secure stabler working conditions and attract more interest from natives.

The type and choice of persons that the C.M.S. sent to Ukaguru were the result of a wide variety of interdependent factors. All recruits were expected to hold Evangelical beliefs, and nearly all were members of the "low" party of the Church. While the range of education and practical training was great, the C.M.S. was sensitive about the fact that its training schools often recruited from the lower social ranks (Holt 1971:127). Those with college degrees, physicians and engineers as well as theologians, were not required to take formal or sustained missionary training. Those without higher education often entered the C.M.S. Training College at Islington in northeast London (Hodge 1971). This mainly involved religious study; only minor attention was paid to more practical skills (*ibid.*:84) since the C.M.S. were suspicious of materialistic life. Native languages were learned in the field, a procedure which consumed vast amounts of time (*ibid.*:95). Nearly all C.M.S. missionaries arrived in Ukaguru almost totally ignorant of the world they would encounter. Ironically, those most likely to hold a higher authority (college graduates) were the least likely to receive rigorous training in practical skills vital to success. The less educated got some foundation at Islington. For field training in evangelizing, overseas candidates practiced on the working class and poor of east London.

Although the C.M.S. was essentially a middle and lower middle class institution, those who volunteered for East Africa were a mixed lot. Volunteers of humbler background often thrived while more educated ministers underwent agonizing obstacles. Those who clung to purely religious conduct, as defined at home, often did not survive or made little headway. Religious dedication allowed missionaries to accept conditions which other Europeans would not, yet survival and presentation of an image of authority and success which Africans would seek to emulate through conversion required secular conduct at odds with missionaries' definition of themselves as primarily spiritual figures. This contradiction appears in the attitudes and conduct of missionaries in the field. Also, rules and aims established by the Home Committee in Britain who were unfamiliar with the realities of life in Africa were not always relevant to workers in the field.

I now consider several facets of missionary life from this pioneer period and from a somewhat later time in order to illustrate these contradictory and at times self-defeating trends.

The Caravans

I begin with each Victorian missionary's *rite de passage* into the reality of the East African field, the caravan. A trek from the coast to Mamboya in central Ukaguru took about sixteen days; to Mpwapwa on the Western border, twenty-one. This varied with a caravan's size and the season. With no roads or bridges, a procession of porters walking Indian-file along bush trails made slow time. In the rainy season they might slog only three or four miles a day waist-deep in water and mud with supplies and weapons hoisted overhead. As late as 1900, Bishop William George Peel, an experienced caravaner, required two weeks to reach Mamboya with 160 porters (*P.C.M.S.* 1900–1901:117–18). Some of the earliest caravans were far larger; and even when conditions were safer, thirty to sixty porters were common (cf. Beidelman 1981). More porters were needed if sick or female missionaries had to be carried.

Assembling caravans involved complex and skilled routines for recruitment, pay, inventory packing, and organization. Recruitment was sometimes difficult; the supply of porters fluctuated due to changing demands for local labor in the agricultural cycle, competition in hiring from other travelers, epidemics, conflicts between different ethnic groups of porters, and availability of desirable trade goods used for payments. Those who led large groups of rough, alien men were constantly faced with dangers of insubordination, defection, and theft, not to mention problems of organizing hygienic, cooking, and quartering facilities for a large number of people vastly different from any that the missionaries had previously encountered. The sheer volume of supplies required was staggering. Each new missionary required over a ton of supplies for a year's stay, including over seven hundred pounds of consumable provisions. Sixty porters were needed for each such lot. One missionary estimated that during a single year he had arranged about a thousand porter-loads from the coast as well as making trips there himself to order shipments, check accounts, and recruit new porters (Pruen 1891:97).

Few missionaries were trained or personally disposed to manage such affairs; they were, therefore, distracted by and impatient with caravan details, considering them impediments to their real work.[3] Yet to an outsider, these secular skills seem among the most impressive of early C.M.S. achievements, especially since they were developed on the spur of the moment and out of necessity. Despite missionary views to the contrary, abilities to control and understand natives were more important to success in the field than any home-taught evangelistic skills could be.

Just managing heathen coastal porters sometimes required conduct which appalled the missionaries. A. M. Mackay, one of the most admired C.M.S. missionaries, shot and wounded several mutinous porters; and the martyred Bishop Hannington hurled firebrands at rebellious workers.[4] Missionaries debated how best to control "a caravan of semi-savage men." Cutting rations did more harm than good as a threat since it weakened porters; avoidance of any threat or punishment led to loss of goods (cf. Watt n.d.:83–85; Ashe 1890:10–17; Pruen 1891:184–85; *C.M.I.* 1890:85).

A crisis over the issue of discipline arose when one C.M.S. missionary, Watt, flogged and tied up several porters caught stealing and one of them subsequently died. The scandal was kept secret and Watt went home, though he later returned to another area to missionize outside the C.M.S. The mission Home Secretary was baffled and shocked that evangelists could defend such apparent brutality (as Watt vehemently did) as essential to their survival.[5]

The problem was never resolved so long as the C.M.S. had to supervise large numbers of men while having few social ties to them. Watt's widow later publicized the problem (though not her husband's case), advocating firm, even harsh, punishment as best for dealing with "these grown-up children of Africa." Apparently, even instructional leaflets informally circulated by the C.M.S. to new recruits contradicted the mission's public policies on the advisability of using force to maintain order among recalcitrant workers (Watt n.d.:83–86).

Sometimes the C.M.S. employed coastal Africans to supervise porters, but this often left them dangerously ignorant of what was actually happening with their goods and men. Ironically, the C.M.S. found that at this period their best caravaner was Stokes, who had been thrown out of the mission on account of his overfamiliarity with Africans (he sometimes wore Arab garb and, far worse, later took an African wife) (Luck 1972 *passim*). Until the end of German rule, the missionaries remained dependent on caravans not only for supplies but for safe transmission of news to and from home. Such services were too important to risk entirely to outsiders, yet clearly required managerial conduct that missionaries never honestly accepted as consistent with their desired image. The immense amount of time that logistics took was time the missionaries considered lost from their true tasks.

Martyrdom

Missionaries often describe their work as sacrifice or as a means of refining character. The C.M.S. believed their suffering and difficulties made them better persons. Thus, it was difficult for them to apply rational, objective standards in determining proper strategies for their work. They were exhorted not to be deterred by failure (though cautioned that some signs of progress in conversion had to be shown if they were to expect further contributions from home). Continued defeats were often considered a means of divine testing and hardly signified a wrong approach.[6] Faced with crushing disappointments, bereavement, and illness, the C.M.S. saw God's ways as

> so mysterious we can only just bow our heads in humble submission to God's will, assured that he makes no mistakes, and what we know not now, we shall know hereafter.[7]

Personal safety was disdained whether from threats of warlike natives or dangerous animals.[8] Missionaries should turn the other cheek *(ibid.)*. One wonders why the missionaries carried arms in the first place.

C.M.S. wrote that "the victories of the church are gained by stepping over the graves of its members" and that "our God bids us build a cemetery before we build a church. The resurrection of East Africa must be effected by our destruction."[9] In 1889, when local Africans and Arabs rebelled against abuses by German traders and others, the C.M.S. refused to flee Ukaguru: "They cannot, however, do anything more than our

God allows them to do. I am not in the least anxious" (*P.C.M.S.* 1892–93:47). Some laymen back in Britain found such desire for martyrdom by Evangelicals to be repellent self-glorification (Bolt 1971:127).

Asceticism

After the 1889 rebellion destroyed or severely damaged all of the C.M.S. buildings and most of their equipment and supplies, the missionaries interpreted this as a sign that God had disapproved of their supposedly excessive interest in material goods and comforts and that they should concentrate more on evangelism and less on constructing a better station: "We needed this purging—we were too comfortable and had too many of this world's goods."[10] "We don't need to be showing these people the way that Europeans live and how many things we have. Other people can introduce civilization and all its good and evil. It is ours to preach Christ. Make Him the Point of attention and interest and the less there is to draw their attention away from Him the better."[11] One C.M.S. missionary feared that "all such displays of superiority and affluence . . . make the native regard the Musungu [European] as a being of a superior order to themselves, and consequently, in a measure, humanly speaking, makes them less willing to believe that our religion is for *them.*"[12] Yet this same writer fretted whether undue disregard for a European style of life was also corrupting: "This is not self-denial, but laziness, and it may easily degenerate into something worse" (Price 1891:252). It is hard to determine when behavior is altruistic and when it is just "going-native."

Ironically, it was precisely the materials and skills of Western modern life that most attracted Kaguru to the C.M.S. Even the missionaries were sometimes aware of this: "They will watch your house-building and gardening etc. etc. and see that you are superior to them in knowledge and energy and are worth listening to therefore on all subjects."[13]

Asceticism was essential to a "Godward life." A missionary should manifest sobriety and seriousness, exhibited through a controlled self, ordered life, and disciplined will. Spiritual dedication and accompanying grace should allow a missionary to surmount whatever deficiencies he had in secular skills. Therefore, during the early period, the C.M.S. sought evangelists rather than builders, foremen, and accountants, though these were needed urgently.[14] Consequently, missionaries often found themselves swamped with secular tasks, which they mastered slowly and painfully. The mission was what Coser terms "a greedy institution" (1974), devouring all aspects of the person's being and time. Such submission was "evidence of the victory of the spiritual over the natural."[15] This sometimes led to psychological and physical conditions inimical to the best service. It also led at times to distruct and conflict within small mission stations where each judged himself and others by unrealistically high standards. Playing down personal welfare led to overwork, malnutrition, improper treatment of illness, loneliness, and depression.[16]

Churchmen found secular tasks tedious and spent so much time constructing buildings and furnishing and supervising African laborers that they hardly had time for evangelizing.[17] Repeatedly, they wrote to the Home Committee pleading for artisans to relieve their secular work. Such pleas were rejected.[18] This was considered an insidious form of secularism,[19] as well as too costly.[20] Establishing a local trading store by which funds or work could be extracted from local Africans, who could also thus be shielded from outside merchants, was viewed as utterly corrupting.[21]

The missionaries wore themselves out, often with secular tasks which they dispiritedly viewed as secondary to their real aims:

> I can honestly say that from 6 o'clock in the morning till 6 P.M. I am busy in mission work, and excepting mealtimes which seldom occupy half an hour during the day simply resting (doing nothing). The calls of the men working on the station, people coming for medicine, or sores to be done up, others with affairs, which have to be heard, calls here and calis there, then some 2 or 3 hours nearly every day with my native teachers besides time taken up in visiting the natives which both Mrs. Last and I attend to as much as possible. For the more we are among them the greater is our influence over them. From 6 to 9 P.M. I am busy reading and writing, so that in each day from 6 A.M. to 9 P.M. there is but little time which is not actually employed and that directly or indirectly in things for or connected with the mission.[22]

> There is a great need for itinerating work [evangelizing] but what am I to do with 200 children on the books besides workmen, and young men to teach and all the services, accounts, and etc. to attend?[23]

The missionaries had selected especially rugged terrain for their stations in Ukaguru, and circuit-preaching added to the strain.[24] Why then did the missionaries not consider passing some secular tasks to others? They hesitated to pass them on to Africans, partly because they feared that teaching Africans such skills would disclose the secular or wrong aspects of the world, aspects that a missionary with his special training and divine inspiration could handle but which the supposedly weaker African would find corrupting. As late as the 1920s, the C.M.S. still taught no skilled trades but only simple tasks in most of its East African schools (Jones 1924:184).[25] This was part of what, as late as 1931, the local C.M.S. bishop could write of as the mission's "trusteeship of the child races of the world" (Chambers 1931:60). Africans were to gain Christian morals and spiritual inspiration first and corrupting, materialistic techniques only later. Nor were nonmissionary Europeans considered for employment, for their conduct was viewed with nearly as much suspicion and revulsion as that of pagan Africans and might set a bad example.

While the C.M.S. missionaries always thought of themselves as living altruistically on meager incomes, their salaries have always been many times higher than those of their African agents. This practice has persisted down to recent times. The double-standard is illustrated by the fact that when Africans were finally ordained as clergy, it was decided that their salary would be less than a fifteenth that of European clergy.[26] All through C.M.S. history, the altruism manifest in standards of living had far different effects from those intended. In terms of the average secular European living in East Africa, C.M.S. missionaries lived frugally. Salaries were far less than those of comparably educated Europeans in government or private enterprise; therefore, standards of living were comparably shabbier. Yet the missionaries invariably possessed items of Western technology unavailable to Africans. During the early period this meant guns, metal goods, cloth, and medicine; later this included automobiles, houses with cement floors and windows, and innumerable other "essential" items. From the African view, the supposedly altruistic missionaries lived incomparably better than their Black brothers and sisters; yet the modesty and frugality of these missionaries' lives appeared seedy and niggardly when compared to other Europeans'.[27] To Africans missionary thrift carried none of the meanings which missionaries themselves assigned to it. For Africans, the missionaries were failed Europeans, demonstrably not as successful as those in government or commerce. Moreover, Africans saw the C.M.S. as apparently not as well off as competing missions such as Roman Catholics. C.M.S. concern over budgets and economizing was interpreted by Africans as miserliness and was measured against the carelessness with money and goods manifested by many in secular colonial society. The C.M.S. did not understand that the image which Africans sought to emulate involved material success and secular power, attributes which the C.M.S. at least formally rejected. The Kaguru wanted missionaries to teach them how to become powerful and prosperous like Europeans, and for that they expected teachers who were themselves powerful and prosperous. Unquestionably, a church more committed to seemingly secular expression of Western beliefs and power would have attracted more attention to its subtler, spiritual messages.

Sexual Asceticism

At first, the C.M.S. considered conditions in East Africa too difficult for women, and only men were sent out. The first C.M.S. missionary to East Africa, Krapf, had lost his wife and child during his first months of work; consequently, both he and the Home Committee insisted upon celibacy for all to follow. Early C.M.S. missionaries were compared to soldiers and their work to combat, tasks inimicable to women.[28] The C.M.S. required all missionaries to East Africa either to leave their families behind in Britain or, if unmarried, to pledge foregoing marriage for some years so they would have no dependents to be supported by the mission in case they died abroad (Stock 1899 III: 355–56).[29] As the years passed, a debate continued as to whether missionaries should be celibate. On the one hand, celibacy was considered a form of altruism and therefore a means for building spiritual character. For the C.M.S., any renunciation, any constriction of the "natural" man, meant a triumph of spirit over flesh. It was also recognized that married couples would require more complex and costly housing. On the other hand, the C.M.S. contrasted itself with Catholics in that their clerics could marry. One of their criticisms of Catholics was that sacerdotal celibacy prevented them from presenting a model family—in the form of a pastor, his wife, and their children—for converts to emulate.[30]

When women were finally encouraged to go to Ukaguru, the Home Committee "would always expect that a missionary wife would do all she could, without question of the source of her husband's income."[31] Missionaries in the field had to petition the Home or Parent Committee for permission to marry.[32] Later, missionaries with five years in the field did not need such permission, but they still required Committee approval to bring wives to the field. The wife also had to pass a physical examination and be judged morally and personally fit. She was expected to serve as an example to the wives of African agents; they, in turn, were to missionize local women.[33] The C.M.S. believed that the pastoral family provided the ideal evangelistic team, especially since the Victorian C.M.S. did not believe that men were suitable evangelists to women.[34] Correspondingly, women were not to deal with African men under most circumstances.[35]

The C.M.S. implicitly feared that celibacy in Africa might be more than some men could bear and that these would be tempted to miscegenation. The missionaries Last and Stokes were both widowed in Ukaguru, and both subsequently slept with African women. For this they were both expelled. It was argued that such conduct was probably the result of an unhinged mind due to sunstroke: "Would a man in his senses work bareheaded from morn til night in the broiling sun, side by side of the natives, and if were compelled to do so would he be likely to retain his reason long?"[36]

On account of these unfortunate lapses, the C.M.S. was urged to reconsider the urgency of encouraging female missionaries.[37] The Home Committee in London insisted that conditions were still too dangerous and unhealthy for women and urged that workers "trust the grace of God to keep them from falling."[38] It was even implied that Africa by its very nature threatened European morality.[39] Yet a decade later a number of female missionaries had worked in Ukaguru. Whether they provided the advantages that their advocates claimed is debatable. Certainly married couples set up households apart from the unmarried missionaries and distant from native settlements; they thus embodied a separation from and autonomy within the community that perhaps discouraged intimate evangelism. Such households also led to the use of servants, a situation which added to feelings of inequality.

Conclusion

The C.M.S. definition of altruism subordinated all aspects of social life and culture to the demands of missionizing. With such ideals in mind, the C.M.S. went to East Africa with unrealistic expectations of how they could exist and flourish in the field. Whatever the temptations and sacrifices, nothing was to stand in the way of spreading the Gospel. All should try to be "good soldiers of Jesus Christ," "True yoke-fellows" harnessed to one work. Recruits were reminded that

> it is most essential that you should all work together, allowing nothing to separate you one from another, but prepared to make any sacrifice, so that union of heart and action, which is strength, may be secured.[40]

In striving to do so, they sometimes made their everyday lives difficult for both themselves and those about them. They repeatedly wrote castigating reports about fellow workers and other Europeans. In any case, such intense efforts to constrain the self produced a rigid and narrow person unlikely to appeal either to other Europeans with whom they had to cooperate or to potential African converts. The C.M.S. group described here appear dour and constricted, even by the standards of Victorian Protestants. The very views which the C.M.S. developed and which encouraged volunteers to risk everything and suffer much in Africa were views that often ill-fitted them to succeed. If antimaterialism drove them from Britain, that same antimaterialism drove the Africans from them as well. Antimaterialism allowed the C.M.S. to penetrate areas where no supportive European power existed, but this later led them to work poorly with such secular powers when they arrived. The C.M.S.'s visions of themselves and their spiritual need for self-sacrifice and self-deprivation constantly got in the way of successful work with both Africans and other Europeans, even though it sustained them through horrific difficulties. The very sources of their interior strengths produced workers illfitted to relate to others in the ways essential to build a successful program for conversion.

5 Colonial History: The German and British Colonial Period, 1891-1961

THIS CHAPTER PROVIDES AN HISTORICAL narrative of the mission during the colonial era which began in 1891 with Germany's declaration that the area was part of what would be the Imperial colony of German East Africa.[1] Emphasis lies on the period of German rule up to the First World War. Relatively little space is devoted to the period of British rule, 1921–61, because it is covered in subsequent chapters.

Many C.M.S. missionaries of this period assumed that their nationality *vis-a-vis* the colonial government was a crucial issue for them; but, ironically, this very negative appraisal of their status proved more significant. Even more crucial was the mission's changing position regarding secular affairs. Both Germans and British impelled the C.M.S. along the same course. So, too, did the Africans, for after 1900, with a decade of brutal military pacification behind them, Kaguru generally recognized domination by Europeans. In seeking accommodation, they began what Maunier terms "spiritual subjugation," in which European culture was applied to many aspects of their lives. The C.M.S. had to follow the secularizing trends, despite misgivings that these might betray the ideals associated with previous years of heroic evangelism. The C.M.S. were relieved when they finally worked under the British, yet they preserved a self-image more consistent with their ideals under German rule, both because the Germans had less time to construct a smooth-running administration before the First World War cut their efforts short, and because the German-British differences in ethnicity allowed the C.M.S. to entertain a sense of alienation from secular power which they had difficulty maintaining with the British.

Imperial Order, Social Unrest, and Growing Colonial Influence: 1891–1907

In an attempt to remedy the inept policies of Peters's company, the new German colonial regime embarked upon a harsh policy of political and economic control. The Germans implemented their policy through coastal and alien African mercenaries (Swahili, Nubians, Zulu) unsympathetic toward the local peoples. Repeated African protests culminated in a full-scale revolt in the southern part of the colony in 1905, the Maji-maji rebellion. Fighting was widespread and continued until 1907. Over a quarter of a million Africans may have died, more from the famine and illness that resulted from the Germans' scorched-earth policy than from combat. Most fighting took place far south of Ukaguru, but toward the end raiding spread to its southern borders. The C.M.S. bishop toured the area frequently during the emergency but sensed little danger. Besides, the missionaries had already survived Bushiri's rebellion only a few years before. In the final fighting in late 1906 the rebels attacked the German fort at Kilosa, only fifty miles southeast of Mamboya. They burned villages near the Roman Catholic station at Ilonga just north of Kilosa and marauded through southern Ukaguru, driving refugees to the C.M.S. stations. The C.M.S. bishop was in the area at the time and fled north to Kenya with his staff. He wrote to the German commandant at Mpwapwa requesting an escort for the remaining missionaries to Kenya, for he advocated temporarily abandoning the station to the care of African converts. The Germans refused military escort, on the Governor's orders, and insisted that the missionaries retire to the fort until they could be sent to the coast. The C.M.S. distrusted the Germans, dreading public association with a regime which they rightly believed had caused disorder through its cruelty. They disobeyed the administration by taking refuge at Kiboriani, in Ugogo, just northwest of Ukaguru. No C.M.S. station was touched by the Maji-maji, but work was set back. The African staff guarded mission property; but without European supervision for five months, they stopped teaching and evangelizing. The rebellion was crushed and the missionaries returned in January 1907.[2] They found their installations so poorly maintained that they were forced to spend a long period rebuilding; they had to postpone the intensive evangelism they had hoped to begin.[3]

Even without such conflict, the mission's future was in jeopardy. In 1897, the Nyanza bishopric (encompassing all of East Africa) was divided: Uganda and northwestern German East Africa remained under Bishop Tucker in Buganda; the remainder, including Kenya, Zanzibar, and the rest of German East Africa, became the Mombasa bishopric, headed in 1899 by Bishop George Peel.[4] Initially, Peel questioned retaining any of the German area, a view endorsed by the Home Committee. His frequent tours of German East Africa in the first decade of the 1900s sprang from doubts as to what to do. Before fleeing to Kenya, Peel had become impressed by the bravery and dedication of the missionaries and urged the Home Committee not to yield the stations in Ukaguru to German Lutherans as had been contemplated.[5]

The proposed transfer of the mission in Ukaguru would have ended the careers of most of the missionaries since there were no ready funds for alternate assignments.[6] Some wrote repeatedly protesting recall home, even for ill health; they preferred to carry on despite the dangers so they would not risk losing their posts. The local mission's unsure status led to policies that exacerbated the very backwardness often cited as the reason for closure. The Home Committee opposed purchase of new land for mission stations, forbade further expenditure for translating or printing works in native languages,[7] and hesitated to replace dwindling staff. They even opposed ordination of Africans on the grounds that the mission might be disbanded, although elsewhere they argued that the lack of African clergy was a symptom of the mission's failure and justified disbandment.

Even without rebellion, possible disbandment, and a chaotic economy, these would have been hard times in Ukaguru. Smallpox, locusts, drought, and resultant famines decimated the population in 1888, 1894, 1895, 1899, and 1908.[8] The droughts were a bitter shock to the missionaries, who had assumed that Mamboya would prove a highland haven.[9] In 1889, the missionaries endured the severest test of all. They completed a large church capable of accommodating 500 worshippers and costing £42; on December 31, during Sunday service, the building collapsed in a windstorm. One Kaguru was killed and many were injured. Kaguru noted that although some mission houses were also damaged, no European was hurt. Some maintained that these were signs that the ancestral ghosts were angered at being neglected in favor of Christianity, and many stopped attending mission services.[10]

Disbandment policies depressed the missionaries in Ukaguru; not only were they dismayed over their failure to convert more, but they were horrified that the Home Committee's withdrawal of support would make their past struggles and sacrifices meaningless. Even worse, they were convinced that their departure would open the way to Islam and Catholics.

Despite serious reservations about a small and unprosperous British mission in German territory, the Home Committee admitted that conversion in Ukaguru was suddenly showing progress, apparently because of the new impetus of German colonialism. Comparison of figures for 1900 and 1907 was most encouraging even though there were still no ordained clergy: from 203 to 612 baptized members, from 3 new baptisms a year to 40, and from 356 students enrolled to 3,603.[11] Furthermore, the C.M.S. was under pressure from a sister British mission, the U.M.C.A., which had expanded its efforts in southern German East Africa and did not want to become the sole British mission in a German colony.[12]

Although it continued the station, the Home Committee pursued a policy of containment, even retrenchment. European staff in Ukaguru declined from 24 in 1905 to 17 in 1908.[13] Those who died or took leave because of illness were rarely replaced. By 1908, Bishop Peel wrote angrily to the Home Committee that soon no clergyman would be available anywhere in the colony. He compared the striking disparities between the C.M.S. allocations to Uganda and Kenya, which were increasing, and those to German East Africa. He rightly noted that retrenchment was assuming self-defeating proportions.[14]

With success in the Mamboya area, each missionary sought to work his own station. (Strayer points out a similar process among C.M.S. in Kenya, 1973b:231.) Three outlying stations were founded in 1900, at Berega, Nyangala, and Itumba. Each was only about eight to ten miles from Mamboya, but the latter two were in the mountains and required twice as long to reach. Thus, the C.M.S. had founded four stations in Ukaguru proper and two on its western borders, Mpwapwa/Kisokwe and Kongwa. Mpwapwa, the original station along the main caravan route, should have retained paramountcy; but because the C.M.S. considered the German garrison at Mpwapwa a harmful influence, in 1900 they switched their concentration to Kongwa, eighteen miles northward over the hills. Before this change, Mpwapwa and its outlying station had 10 African teachers, 150 baptized Christians, 27 catechumens, and 96 students attending 5 schools. Yet its African members contributed only 43 rupees, barely enough to pay for a porter to bring five loads up from the coast (over 60 such loads were needed just to outfit and supply one missionary for a year). In contrast, Mamboya had 2 teachers, 33 baptized Christians, 7 catechumens, and 118 students attending 4 schools. It provided only 16 rupees. The three new stations, Nyangala, Berega, and Itumba, had a total of 4 teachers, 17 baptized Christians, 9 catechumens, and 71 students in 6 schools; they contributed only 15 rupees.[15] Africans also built traditional structures elsewhere in order to encourage touring missionaries and their agents to teach and preach.

Unfortunately, just as some of these stations became well established, they had to be phased out. Kaguru had preferred the mountains mainly for defense; with stabler political conditions after German pacification, ever-increasing numbers migrated from the cool, damp, uncomfortable mountains to the plateau and valleys. As a result, by 1904, the mountain station at Itumba was in decline and the original hill station at Mamboya reduced to secondary status as the Europeans moved to Berega.[16] The senility of the reigning chief at Mamboya further encouraged Kaguru to move to Berega, where his more adept prospective heir had settled.[17]

With this proliferation and shift of stations, unified and coordinated activities became increasingly difficult to maintain. By 1894, the missionaries in Ukaguru began holding periodic conferences, at first two a year, which everyone attended, and later two more, to which only those from the Mpwapwa area came. The smaller stations formed satellites around Mpwapwa (later Kongwa) and Mamboya (later Berega), with the western branch retaining seniority. By the 1900s, conferences were regular, even though attendance involved great inconvenience. These conferences drew up local budgets; they also decided postings of staff and adopted policies. Theoretically, such issues should have been determined by the bishop and Home Committee, but this was far from realistic. There was repeated conflict and misunderstanding between those in the field and those at home as to how far local workers should decide their affairs. Missionaries scattered across nearly eighty miles of rough and varied country were bound to perceive things differently and have competing needs; it was bound to be difficult to coordinate their aims and methods. Achieving local coordination and control was a permanent C.M.S. problem, just as it plagued secular colonial administrators.[18]

After 1907, the Germans attempted various administrative reforms and poured in funds for development. The most striking measure was the commencement in 1907 of a railway stretching over seven hundred miles westward from Dar es Salaam to Lake Tanganyika. The railway passed through Kilosa and along the southern border of Ukaguru.[19] It encouraged Germans to attempt plantations in the lowlands south and east of Ukaguru; they farmed first cotton and kapok and later sisal. With them came an influx of Swahili-speaking workers and traders from the coast; all were more sophisticated than Kaguru, and most were Muslim.

Africans were beginning to recognize that they would have to accommodate themselves as best they could to an enduring colonial structure, however much they might resent it. Rapidly expanding opportunities for African employment in colonial institutions and a new demand that taxes and purchases be paid in cash, rather than through produce as before, forced Africans into a European-controlled market for labor and goods. When Africans and Germans pressed for an increase in educational facilities, the C.M.S. found itself the center of growing secular interests which perplexed and worried them.

German and Mission Relations: 1907–13

Before the Germans began pacification in earnest, the C.M.S. record in Ukaguru was dim. In 1904, after nearly twenty-eight years of struggle, they could report no better than this:

	African Teachers	*Baptized Members*	*Catechists*	*Schools*	*Students*	*Contributions (rupees)*
Mamboya	4	67	8	9	249	39
Itumba	4	33	11	13	390	38
Berega	4	27	1	15	298	35
Nyangala	3	25	5	8	191	22
Mpwapwa-Kisokwe	8	234	45	6	335	49

P.C.M.S. 1904–1905:91

In part, this was due to the initial difficulties of subduing an alien and hostile environment. It was also due to appalling staffing problems. For example, at one point a single missionary stationed at Mpwapwa supervised work at Berega and Nyangala by fortnightly hikes (over fifty miles each way); for eight months a single woman worked the remote station at Nyangala; and sometimes stations had no missionaries at all for months or even a year at a time. Furthermore, German colonial expansion was beginning to drive up costs of goods and labor; this created problems for poorly funded missionaries such as the C.M.S. A strike by the African teachers at Mamboya astounded the missionaries but merely underscored the growing inflation that colonial development brought.

Yet it was precisely the secular demands of German colonial expansion, the same forces that inflicted burdensome inflation, that were to skyrocket C.M.S. conversions. If the C.M.S. record had been dismal until now, it was because very few Kaguru could discern any realistic advantage in adapting European culture. Now the Germans pressed to secure a literate and skilled supply of Africans who could facilitate their task of organizing and exploiting the colony. They saw missionary education as the cheapest and readiest means available; denomination did not matter. In 1910, the Germans made education compulsory for Africans, particularly for heirs of chiefs and headmen, where it was available. They even agreed to provide limited funds to support educational and medical work by missions. By 1912, the C.M.S. was issuing certificates to the qualified African teachers whom it employed in an expanding system of small bush schools scattered out from supervisory mission stations. Actual teaching was almost entirely by African agents and was of inconsistent quality. For example, schools near a station might be taught three times a week, while others met only once every few weeks or once a month.[20]

The C.M.S. tried feverishly to expand its already overextended program, hoping to obstruct encroachment by rival missions and to discourage local construction of government secular schools. There were harsh conflicts between the C.M.S. and its rivals, especially the Roman Catholics, as they competed for government support and domination of a population now clamoring to acquire European skills. The intensity of these changes may be appreciated from the fact that in a single year students in the C.M.S. schools in Ukaguru and Ugogo went from 7,200 to 17,200 (*P.C.M.S.* 1912–13:53). As the Rev. T. B. R. Westgate observed:

> The fact also that many of their own complexion, trained in the highly-efficient German schools at the coast, and now occupying positions of considerable responsibility in both the Government and railway services has fired them with the hope that they also may attain to greater and better things. [1913a:56]

Westgate goes on to plead frantically for more funds and staff to prevent Africans from falling "either under the blighting blast of Islam or the erroneous teaching of Roman Catholicism" *(ibid.)*.

These changes are dramatically illustrated by the final C.M.S. report for Ukaguru before World War I broke out. Despite loss of staff, shortage of funds, closing of some schools, and a dislocative transfer of the center of operations from Mpwapwa to Kongwa, student enrollment had increased spectacularly:

	African Teachers	*Baptized Members*	*Catechists*	*Schools*	*Students*
Mamboya	6	79	155	8	417
Berega	50	160	786	76	3,701
Nyangala	18	117	106	41	1,959
Kongwa	23	389	387	60	4,161[21]

The First World War

Encouraging trends were cut short by the First World War. At first the missionaries were merely confined to their stations; the women were allowed to work, but the men were restricted indoors. Later all were under guard, and overcrowded when other British missionaries (U.M.-C.A.) were brought up from the south. Then men were forced to make boot-pegs and the women to knit and sew for enemy troops. Two missionaries were repeatedly accused of encouraging Africans to spy on the Germans and were threatened with death. It was a harrowing experience of hunger, illness, and privation; apparently the possibility of death was real since the Germans eventually did shoot a Greek quartered with the C.M.S. The society's original misgivings about work in a non-British territory were justified. Finally the missionaries were shipped several hundred miles west by rail to the German fort at Tabora; there the Belgians found and liberated them on 19 September 1916. For a short time, after the missionaries left, a German Protestant missionary manned the station at Mamboya. After he left, some African staff continued to teach, hold services, and evangelize (*P.C.M.S.* 1916–17:35). In February 1917, two missionaries from British East Africa toured Ukaguru briefly to encourage the remaining African workers to continue work until the recuperating C.M.S. returned. Unfortunately, illness and poor transportation kept the missionaries from resuming work until 1919.[22]

Kaguru converts suffered far more than the missionaries. Many were impressed into porterage (from which they often died), and later fighting disrupted agricultural work. During the German retreat, some mission employees were harassed by German troops and some of the mission buildings were burned. The most serious hindrance to resuming full-scale work was, however, the epidemic of influenza which followed the war; it brought not only illness but also famine since few were able to cultivate.

British Rule

Under British colonial authority, the C.M.S. resumed work with increased confidence. Many missionaries felt it a propitious sign that soon after their return, on 21 August 1921, the first Africans were ordained, Haruni Mbegu and Andrea Mwaka. They had been candidates for ordination ever since the grim days when the mission was considering disbanding.[23]

African agents continued to do most of the actual teaching and evangelism at low pay, under the supervision of Europeans; for example, the C.M.S. in Ukaguru and Ugogo combined was run in 1924 on about $6,000. Yet even this modest sum was difficult for the C.M.S. to sustain. In that same year, prospects brightened for support of mission work: members of the Phelps Stokes Commission, whose purpose was to study educational policies in Africa, toured Ukaguru and Ugogo in connection with proposals by the British colonial government to subsidize missionary enterprise in education. The C.M.S. in Ukaguru may not have been able to survive without such government support, yet later chapters will reveal that this posed as many problems as it solved. Even in 1925, when government subsidization of mission education began, the C.M.S. still considered abandoning Ukaguru both because of their dwindling staff and funds and because of the kinds of secularizing changes and controls that government support would entail.[24] In 1926, various missionary bodies with work in Africa held an international conference at La Zoute, Belgium. Despite protests from a conservative Evangelical minority, the participants reaffirmed that missionaries would provide secular services in order to secure outside support. However uneasy some might feel, secularization appeared a universal trend which almost all missions were following and which the C.M.S. could hardly reject if it was to compete with others. Despite its new co-optation by government, British C.M.S. still found themselves strained beyond their resources in both volunteers and funds. Consequently, in 1927 the C.M.S. of Australia was invited to undertake all work in East Africa. Ukaguru was placed in a new Diocese of Central Tanganyika under an Australian Bishop, the Rev. G. A. Chambers, who arrived the following year.[25] The Australian C.M.S. appeared even more conservatively Evangelical than their British cohorts; and this, as well as their nationality, set considerable cultural distance between them and the British administration. Although in perennial economic straits, the mission persisted in considering expansion into other areas and in 1933 built an impressive and costly cathedral in Dodoma. In doing so, it showed a poor calculation of its economic needs, especially since the current worldwide depression in the 1930s hit all the world missions severely. Max A. C. Warren, a former Secretary of the C.M.S., estimates that between 1929 and 1933 funds dropped by half and were further jeopardized abroad by wild fluctuations in the exchange rates.[26] The mission intensified its call for African free-will offerings for medical treatment and at *rites de passage* such as baptism, confirmation, and marriage. No new out-stations were to be built without firm local funding. There was a 10 percent cut in all missionary salaries, and many senior missionaries were retired early. African clergy were limited to 35 shillings per month ($5) for priest and 30 shillings for deacons.

From economic disaster, the British and Australians plunged into the Second World War. Staff became even more scarce, and subsidization and support from home were cut to almost nothing. Even some of the African staff left to serve in the armed forces.

After the war, Ugogo and western Ukaguru were thrown into turmoil by the gigantic Groundnut Scheme, an ill-planned multimillion-pound fiasco which had its headquarters at Kongwa, alongside the C.M.S. center, and which adversely affected the mission by drastically inflating the local cost of living (Wood 1950).

In 1947, Chambers was replaced by the Rev. W. Wyne Jones, who died only three years after taking office. He was succeeded in 1950 by the Rev. Alfred Stanway. In 1955, an African Assistant Bishop, Yohanna Omari (ordained 1938), was appointed. Yet no general Africanization of the mission occurred by Tanzanian independence in 1961, even though this had been a goal ever since the mission's founding.

6 The Mission and Its Sacred and Secular Competitors: Islam, Competing Christian Missions, and Secular Colonial Society

THE PRECEDING CHAPTER TOUCHED briefly on this one's theme, the growing secular influences which threatened to alter the C.M.S.'s picture of themselves and of the world they hoped to establish. Here I discuss this change in terms of the C.M.S. view of and response to rival colonial institutions which presented alternate, competing interpretations of material progress—first the Muslims; then other Christian missions, especially the Roman Catholics; and finally the German colonial administration. C.M.S. relationships with other colonial institutions were determined not only by the stereotypes which the C.M.S. held about both themselves and these other groups but also by the fact that the German administration utilized its paramount position to force responses that would further its own vision of what progressive development should be.

The C.M.S. View of Arabs and Islam

The C.M.S. associated the Arabs of East Africa with two abominations, the slave trade and Islam. Negative accounts of Islam appear frequently in C.M.S. journals during this period.[1] Arabs were the major agents in the slave trade, which was often financed by Indians and abetted by Africans who manned the caravans and sold slaves and supplies. Hostility to Arabs rather than Indians and Africans was religiously convenient to the C.M.S. and enabled missionaries to displace some of their own collective guilt for the part Europeans had earlier played in slaving.[2] Yet the slave trade formed the foundation of the networks on which the C.M.S. relied. The same porters, paths, and supply points used by Arabs also served the missionaries. Missionaries, at first, were often befriended and protected by Arabs. The Rev. Ashe describes several such situations.[3] One C.M.S.

writer admits that "the Englishman who has troubled himself little about manners in his own country, will find himself much at a disadvantage in dealing with the polished, dignified Arab, even in the wilds of Central Africa" (Pruen 1891:254).

The missionaries considered Islam more dangerous than heathenism since it involved a supposedly degraded monotheism. Islam was associated with a "higher" culture. Conversion provided an impetus to literacy; interest in trade, crafts, and skills; and even improved hygiene, dress, and housing. To the C.M.S., Islam was demonstrably inferior to Christianity because it flourished in lands which had been subjected by Europeans. "The Arab, unlike the missionary, does not take much civilization with him, and his converts consequently get practically none" (*ibid.*:298).

Although I use the term *Islam,* this rarely appears in early C.M.S. writings which favor the term *Mohammedanism,* indicating a misconception that Muhammed had a religious function equivalent to Christ. Islam was characterized as a religion of mere form, of prohibitions rather than spiritual sincerity. "We know that Mohammedanism will give [Africans] far more license in the sins they love and cling to, than Christianity can."[4] "No doubt it is easier for the African to govern himself by the few rules set forth by Mohammeddanism [*sic*], and to control the few passions which the system insists shall be controlled, than to govern himself by the all-embracing stringent laws of Christianity" (Pruen 1891:298). Christians, because of God's favor, surpass human limitations:

> Now Mohammedanism, though it does not give its devotees the strength to fulfil its commands, yet only gives such commands as are compatible with even an African's moral strength; but Christianity, which gives commands far beyond the power of natural man to fulfil, does give with them the strength necessary for their fulfilment. God gives grace to His followers in proportion to their needs, and has promised His Holy Spirit to those of His children who ask Him. [*ibid.*:299]

Because Islam offered an "easier path" to the supposedly unrigorous and callow African, it had to be vigilantly opposed (*P.C.M.S.* 1907–1908:62). And

> it is infinitely better for the African to remain a pagan than to be given Islam as a new religion. Islam leads to the hardening of the soul, self-

righteousness, spiritual pride, a low esteem of womanhood, social disregard for non-Moslems, and a system of thought that is itself crumbling to pieces even in its strongholds before the advances of modern knowledge. [Chambers 1921:58]

C.M.S. missionaries went to some lengths to obstruct the Arab slave trade. Baxter writes from Mpwapwa:

Whenever slave caravans pass through, of which there have been several lately, and many more are expected, a few slaves generally manage to escape to us; and of course we refuse to give them up, if the Arabs ask for them, which, however, is very seldom. We have sent the names of several slave dealers who have passed on to the coast to Dr. Kirk [the consul at Zanzibar], and as a result, one, if not more, has been arrested and tried.[5]

The C.M.S. was cautioned that this might expose them to dangers that the Consul or even the Sultan himself might not be able to avert.[6] They continued to shelter sick and runaway slaves, but found it burdensome to maintain them with their scant provisions.[7] Sometimes Arabs themselves gave sick slaves to the missionaries, assuming that once these recuperated, they could be retaken since they could neither make their way home alone nor find ready acceptance locally. Female slaves posed a dilemma for the C.M.S., for "we don't know what we are to do with the women there being no ladies here to look after them."[8]

Kaguru urged the C.M.S. to fly the British flag in order to intimidate caravans,[9] but the missionaries avoided taking sides in quarrels between Arabs and Africans. When Africans pilfered Arab caravans, they asked the missionaries to defend them against reprisals, but the C.M.S. refused; to them, theft was theft. As a result, some Africans were killed. When porters in Arab caravans stole local livestock and goods, the C.M.S. dissuaded Kaguru from retaliating[10] by counselling avoidance and turning the other cheek:

On Sunday last like the Scottish covenentors of old, we had our Swahili services high up on the hills, where our poor people had to hide 3 days for fear of being taken into slavery by the Arabs who had arrived in huge numbers viz 10 with I should think between 2,000 and 3,000 porters from count.[11]

To maintain order, for a time the Sultan of Zanzibar sent small contingents of Muslim troops to Mpwapwa and later Mamboya, but their dissolute conduct and pilfering upset the missionaries nearly as much as the caravaners.[12]

Inveighing against the slave trade, the C.M.S. were perplexed that the supposedly iniquitous Arabs often still retained considerable loyalty from Africans. Pruen shrewdly observed:

> They prefer their Arab masters to their English or German deliverers, who want them to work hard, and who do not treat them as if they were fellow-country men. Their Arab masters, if already possessed of many slaves, do not require much from them; and though they will kick them one day, will sit down to a meal with them on the next, and behave as their brother or father. There is a good deal of human nature in such a preference. People of any colour prefer those who treat them as brothers to those who treat them as servants only, even though the brother be hasty and bad-tempered, and the master just and good tempered. [Pruen 1891:241–42]

When missionaries and Arabs clashed, as in Bushiri's rebellion, Muslim porters from the coast refused to help their C.M.S. employers. To the missionaries, this indicated the base nature of Islam.[13] In contrast, Bushiri considered himself a friend to the Roman Catholics east of the C.M.S., and it was through their efforts that the captured C.M.S. missionaries, Roscoe and his wife, were released (Kieran 1970). The Alsatian fathers made no formal opposition to slavery, and even bought slaves from Arabs in order to convert them.[14] In contrast to the C.M.S., they maintained self-contained stations rather than bases from which clergy would itinerate and thereby disturb local affairs. The C.M.S. saw this as a further sign that Catholics were not interested in stemming the slave trade (Bolt 1971:112).

Despite C.M.S.'s preoccupation with attacking slavery, they mainly interfered with Arabs as competitors in distributing trade goods, job opportunities, and other economic benefits. By this they disrupted a complex network of local dependencies and deterred slaving far more than by direct opposition.[15]

Whatever the reality, the C.M.S. considered its stand against slavery as proof that its motivations were altruistic and uncolonialistic:

> . . . it is from the slave-hunters among the Arabs, and not from the natives, that we wrest the authority. We dispossess no chief, subvert no humane laws, take no foot of occupied land, but replace the cruel power and overlordship of the slave-hunter by the fostering care and gentle control of a firm but tender government which gives equal rights to all its subjects. [Pruen 1891:230]

Some went so far as to argue that slavery itself was part of God's greater plan for fostering evangelism: "Humanly speaking, had they not fallen into the clutches of the cruel man-stealer, they would never have come under the sound of the Gospel" (Price 1891:21).

The C.M.S. continued to fear Islam long after the Arabs lost political and economic power. At the turn of the century, their concern was founded on the fact that for many decades the better educated Muslim coast provided the illiterate and underdeveloped upcountry with clerks, artisans, and teachers. Although Muslims were described as backward in civilization, their greater willingness to become involved in trade and other secular activities made them at first better adapted to the needs of a developing colonialism than were the C.M.S.[16]

The C.M.S. and Other Missions

The Holy Ghost fathers (or *Pères Blancs*) were the first Christian missionaries in Tanzania; these Alsatians established their station at Bagamoyo in 1863. The German Benedictines arrived on the coast in 1887 and with government encouragement set up stations both south and west of the C.M.S. They maintained that, since the C.M.S. had not yet established stations in these areas, Germans should be allowed. The Benedictines had strong backing in Germany, but the Alsatians were tolerated by the administration only after it failed to persuade church officials in Rome to replace them with Germans.[17]

The C.M.S., like all English Evangelicals, entertained a consuming hatred of the Roman Catholic Church (cf. Norman 1968:20). They contrasted "people of the Pope and people of the Book [C.M.S.]," and they referred to the Pope as a devil, to the beliefs of Catholics as "tyrannical" and "superstitious," and to Catholic missionizing as "Jesuit aggression."[18] One account even compares Jesuits to Turkish Janissaries. Another C.M.S. writer wonders whether any are under any conceivable delusions, [that] Romish missionaries are looked upon as "fellow helpers to the truth." How can this be if what they present is a caricature of the truth? [*C.M.I.* 1880:139]

casting aside all that maundering cant which labours to make out that Rome is a portion of genuine Christianity, she should be recognized in her true aspects as its avowed and persistent antagonist. [*C.M.I.* 1880:156]

Like Islam, Catholicism was thought to appeal to the Africans' weakest side:

Romanism is to a very large extent, and indeed for the mass of its adherents, a religion of rites and ceremonies, the spiritual purpose of which, when there happens to be any, the vulgar herd very dimly appreciate.[19]

Until 1912, in East Africa the Roman Catholics required only a short catechism before baptism (Richter 1934:39–40). A C.M.S. missionary once confronted a Roman Catholic priest from Ilonga (just southeast of Ukaguru) with the fact that while the Catholics did have 440 converts (far more than the handful in the C.M.S. at that time), only 20 were literate. The Protestant claimed this reflected shoddy standards. The priest retorted that one did not have to read to enter heaven.[20] The C.M.S. could not conceive of conversion without literacy since they set such store on reading Scripture, especially the New Testament. Despite this, as the years passed, Roman Catholics developed impressive educational facilities while the C.M.S. fell behind. In large part, this change in Catholic policy toward literacy relates to their quick response to the obvious demands for education set by colonial administrators, even when this might inhibit attention to evangelism. After 1912, the Church required three-year prebaptismal training (the C.M.S. never stipulated a time period) and in general considered conversion to be a gradual affair. The C.M.S., in contrast, demanded a radical alteration in Africans' lifestyle as a sign of grace and was unforgiving over serious moral lapses. Catholics set greater store in teaching the formal ideas and practices of the Church and expected occasional lapses which the institution of priestly confession was ordained to administer.[21] Leys is more critical, suggesting that because Catholics did not circulate Scripture (the New Testament being essentially radical and egalitarian), the Church could "teach an ethic suitable to the circumstances and social conditions of Africans" (Leys 1926:257). The Catholics were less involved in the open evangelism so dear to the C.M.S. but instead emphasized formal schooling. Because of the Catholic sacerdotal tradition of lifetime obedience and celibacy, a missionary might spend nearly an entire career in Africa with few if any home leaves and no distracting family. Also, unlike the C.M.S. Catholics did not hold secular life in contempt. As a telling example, the Roman Catholic church built in 1886 still stands in Morogoro, the provincial capital to which Ukaguru is attached (Johnson 1967:195), while only in the 1960s did the C.M.S. begin construction of a comparably substantial church in Ukaguru (ironically, even then it was not completed before the Catholics, who had finally gained permission to break the C.M.S. monopoly, finished an even finer building in Ukaguru).

The Roman Catholics thus contrast with the more antisecular Evangelicals such as the C.M.S. Their stations, such as the one at Bagamoyo, are described as "practical" places (Anderson 1977:10–11). By the First World War Catholic willingness to recognize materialistic needs of both Africans and administrators, as well, apparently, as better funding and staffing, led to there being six times more African Catholics than Protestants in German East Africa, even though there were only three times more Catholic missionaries (Gann and Duignan 1977:212).

The C.M.S. repeatedly published warnings of the potential dangers from Catholic inroads into East Africa, and they argued for new stations to stem the Catholic tide.[22] It was the German administration's growing encouragement of mission education which led the Roman Catholics to expand their operations. The German Governor Albrecht Freiherr [Baron] von Rechenberg was himself a Roman Catholic but seemed to care little what denomination worked an area so long as it promoted education and other practical services. In view of the C.M.S. failure to expand, he allowed the Benedictines competitive leeway. Some accounts of the resultant competition between the C.M.S. and the White Fathers and Benedictines resemble battle reports:

> . . . the old-established Roman Catholic missions at Kilossa and on the Nguru mountains became very aggressive and invaded the C.M.S. sphere of Ukaguru from the south and from the east. A determined attempt was made by them to capture many of the C.M.S. village schools, and to break up the work which the teachers were doing by means of the weekly itinerations mentioned above. At times the Roman Catholics even resorted to violence, beating the children for attending the schools of the English

> Mission, and going to such lengths as to enter the school houses and throw the books and slates they found there into the forest.
>
> The very great superiority in numbers of their European staff enabled them to have one of their missionaries always on the spot, thus placing the English Mission at a great disadvantage, since it could rarely be represented save by African teachers. The people, however, in these two countries were staunch in their adherents [*sic*] to the English Mission which had worked so long among them, and they declined to be intimidated into accepting a faith which was new to them. The teachers, too, were surprisingly bold in challenging the right of the Roman Catholic priests to fill their schools by emptying those of the C.M.S. and to make converts by force from an unwilling people; and one of their number, Marko Mutita, of Itumba, was in consequence arrested on a false charge preferred against him by Roman Catholic agents, and sentenced to a month's imprisonment. Although he had to suffer this injustice, his intervention was successful in rendering nugatory that attempt at proselytizing.[23]
>
> ... marshalling and organizing all the forces of knavery, an art in which they are thoroughly accomplished, they [Roman Catholics] seem to have deliberately set themselves the task of checkmating and confusing our every effort.
>
> ... the Roman Catholics have bribed many of the chiefs to allow them to open little preaching places and locate African agents in their villages, but ... some chiefs have refused to accept the inducements thus offered.
>
> ... in certain villages in the neighbourhood of Mamboya the Romanists have even taken possession of C.M.S. preaching places, planting small crosses on the doors to show that they have done so. Efforts were made to arrive at some agreement with the Roman Catholics as to a delimitation of spheres, but the conference arranged with the object in view proved abortive, owing to the excessive demands of the Romanists. [*P.C.M.S.* 1912–13:53]

The C.M.S. believed the Catholics were trying to cut them out of areas where they had first claims to convert (Stock 1916 IV:80). To deal with such alleged poaching, the C.M.S. decided that

> owing to the activity of the Roman Catholics it has been found necessary to establish a line of out-stations along the frontiers affected, somewhat after the fashion of the blockhouse system.[24]

The Home Committee granted extra funds for the emergency, a measure rarely taken.[25] These intense antagonisms persisted and characterized much of East African life, not just that in Ukaguru:

> It is greatly to be regretted that a spirit of jealous rivalry has manifested itself in certain districts between the Christian missions of different denominations. [*Tanganyika Report to the League of Nations for 1921:11*]

The German administration tried to reduce conflict by calling a series of meetings at Dodoma between the C.M.S. and the Roman Catholics.[26] As a result, Germans (and later the British) set up comity, or spheres of influence, for each mission group. Such partitioning by denominations had the effect of equating denominations with tribes (cf. Sundkler 1966:114–15).

In contrast to their hostility toward Catholics, the C.M.S. had civil but scant relations with some Protestant groups. For example, they were on fair terms with the U.M.C.A., which was also a branch of the Church of England, although "high" church, and which worked far to the south, though some competitive conflict is reported even between them (Bennett 1971:85). The C.M.S. also sided with German Protestants against Roman Catholics and tried to use the Berlin Mission to lodge complaints about Catholic expansion.[27] Protestant solidarity was encouraged by the Berlin Conference on Colonial Questions in 1910. That meeting led directly in 1911 to an ecumenical conference in Dar es Salaam in which the various Protestant missions in German East Africa tried to find common grounds. In the hope of promoting missionary cooperation, the German Governor gave the conference a reception at Government House and even promised some aid. The C.M.S. had sent a representative to the conference, but his reactions were uncooperatively Evangelical: for example, he feared C.M.S. converts would be corrupted by contact with missionaries who smoked and drank.[28] C.M.S. relations with other Protestant missions are unimportant in comparison with their hostility toward Catholics. This is not, however, entirely due to Evangelical anti-Catholicism. C.M.S. stations in Ukaguru and Ugogo are bounded by Catholic, rather than other Protestant, areas of comity. To the C.M.S. this appeared to be the result of deliberate attempts by Catholics to encircle them. This meant that any C.M.S. attempt to expand beyond their original area led to confrontation and complaints by Catholics. It was territoriality as much as ethnicity and dogma that divided the missions.

The C.M.S. and the Germans

Three factors accounted for the tensions that developed between the C.M.S. missionaries and the German colonialists. The most obvious was the ethnic distance epitomized by language and, more important, the chauvinistic hostilities that were long felt between British and continental Europeans. Less important was the fact that few German colonialists represented a social class comparable to that of the C.M.S. The most important factor, however, had to do with differences of aim and perspective that would have separated the C.M.S. from any government or business; that gulf separated Evangelicals from all those engaged in development of secular skills and needs. In this last respect, the alien nationality of the colonialists had a masking effect that allowed the C.M.S. to entertain the illusion that matters might be different under the British. In fact, conflicts between sacred and secular views continued and even intensified with British rule. Differences were most strikingly expressed in the educational demands which colonial governments made. An expanding administration exerted support of and controls on subservient institutions such as missions, and the overall, inevitable trend to secularization was the inevitable result of both colonial pacification and modernization in general.

When the C.M.S. arrived in East Africa, they assumed that the entire area would eventually fall under British rule as, indeed, Zanzibar, Kenya, and Uganda did. The unexpected rule of the Germans led to serious doubts about the feasibility of continuing as the only branch of the C.M.S. in Africa working outside British protection. Bishop Tucker felt that "there is reasonable fear that ultimately we may be compelled to withdraw [which] makes any considerable expenditure in this way of extension a very unwise proceeding."[29] Furthermore, there was at the time considerable anti-German feeling back in Britain.

Recent historians have characterized the early German colonial service as "unsavory" (Gann and Duignan 1977:16, 90) and observed that those in Peters's trading company and in the first wave of lower-level administration all came from the poor sectors of German society (*ibid.*:88–90). That the Germans allocated mainly military men to the early East African colonial staff probably also accounts for the harshness of their policies. Bishop Tucker complained about "the high handed way in which this country is ruled, the harsh manner in which the people are treated, the immoral way in which some Germans act in their relation with the women of this country."[30] From the first, the Germans responded vigorously to African insubordination. They believed in forced labor, in confiscation of supplies when needed, and in harsh punishment, usually public beating or hanging. The C.M.S. was appalled.[31]

Because the actual number of German officers was very few, they had to rely upon local African assistants, mainly coastal Muslims. This thin spread of personnel led to considerable discontinuity of staff, poor supervision, and a sense of distance between the senior German officers (often of the aristocracy) and their underlings (*ibid.*:88–89, 102). The Germans sought to counter their deficiencies by allowing vast discriminatory powers to local officers. In the view of the C.M.S., a few arrogant officers ruled harshly and allowed henchmen, very often coastal Swahili, to assume many powers, even to exploit local people.

Some Africans sought the missionaries as allies against the Germans. While the C.M.S. themselves emphasized that they were not Germans, they tried to serve as mediators, interpreting Germans to natives and explaining local realities to the new strangers. As one Kaguru observed, "You are different but you are the same colour and will be listened to and honoured by them whenever they meet you."[32] (Yet the C.M.S. were cautious because they had recently been expelled from the important Kilimanjaro area for just such involvement in local politics.[33] Price was typical in expressing disdain for German opinion: "I consider it rather a questionable sign when worldly men patronize and praise us or our work."[34]

Under German rule, the C.M.S. led safer lives than before but were less free. They no longer controlled their mails, could not fly the Union Jack, required government permission to travel, depended upon German goodwill for waivers of import duties, and could not harbor runaway slaves. (Germans did introduce the issuance of manumission papers to mistreated slaves.) The missionaries were required to report marriages for recording purposes and to refer all local legal disputes to the Germans or their agents. In practice, the C.M.S. tried to deal privately with petty crimes, such as theft and immorality.[35] German legal policy was a mixed blessing; earlier missionaries could try and punish their own converts within the little theocratic community of their station; but C.M.S. were wary of assuming anything approaching secular authority and in fact, had been criticized back home for doing so. Their mixture of sacred and secular aims and means were unresolvable; and although the C.M.S. carped at the Germans, nothing short of a government staffed by C.M.S. laymen would have eased their dilemma.

As the German stations at Mpwapwa and Mamboya grew in men, shops, markets, courts (with accompanying floggings), beer clubs (with the inevitable brawls), and other conveniences, the C.M.S. retreated to a greater distance both because of behavior offensive to lady missionaries and "because of the temptations to which [converts] were exposed."[36] A C.M.S. Secretary wrote that "the greatest obstacle to the reception of the Gospel by non-Christians in lands where whites live is the inconsistent lives of those whites, whom the natives naturally regard as object lessons of Christianity" (Hooper 1911:79). The new railway accelerated change, and the C.M.S. felt misgivings at the fostering of a cash economy. German control of markets and issuance of money meant new dependence for the C.M.S.[37]

Starting with von Wissmann, German administrators tended to advocate the use of indigenous Swahili institutions and language and spread them inland as useful means for subcolonization (Gann and Duignan 1977:65–66). The Germans' reliance upon Muslim agents particularly irked the C.M.S. Yet they preferred the Nubian Muslims to local Swahili since aliens were less likely to promote conversion.[38] Muslim agents frustrated C.M.S. hopes to promote a new Christian elite who would serve as role-models for Christianity. The C.M.S. maintained that African Christians had "intellectual and moral superiority . . . above the heathen and so [were] deserving different treatment from [the Germans]."[39] "It should never be possible, e.g. for Soldiers who are frequently Mohammedans and very cruel to ill-treat these people, speak ill of their education and even of the Christian Religion."[40] The C.M.S. insisted that the Germans should ask them, and not alien native agents, to enlist local labor and to distribute food during famine. They did not, however, suggest that they would help collect taxes.[41]

All negotiations between Germans and the C.M.S. were carried out in Swahili, for although the Germans had been in the area for over twenty years, the C.M.S. had made no attempt to learn their language.[42] The Bishop received a scathing reproof from the German Governor pointing out that "however suitable to the comprehension of the natives, [Swahili] is not always adapted to the clear statement of more weighty official matters amongst Europeans. . . ." He implied that the C.M.S. could not expect continued protection if they did not learn German.[43] The C.M.S. agreed to send a man to Germany for training, gratuitously adding that lady missionaries should not learn German since that would put them "in danger of being insulted, [and] at any rate they could not with propriety have business relations with such."[44] This seems odd given the high social standing of German officers by that time and their general deference toward European ladies, not to mention the freedom which lady missionaries had to interact with African servants (Gann and Duignan 1977:5, 111).

The Germans and Education

The C.M.S. feared that the Germans would promote Islam; and indeed administrators found the coastal Muslims useful since they were literate and spoke Swahili, the *lingua franca* (Iliffe 1969:52–53, 199–200; Gann and Duignan 1977:209).

> The Africans at present employed by the Government as soldiers, teachers or subordinate officials, are for the most part Swahilis and also zealous propagandists of Islam, and they carry on their propaganda all the more effectively because their official position gives them, in the eyes of the natives, the weight of authority. To remedy this state of affairs and erect a strong bulwark against the advance of Islam it is necessary that Christians should be substituted for Mohammedans as teachers, clerks, and civil servants throughout the Colony, and the Government has expressed its willingness to appoint them provided qualified men can be provided.[45]

Up to then, the C.M.S. had been criticized for paying too much attention to spiritual matters and not enough to useful skills (cf. Oliver 1952:179–80). There are frequent C.M.S. denunciations of the growing secularism within the mission, which should be "primarily and dominantly evangelistic."[46] The Germans were prepared to encourage and even to subsidize mission education if missionaries would better relate their work to secular needs for staff and would serve towns and trading centers where so far mainly Muslims seemed attentive. In 1900 the government agreed to cooperate with missions and make modest subsidies provided the mission followed a syllabus designed for training government servants and provided graduate teachers be supplied to government schools. Up to then, the C.M.S. had employed nearly all their graduates as mission teachers and evangelists, discouraging them from working elsewhere. It was this parochiality of the C.M.S., their absorption with natives in the bush areas, their mixing of evangelical with secular needs, and their formation of insulated stations that led Governor von Rechenberg to prefer Muslims to Christians (Iliffe 1969:199–200). Where missions refused to modify their aims to comply with secular needs, the government threatened to set up government schools in mission areas, staffed with coastal Muslims (P.C.M.S. 1909–10:56; cf Austen 1968:7; von Sicard 1968:330). Such government schools were more practical than those of missions (Gann and Duignan 1977:210).

Once regular colonial rule prevailed, the Germans themselves "missionized" for education. The C.M.S. wrote from Mpwapwa: "A considerable increase in the number of scholars took place in the autumn. It was due chiefly to the action of Captain Fonck, the German officer in charge of the district and a good friend of the missionaries, who continually impressed upon the Natives the advantage of being able to read and write, and urged them to attend the mission school."[47] Fonck also established a secular school at the fort and compelled some local youths to attend if they were not already in the mission.[48] In 1910 the government commanded all chiefs and their heirs to place themselves under instruction to read and write (*P.C.M.S.* 1910–11:57), and a C.M.S. missionary could remark:

> The attitude of the Government towards education has caused a widespread desire to read, and there is also a wish for the positions of influence which knowledge opens before the Africans. The result is that the people are clamouring for teachers on all sides. [*P.C.M.S.* 1912–13:51][49]

The Germans urged the C.M.S. to teach in Swahili, but Ukaguru and Ugogo were so backward that this was not always practical. At Mpwapwa the German school taught Swahili, but the nearby C.M.S. used mainly Cigogo and Chikaguru (Briggs 1918:44). The missionaries had invested much time and money in texts in the local vernacular and perhaps balked at now abandoning them. More important, however, was apparently the C.M.S. implicit association of Swahili with both Islam and secularism.[50] The administration also wanted some German taught; but since no C.M.S. knew it, this was impossible.[51] The C.M.S. hoped that the newly educated Christians might replace Muslims as government agents, forming a special "Christian Corps" segregated from both Muslim agents and other secular influences. It was expected that these agents would use their new secular prestige to facilitate evangelism, even though comparable conduct by Muslims outraged missionaries. The ensuing conflicts led the Germans to insist that Christian agents renounce all intentions of evangelizing while in government service. No such ban was ever deemed necessary against Muslims (von Sicard 1970:179).[52] Certainly C.M.S. held no respect for any ideological rights of non-C.M.S. living in their area of comity:

> Alive to the importance of having their children learn to read and write, Mohammedans asked if we would consent to teach them, minus religion, to which, of course, we could not accede, with the result that we got the children on our own conditions. [Res 1913a:154]

The C.M.S. even made the extraordinary request that Christian employees receive lower wages than other government agents so that they would not be corrupted.[53] In 1907 the administration introduced a system of local agents *(akidas)* as para-chiefly officials and asked the C.M.S. for recruits, awarding three out of five appointments to Christians.

Conclusion

The C.M.S. became ever more involved in secular affairs through its acceptance of education as the key to missionary work. The co-optation of the missions by colonial governments had two opposite effects: it made all missions more alike by making them profoundly dependent upon government for funds and even for permission to function; yet the various missions, now drawn into competition, not only among themselves but also against Muslims and purely secular institutions, sought repeatedly to describe themselves as unique in having some special spiritual and social message. The more they began to resemble one another in terms of their broader social structural positions, the more they maintained their ideological differences. In this sense, their profession of ideological differences masked their growing similarities as they were co-opted into a growing colonial infrastructure. Conversely, ethnic differences between missionaries and secular powers did facilitate the maintenance of ideological differences. It was easier for British or even Alsatian missionaries to criticize a German regime than it was for Germans, or than it would be later for British to criticize British. Although many missionary groups frequently proclaimed their liberal impulses and disassociation from secular colonialism, this alienation was easier for ethnic outsiders to manage, not only because of their national outlook but also (and more important) because those at home who supported them were hostile to national self-criticism.

7 Missionizing: Sacred and Secular Strategies and the Missionary Self-Image

THE C.M.S. ARRIVED WITH PRECONCEPTIONS about what it meant to be missionaries, about what kind of activities constituted proper evangelism, and about how to measure success. The missionaries' ideas about themselves were in part projected onto Africans and in part marshalled to define themselves as patrons to their converts. They were troubled that medical work, education, and material development related to their work, for their Evangelical character led them to dismiss broad sectors of modern life as unworthy. Yet Christianity unmistakably preaches a total commitment in social life that makes it difficult to dismiss the larger world. The C.M.S. call to evangelize abroad was rooted in spiritual revival and rejection of materialism, yet their appeal to Africans was rooted in the secular powers of the growing colonial state. Conversion, the aim and measure of mission endeavor, was an activity embodying a dangerous mixture of sacred and secular affairs, as well as a process inextricably linked to the ways missionaries defined the person. In this chapter I examine the concept of conversion mainly in terms of the missionaries' vision of themselves and their work as reflected in their policies. I postpone until later chapters consideration of how they stereotyped Africans and how they actually worked.

Missionizing and Character: the Significance of Success and Failure

Although many C.M.S. accounts convey a tone of sacrifice and altruism, strictly considered the missionaries were in the field to save themselves. Their evangelism was inextricable from their own conversion to born-again Evangelical Christianity: "Souls are dying in ignorance and sin, souls for whom Christ died. He has saved you, and has entrusted to you His remedy for their souls' sickness, and it is at His bidding you go . . ."[1] Evangelism was thus as much to build character as to convert. Failure to convert, even for decades, was seen as God's will, as a test of faith, and not as a reason either to abandon an area or to reassess methods:[2] "God knows how much humbling we need. May He have all the glory."[3] Yet some were disturbed about failure and urged moving elsewhere: "There is also this lamentable fact that although this year is the 20th anniversary of the opening of Mpwapwa as a Mission Station there is, as yet, no adult Christian or Catechumen, a native of the place."[4] In a pamphlet enlisting recruits, Cust observes that "We must find our reward in the work itself" (1892:23). One C.M.S. essay maintains that even failure confirms God's greatness (Steward 1891). Yet C.M.S. missionaries in Ukaguru were discouraged by their slow progress.[5]

Conversion itself was considered due to God's intervention rather than missionary skill:

> Had we anything short of the mighty power of the Holy Ghost to rest upon to change these people's hearts, and to draw up their minds to high and heavenly things it is abundantly evident that the task would be hopeless. But blessed be God that this is *His* work not ours. Ours is to sow the seed, *His* to make it grow.[6]

A C.M.S. Secretary contradicted himself when he compared missionizing to a well-organized military campaign, yet maintained that all strategies and mundane issues of funding and staffing were irrelevant in the face of God's will (Hooper 1911; cf. White 1977:80).

Preaching, the Holy Spirit, and the Divine Message

Evangelism involved the same steps in Africa as in England: God's word, especially scripture, was made known through preaching. The fervor and conviction behind the words were thought to convince a listener even when words were poorly understood. Even when they could not speak any African language, the C.M.S. held services and preached "the good news" (in Chikaguru, *nsachilo uswamu*).[7] Prayers, hymn singing, and the fellowship of other Christians were also thought efficacious preparation for receiving the gift of belief. The missionary's own conduct was to be exemplary so that outsiders would seek to learn what inner inspiration accounted for it; he was thus perpetually on display. Yet none of this was thought useful unless the Holy Spirit descended on both the missionary and the potential convert.[8]

> And I am especially glad to observe the very cordial and hearty way in which you seem to meet the Africans—as you very well know the human heart responds to a frank and cordial[?] manner accompanied by kind words and supported by kind action. And a thoroughly honourable conduct will go far to recommend the Gospel.
>
> Bear in mind dear Friend that the initial ideas of Christianity will probably penetrate into the minds of the heathen by examples of its life giving power. The domestic happiness of your Home will be a powerful means of touching the affectionate hearts of the people. Awaken an inspiration first in the women after a higher kind of life and the men must follow. Win the women through the children.[9]
>
> . . . these people are accustomed to get ideas into their minds through their eyes more than through their ears. Also their mutual distrust of all men leads them to attach more weight to what they see than to what they simply hear. They will watch your unwearied plodding at their language and gradual improvement in it. Your patience in conversing with them and attending to their sickness and visiting them in the villages or talking with them in the shambaas (fields) and thus by your acts rather than by your words will you convince them of your real interest in them. They will notice your evident interest in the Bible and your persistent study of it and your daily prayers and hymn singing and your readiness to give up your time to any who wish to learn to read and they will *see* how you differ from traders and themselves. They will watch your house-building and gardening etc. etc. and see that you are superior to them in knowledge and energy and are worth listening to therefore on all subjects. They will watch your treatment of your boys and men. I would therefore let them *see* what you are and how you live and I believe the Holy Spirit will in time enable them to learn such lessons through their eyes as will surprise you.[10]

The missionaries impressed Kaguru through magic-lantern shows, melodeon playing, and such wonders as pocket watches, field glasses, and guns.[11] One magic-lantern show drew three thousand.[12] Hymns and prayers were often arranged for unconverted workers employed in building.[13]

The Rev. Price describes his first halting efforts:

> I long to be able to tell you of actual missionary work. Meanwhile, we must pray the Holy Spirit to *prepare* the hearts of these people to receive the good seed. I have got quite to love the people especially the children. Some of the happiest hours I spend are when going round to the tembes [houses] trying to make myself "at home" with the people. Although I cannot say much to them, this is useful work, for it is thus we can best gain the confidence and interest of the people. Even now in some of the out-of-the-way tembes, where the white man seldom goes, the children run away terribly frightened when they see me coming. But after a bit of fun with them we soon become good friends. One little girl who was working the shamba [garden] close to the tembe where she lived upon seeing me, threw down her jembe (native hoe) and ran. I went and took up her jembe and began working a bit for her. This seemed to please her and especially her mother who was looking on, and afterwards she was well laughed at for running away. I am trying to make a regular visitation to all the tembes about here just for the reason above mentioned. You know they lie very much scattered. Of course, I am in a way "killing two birds with one stone" for one is able to get hold of a few words here and there in this way. I am afraid we have not made so much progress in the systematic study of the language just lately as I should have wished.[14]

Differences in language led to different techniques for conversation. At ethnically heterogeneous locales, formal techniques were applied to coastal Swahili speakers and caravaners; at the same time, informal, more spirit-directed techniques were applied to Kaguru whose language was poorly grasped.

> Less time than one could wish has been given to work amongst the Natives of the place, owing to our having the slave refugees and other (coast people) connected with the Mission. Although such a collection of representatives of so many tribes, most of them know more or less of Kiswahili, and in this language we convey our instructions. This consists of two services on Sundays when I use Bishop Steere's translation of the Prayer-book and Scriptures, and give them a simple address, generally on the Gospel for the day, in the morning and in the afternoon questioning them on it or other subjects.
>
> My work amongst the Wagogo and Wasagara [Kaguru] Natives of Mpwapwa has hitherto been only of the simplest character, viz. going about amongst the various scattered tembes (or as some have improperly called them villages) and talking to the little knots of people which may be found sitting about gossiping, or making their hoes and other implements.

> That great, glorious fact which was the centre of the apostles' teaching —the Resurrection, I find always secures their attention, if nothing else will. It is just the kind of thing to interest these wonder-loving people, with their ideas of magic, witchcraft, and rainmaking. To be told that a man was put to death by wicked men and then rose again, and ascended visibly into heaven, and will come again and raise them all in like manner, is so altogether new to them that their ears are at once secured, and they often repeat what I have told them to each other, as though they have really heard something new. [*P.C.M.S.* 1881–82:41]

As Rees observes, "It was not the Cross but the Resurrection which was accounted foolishness" (*P.C.M.S.* 1902–1903:102). One attempt to explain this was by analogy to the Kaguru custom of pawning kin for debts: "We know the Wamegi [Kaguru] give cows for the redemption of men, but God gave His son" (*ibid.:*103). Kaguru were called "God's runaway slaves" (*P.C.M.S.* 1884–85:42–43). Some of the missionaries even relished opposition, such as they probably encountered when evangelizing back home (*P.C.M.S.* 1892–93:45). Kaguru did find it difficult to believe in a kindly supernatural being, especially considering the frequent famines and plagues of locusts: "Our God has doubtless some wise and loving purpose in it all, but it is hard for the people to believe that He loves them under such circumstances, and one feels *so* helpless" (*P.C.M.S.* 1894–95:88).

Once converts were made, they were expected to evangelize others, presumably because they were more adept than Whites at posing doctrine in a manner consistent with local patterns of thought. The word of God was compared to the medicine of diviners (*P.C.M.S.* 1900–1901:120) or to a lighted lamp. "Even as we prepare porridge, and reserve some to eat cold on the morrow, so may this teaching give us life beyond to-day." "The things that have been taught us, help us to pick up, one by one, as does a chicken, and put them into our hearts" (*P.C.M.S.* 1902–1903:103); "Which is the better, to have a pot of boiling water and flour, or to have the pot and boiling water only? We are like the people who have the food, —you have nothing but the pot of water, which will never satisfy you" (*P.C.M.S.* 1904–1905:86). "We have brought our broken staff to Thee to be mended." "The blood of Jesus Christ is a rope that raises us up to God." "He is the hoe [preacher], Thou [God] art the Cultivator's hand upon it" (*P.C.M.S.* 1911–12:51). "May the bullet of the Word pierce and smash their bones." "We are churned now by joy, now by sorrow, like milk, out of which comes 'butter.' "[15] "In our country Darkness has long dwelt."[16] One missionary compared Jesus and converts to a chief who has his subjects cultivate his fields and then gives them a feast as a reward.[17] It was thought to be the Holy Spirit that gave these evangelists eloquence:

> Could an Atheist or unbeliever have seen that wild dance stilled simply by a man preaching the Gospel of peace, and that man an African, with no English missionary there, he could no longer doubt the power of God the Holy Spirit living in a converted Heathen. That teacher is a Mnyamwezi too (not an Mmege [Kaguru]), a fact which testifies still more that it was God alone who did the work that afternoon in the midst of all those Wamegi. [*P.C.M.S.* 1903–1904:95]

Public Confession and Revival

True conversion involved people "demonstrating their change of heart by a change of life and action,"[18] an expectation which Harries associates with Protestants more than Catholics (1953:343).[19] Since this was characteristic of Evangelicals everywhere, it set the C.M.S. somewhat apart from other Anglicans. Many C.M.S. missionaries had themselves experienced dramatic conversion or religious rebirth at revival meetings. Mrs. Watt maintained that unless one was regenerated in such a way, one should not missionize (Watt n.d.:22). Her husband had earlier been reborn at a revival led by D. L. Moody:

> My husband rejoiced daily more and more in his newly-found Saviour, and, as he travelled on railway trains and mingled with fellow-travellers in the commercial rooms of hotels throughout the country, he found great joy in humbly testifying to the power of Christ to save unto the uttermost all who would come unto Him. [*ibid.*:21]

Romans 8.16 was cited to support revival: The Spirit itself beareth witness with our Spirit, that we are children of God." As the *Book of Common Prayer* stated, "The Scripture moveth us in sundry places to acknowledge and confess our manifold sins and wickedness" *(Morning Prayer).*

To Evangelicals revival was the most dramatic way of determining whether the Holy Spirit had truly touched a person. Revival involved self-confession and often denunciation of others' misconduct. Evangelicals are a censorious lot. As Bradley writes: "Readiness to reprove any defect which one might observe in others was one of the hallmarks of true Evangelical seriousness" (1976:31). At home, the C.M.S. interpreted such behavior as rebirth of someone who was already a Christian but had grown lax or even fallen. In East Africa public confession was essential as a *rite de passage* between pagan African culture and Christianity. It was essential before a candidate would be admitted as a catechumen:

> Many very bright and encouraging testimonies were given, but what struck me as one of the most hopeful signs of a real work going on amongst them, was the humble way in which some of them spoke, and confessed that in the past they had despised and refused God. . . .[20]
>
> . . . we had special Meetings at Pentecost, and it was a time of blessing to many. One felt as if he were in a "Revival" meeting at home the workings of the Spirit and the testimonies of the people there being so similar. It was a new experience to us to see the people under evident conviction of sin, and they were wont to express their faith in it without showing any signs of penitence; but now under the teaching of the Spirit they are broken down seeking for forgiveness.[21]

Bishop Chambers lists the questions put to a catechumen, and one may readily discern how these were designed to prompt confession and denunciations:

> Do you renounce false gods and evil spirits and cleave unto the one true God and worship Him?
>
> Do you renounce sacrifice to idols, fortune telling, charms, witchcraft, heathen medicine men, the pretence of rain-making, the worship of trees and snakes, that you may worship God in spirit and truth?
>
> Do you realize that lying, thieving, blasphemy, drunkenness, adultery, and such are evil, and have you decided to foresake them and live a new life?
>
> Will you seek the quietness of a holy life instead of a life according to the lusts of the world?
>
> Will you try to bring your family and relatives to the Christian religion and earnestly endeavour to come every Sunday to hear the word of God, and mould your life and that of your family according to the teaching of Christ?
>
> Do you truly repent of all your sins, and is it your earnest desire to foresake all that is contrary to God's will and commandments?

> Do you believe on the Lord Jesus Christ as your Saviour, and do you desire to learn His doctrine and be baptized and enter His fold. [Chambers 1931:28]

Further public confession and protestation were repeated at baptism. Once the missionaries had established a body of local followers, two African members of the congregation were also asked to testify publicly to the candidates' sincerity and worth and to pledge supervision of their continued moral development.

> After services in the church, we went to the river, where a place had been deepened in the sandy bed for the purpose.[22] After prayer, singing, and a short address, the Christians took their places on one side of the river, and the candidates and every one else on the opposite bank. I then asked them the usual questions, explaining that the "works of the devil" included all their heathen customs, rites, and beliefs, and after each had given a satisfactory answer, I stood in the water and called them to me one by one. They knelt down in the water, and after the baptismal formula, were put completely under water; then after being signed with the cross, went over to join the band of Christians on the other side. (*P.C.M.S.* 1892–93:45)

The service closed with the hymn, "O happy day that fixed my choice."

While public confession was essential to denote proper conversion, it was equally important in revival. "There must first be tired believers before they can be revived" (McGavran 1970:170). In this sense, revival comparable to that in Britain and America could occur only after Africans had been converted and then strayed. ". . . joy shall be in heaven over one sinner that repenteth, more than over ninety and nine just persons, which need no repentence" (Luke 15.7). Revival allowed a congregation to revalidate publicly certain norms which had been threatened; it also allowed readmission of persons who had been judged unfit for mission life, but whose skills were essential. More recently, it had allowed ambitious and aggressive members to question the existing system of rank and influence within the mission.

Public confession of sin reminds everyone of the conduct which defines group membership. It thus resembles traditional Kaguru confession of witchcraft and sorcery and public rectification of slights and wrongs during divination of misfortune and at funerals. In the case below, the mission saw such confession in terms of reaffirming morality. The dismissed teacher probably agreed to public humiliation in hope that at a later time he might be readmitted to the mission (in that time the mission could prevent him from finding comparable employment with government):

> There reaches me to-day the sad news that one of our teachers has been dismissed from his office for adultery. "It was the only thing that I could do," writes the missionary, "as there were all the students to think of and his example counted for so much. There was no doubt about his guilt. I took him and his wife to the station to send them to their home by train. Before we went we had a service of humiliation and warning for I felt the shame of it all before the local people. All the students met in the chapel. I spoke and then the two native assistant teachers spoke. We then read the Litany and had special prayer with an hour of absolute silence, until evening chapel. I think an impression was made." [Chambers 1931:34–35]

From the earliest days of mission work in Ukaguru, Africans working for the mission occasionally lapsed from the strict standards set by the mission.[23] After public confession they were forgiven and sometimes given back their jobs. If they refused, they were expelled.

The local mission council passed repeated resolutions demanding that employees abstain from alcohol and use of native medicines and that all Christians avoid dances and other traditional ceremonies (*P.C.M.S.* 1924–25:15). The mission encouraged drinking tea in place of beer.[24] Teachers were not allowed even to be present where beer was drunk. First offenders were sometimes put on a year's probation if they publicly confessed.[25] At the first interdenominational missionary conference held in German East Africa in 1911, only the C.M.S. was adamant that no teacher convicted of adultery be allowed ever to teach (Wright 1971:127–28). The C.M.S. insisted on observation of the Sabbath, urging even those who were still unconverted not to work or feast (*P.C.M.S.* 1882–83:42). In short, the C.M.S. enforced a "serious" life of abstinence and rectitude on all employees.

More recently, Kaguru teachers convicted of sin (drink and adultery) were dismissed only to be readmitted after they exhibited remorse by publicly proclaiming their sins during revival meetings (Beidelman 1971b:123–25). The C.M.S. could in this way readmit useful members of the native staff without jeopardizing their high moral standards. Indeed, they could cite the parable of the prodigal son, more cherished than his brothers because he returned from sin.

Revival also served as spectacle and in this sense excited keen interest in Christian congregations. A former General Secretary of the C.M.S. even admitted: "Long Christian experience suggests that exhibitionism, prurience and superficiality lurk in the shadows of this particular discipline" (Warren 1954:73).

Although public confession has always been a feature of C.M.S. work in East Africa, revival took on special prominence in the 1930s and again in the 1940s; that prominence has continued into the present.[26] Spurts of revival appear related to tensions within the local missionary church, the result of dissatisfaction and frustration among local, ambitious African Christians who feel they have not received sufficient rewards or recognition within the church. Through revival and the resultant assumption of new, superior moral status as "saved" or "reborn" Christians—Kaguru referred to themselves in 1958 as *wangofu* (Swahili, "ones who have been broken down")—local Africans could sometimes compete with local African pastors, catechists, and even European missionaries as the type of Christian most fit to judge and lead others.[27] As Evangelicals, the C.M.S. were ideologically committed to revival, yet they could not easily control such activities. Revivals were led by those who themselves had been redeemed by revival, but European missionaries were reluctant to confess serious error and could not therefore be revived in the spectacular manner some Kaguru chose.

The first mention of C.M.S. revival in East Africa comes from Buganda in 1894; by then a sufficient number of Africans were converted and restless within the conventional mold of the mission church (Tucker 1911:143). In the 1930s, after the turmoil of the First World War and with the difficulties of the depression, the C.M.S. experienced "conventions for the deepening of spiritual life" (*P.C.M.S.* 1932–33:7). Local groups gathered to pray, fast, confess, and urge a return to simplicity. Revivalists moved about the countryside with their followers, relatively independent of either local African pastors or missionaries. Bishop Chambers of Tanganyika was so uneasy about this threat to authority that in 1939 he toured the spiritually agitated areas to dampen enthusiasm (Sibtain 1968:84–86).

Attending a Kaguru revival is similar to attending pagan Kaguru therapeutic conventions, such as a meeting where witch finders seek out supposed witches. Both pagans and Christians reflect diverse motives. For some, meetings are cathartic, allowing confession and recommitment to the group; for others, the meetings exacerbate antagonisms and further separate competing and dissident individuals. The C.M.S. writer Taylor praises revivalism's reaffirmation of the laity and attack on the conventional clerical hierarchy. The Holy Ghost can possess anyone regardless of rank; to Taylor, this represents a local protest against a centralized, diocesan structure (1958a:101–104; 1958b:16). Warren expressed misgivings over the danger of setting up an exclusive, "spiritual elite" within a larger church. During the last World War, some East African revivalists professed pacifism despite Anglican support of the war effort. Warren, like Taylor, notes revivalism's divisive results (Warren 1954:25, 68–69, 81; 1974:200).[28] The Catholic writer Jassy notes that revivalism has hurt East African Anglicans since revivalists conceive of themselves as superior to local pastors or diocesan authorities (1973:67–68). Certainly revival in Ukaguru frequently bypassed European control. When it did so, it was through traveling, charismatic leaders who exploited local dissension which African pastors had been keeping under precarious control.

Contradictory interpretations of revival are consistent with the C.M.S.'s and other Evangelicals' own ambivalence. One part of the C.M.S., that which was committed to the Holy Ghost's divine intervention over reason and hierarchy, endorsed revival. Another side, that associated with paternalism and colonialism, distrusted any egalitarian, popular movement. Revival may have heightened ties within some local groups, but it weakened the broader fabric of the church. Its most useful function was in allowing the C.M.S. to readmit lapsed but needed members, such as teachers and artisans, without apparently taking a lax position on morals.

Healing: Science and Religion Conjoined

Missionary medical practices provide a useful area for examining the relationship between modern, scientific technology and the religious faith to which it is often assumed to be antithetical. Although the C.M.S. resisted modern education and technical training, the mission provided medical care as part of its work (Stock 1899 III:309–10). As early as 1892, the C.M.S. had a medical secretary supervising such work (Anderson 1948:5). For Christians, health and wholeness involve both physical and spiritual well-being; and for many C.M.S., moral and spiritual inadequacies were reflected in physical ills. Medical skills were always considered subordinate to those of "Christ Himself the Good Physician,"[29] and illness was "the sweat of Sin in Adam" (*P.C.M.S.* 1906–1907:76). Health was thus an external sign of inner salvation (Dougall 1946). Missionaries' conflation of physical and moral states parallels ideas of African and other preliterate societies.[30]

Medical work was presented as the kind of selfless labor which epitomized Christian life and set an example to the heathen (Tucker 1911:237). It also served as an opportunity to evangelize. The C.M.S. assumed that a missionary doctor was able "by caring for the bodies and by alleviating the pain and suffering, to incline the hearts of the people to receive the World of Life for their souls. . . ."[31] Medicine was combined with prayer and the expectation of miraculous phenomena:

> All medical mission work is but part of the Gospel of full redemption of body, mind, and spirit. As the patients wait to be treated, the opportunity is taken to set before them the way of life in Christ Jesus. The love of Christ is revealed to them in the New Testament which is read and explained, and God's help is sought in prayer for His blessing on the sick, for guidance in every operation and for the effective use of the medicines given. When patients are past human aid, the direct and immediate healing power of God is asked for, often with results which to the world are inexplicable. . . . Sometimes in accordance with apostolic practice the laying on of hands accompanies prayer, and health of body and mind as well as of soul and spirit is restored. [Chambers 1931:52]

The official C.M.S. position was put in its medical journal, *Mercy and Truth* (Lankester 1897:247):

> They will not object to a prayer to God to give the physician skill and bless the medicine, and in the course of days, rather than months or years, large numbers will come to the dispensary. A small charge for medicine supplied often tends, if anything, to give more confidence, and the amount received is often a real help toward defraying the cost of the work. As the demand for his services increases, he is able to lay down more definite conditions as to the preaching of the Gospel before the patients are seen, and thus very soon the doctor has a daily opportunity of making his message known, it may be, to a hundred people, seated quietly in a room, who either have already good reason to be grateful to him, or who are expecting him to do something for them. . . .

Medical work was subsidiary to the real work of proselytizing, and medical missionaries were cautioned not to confuse their priorities by curing more at the cost of converting less (Lankester and Broune 1897:219).

In Ukaguru the missionary doctor was expected to preach and provide religious instruction along with medical care, to use

> the opportunities afforded him by his medical practice . . . to "point out the deadly character of sin's disease, and the need of the Great Physician" (*P.C.M.S.* 1882–83:52).[32]

Outpatients were assembled for a short Gospel service before treatment, and the doctor and African staff conducted services and Bible-reading classes each morning and evening. Patients were encouraged to declare their faith and admit their sins with the implication that these were related to their ill health (*Mercy and Truth* 1898:193–94; 1903:229–30; 1913:88–91).[33] Such practices could still be observed in 1957–58.

Smallpox epidemics in 1892 and 1909 afforded the C.M.S. exceptional opportunities for preaching. Dr. Baxter and his native assistants vaccinated and preached to between eight and ten thousand during the second epidemic (*Mercy and Truth* 1911:204–205).[34] Yet Kaguru were suspicious and at times "hardly any gratitude was shown by the patients" (*P.C.M.S.* 1903–1904:96). Kaguru better understood paying for such services and traditionally saw no enduring moral relation between patient and curer. Still, for a long time the aged and sick were the majority of C.M.S. converts in Ukaguru and Ugogo (*P.C.M.S.* 1906–1907:76).

Medical work involved far more than costs of staff, medicine, and equipment; missionaries provided housing, food, and clothing for patients and staff and accommodated patients' kin who came to tend them. A doctor was expected to supervise the construction of facilities (Pruen 1891:307,cf. *P.C.M.S.* 1901–1902:108). Until long after World War I, wards, dispensaries, and staff housing were mud-and-wattle buildings. Outpatients were interviewed outdoors, and a bedstead with a door atop was an operating table. At this time, the C.M.S. tried to provide medical services outside the immediate mission area, first by an itinerating doctor and later through native assistants with rudimentary training. At the outbreak of the First World War, the hospital at Mamboya had 12 beds, served 24 inpatients and 2,582 outpatients, and performed 61 operations a year (*P.C.M.S.* 1912–13:254). After the war the Mamboya hospital was abandoned for ones at Kongwa and later Berega. In recent times, medical services were concentrated at those two hospitals; and with improved transportation, outpatient attendance increased vastly. During British rule, the C.M.S. set up leper treatment stations on the fringes of southeastern Ukaguru. Shortage of funds hindered development although both Germans and British contributed modest subsidies for C.M.S. medical work.

After World War II, the C.M.S. rethought its medical policies since they could not compete with government, even with government support (Anderson 1948:15–23). Many held to the long criticized notion that medical service, in and of itself, justified such work (Anderson 1956:3). An official position-paper urged workers to return to "medical evangelism" (Anderson 1948:15) and to strive for "spiritual healing" of the "whole man" (Anderson 1956:22–23). The C.M.S. continued to maintain its hospital and dispensary at Berega; indeed, they expanded and improved their facilities during the time of my fieldwork (1957–58, 1961–63). Paul White's long series of Jungle Doctor books (all set in Tanganyika and most in Ukaguru and Ugogo) are the most popular and compelling propaganda works in C.M.S. literature. The idea of healing, manifested in Christ's example, the body as well as the soul, remains a central theme in C.M.S. thought. Yet medical staff are still warned never to let medical values subsume religious ones. In this, C.M.S. appear at odds with all but the most radical forms of contemporary medicine. However, perhaps they are not so different in actual practice since medicine is always applied in the context of broader social values.

Education and Its Relation to Evangelism

Since the C.M.S. considered daily reading of the Bible and related works essential to Christian life, converts had to be taught to read. It was further assumed that such study would involve a Bible written in an African vernacular and not in English. Consequently, the first missionaries hastened to learn local languages not only so that they could preach to and converse with natives, but also so that they could translate Scripture. Ideally, the Bible would be translated into every language spoken where the C.M.S. worked. In practice, this was done only when sufficient numbers existed to merit it. By 1879, Baxter and Last claimed to have "mastered" Chikaguru (*P.C.M.S.* 1879–80:27), but it was eventually decided that too few Kaguru existed to justify such labor.[35] Although early workers translated parts of the New Testament, the catechism, hymns, and prayers, it was finally decided that Swahili should serve workers in Ukaguru.[36] Before that time, simple texts were printed locally in both Chikaguru and neighboring Cigogo, on a press which the mission acquired at Mamboya in 1883 (*P.C.M.S.* 1883–84:48). The extensive ethnic mixture in Ukaguru encouraged missionaries to consider the *lingua franca* Swahili the best choice. By 1910, although some sermons at Mamboya were delivered in Chikaguru, the sacraments and other rituals were in Swahili, based on standardized translations of texts.[37] Another reason for preferring Swahili was that if a missionary were transferred, Swahili could still be used; a local language could not. By the time of British rule, almost no mission work was carried out in Chikaguru, and even in Ugogo most C.M.S. worked exclusively in Swahili. By 1925, Swahili became the government-sanctioned language for all education (Buell 1965 I:478–79).

It is odd that few C.M.S. missionaries in Ukaguru raised the question of using a European language for instruction.[38] The German colonial administration had urged that some natives receive instruction in German, but nothing came of this. With British rule, the C.M.S. taught some English at the higher levels (Standard IV and beyond),[39] but this was no result of mission policy. The mission associated European languages with the corrupting forces of materialism which the African would find difficult to handle. When English entered the C.M.S. curriculum in Ukaguru, it did so because of government pressure. Like the Germans, the British required literate natives to assist administration. Fostering local languages was antithetical to a useful labor force that might be transferred about the country and had to work with a European staff. In keeping with the British notion of Indirect Rule, the *lingua franca* Swahili served such purposes while allowing some barrier between Africans and European culture. Thus, even when English was taught, nowhere in Africa did the British encourage a commitment to a European language in the way that the French or Portuguese had done (Crowder 1964).

Reluctance to promote English was a symptom of a wider C.M.S. attitude toward "advanced" education. Basic reading and writing skills in Swahili sufficed for Bible-reading and religious study. Knowledge of

Swahili also facilitated learning the simpler skills in farming, animal husbandry, and crafts which were considered the proper domain of Africans.[40] It, along with some arithmetic, was sufficient for the convert's needs toward an anti-materialistic, Christian life. While the mission justifiably feared the intrusion of modern education into their assigned tasks, even government agreed with Bishop Chambers that "religion is the fundamental element in all true education" (Chambers 1931:49). The Education Conference in Dar es Salaam, which was held to consider greater government support for missions, stated that religious education was essential to ensure "the formation of character and habits of discipline" (*P.C.M.S* 1903–1904:98).

From the beginning, the C.M.S. saw its new literate converts not as fodder for a growing administrative and mercantile organization but as new missionaries, as hoes preparing the soil of conversion for their fellows.[41] They were sent to preach and teach. Small huts were built for itinerating workers; that Kaguru erected these voluntarily indicated their desire for education more than eagerness for the gospel. In the dry season, classes were held outdoors where large cloths were hung bearing printed letters and syllabic exercises. By 1903 there were thirteen schools in central Ukaguru besides the one at Mamboya. These out-schools varied in quality with their distance from the mission station: those that were closest met three times a week; those farther away, weekly; those most distant, only fortnightly. By 1909 seventeen schools outlay Mamboya. Outstation work was almost entirely by native teachers.[42] Itinerators went on monthly circuits, spending insufficient time in any place to establish rapport.[43] As a result there was a growing gap between mission doctrine and what was locally believed.

A review of the C.M.S. (Ukaguru) educational syllabus for 1909 provides a guide to what the C.M.S. considered sufficient for Kaguru needs when the C.M.S. was under only moderate pressure from administration to provide secular skills. (The syllabus is discussed in detail in an appendix to this chapter.)[44] The students were divided into four grades; those led to admission to the church.

Those who sought instruction were considered to be on moral probation; religious beliefs and character were emphasized as much as reading, writing, and arithmetic (C.M.G. 1887:40). Pruen gives a vivid account of early classes:

> When a native becomes an inquirer, the usual plan is for him to join a Bible class for beginners, which would meet perhaps twice a week for the purpose of reading the Bible together and of prayer. The class for men and boys would be conducted by the missionary, and for women and girls by his wife. Both men and boys take their turn in reading and in leading prayer—very different from the practice in England, where a boy's shyness and self-consciousness would usually keep him from praying in front of others. But natives, as we have seen, are quite accustomed to living their whole lives in front of others, and have never yet heard of people being ridiculed for religious beliefs or observances whether these observances be heathen, Mohammedan, or Christian. [Pruen 1891:281]

The terms which the missionaries used for different stages of Christianized Africans changed through the years. Here is the clearest account:

> In the diocese we have four classes of men and women who are definitely distinguished from the pure heathen folk:—(1) The hearer, who comes for instruction but is not ready to avow himself an inquirer, and to renounce Heathenism publicly at a service. (2) The inquirer [sometimes also called a probationary agent] who has openly made a renunciation of idolatry, witchcraft, and so forth, and professed, in a public service, an earnest desire to find God and to be saved by His Blessed Son. (3) The catechumen who has gone much further, publicly, at the service for admission of catechumens, and stands before men as a Christian in life and profession though not admitted to the privileges of the Church. (4) After six months of probation the catechumen is baptized and enters the fourth great class of Christian. This extreme care to keep the Sacrament of Baptism from being dishonoured by seemingly fit but really unready "inquirers," as in days gone by, will, we trust, bear fruit, and give, perhaps, a better chance of reading a man's character, as well as of testing his steadiness in the face of the sensual temptations which are Africa's great snare. [*C.M.I.* 1904:119]

Earlier it had not been clear whether newly baptized Africans should be automatically admitted to the Eucharist[45] since the C.M.S. prided itself on setting what it considered to be higher standards than those of the Roman Catholics. They considered that the Catholics baptized too freely.

As the 1909 syllabus indicates, educational emphasis—even when the subjects taught were Swahili, geography, and history—was religious. Lack of Chikaguru translations for most Christian texts, as well as absence of general textbooks in Chikaguru, made it inevitable that after preliminary studies, work was in Swahili. Therefore successful Kaguru converts were fairly sophisticated in Swahili. This was the most powerful tool which missionaries provided Kaguru and their neighbors for understanding the outside world.[46]

C.M.S. educational standards applied essentially to men. While women were encouraged to read and write so that they could study scripture, they received instruction mainly in "mothercraft," tasks related to domestic life (Hodgshon 1928:32). Furthermore, it was considered unseemly to teach the opposite sex, so girls' education languished when women teachers were few. When the first missionary-wife (Mrs. Last) arrived, she began teaching sewing,[47] which was considered important since the missionaries were keen to see the seminude Kaguru clad in cottons. Child care was also stressed:

> A mother's meeting is held most Tuesday mornings when, after instruction has been given in sewing, the meeting goes with a short talk to women on the homelife and the bringing up of their children. A junior class is also held the same day with instruction in sewing and a little talk after, sometimes some singing of the Canticles to help them to join in the Service on Sunday morning.[48]

> One cause for thankfulness is that the women of our Mission Station have at last learned to feed their new-born infants properly. Hundreds of infants die through the old women insisting on their being fed on porridge of flour and water which is forced into their mouths, but thank God our Christian women have learnt that this is unnatural wrong and cruel. . . .[49]

In general, female education fell behind that for males; as late as 1937 there was no girls' secondary school in all of the colony (Hailey 1938:1242).

Materialistic Enterprise and Its Relation to Evangelism

Although no missionaries questioned the evangelistic value of some work in medicine and education (cf. Anonymous *C.M.G.* 1920:57), the C.M.S. resisted any endeavor related to commerce or industry. Some even sought special guidance, through prayer and Bible study, in how to handle money without becoming mercenary (*C.M.G.* 1907:179). Today the

C.M.S. runs modest shops, originally intended to sell educational or medical supplies but now also carrying other items. When compared with huge Roman Catholic stations with their own electric plants, lumber mills, furniture shops, and stores, C.M.S. ventures into trade and commerce appear timid. Yet from their arrival, it was clear to the C.M.S. that Kaguru sought contact in order to gain access to European goods and skills and that displays of material benefits served as powerful magnets to attract potential converts.[50]

When the mission work expanded, local workers suggested that they might be better employed teaching, preaching, and administering than in supervising construction work. The Rev. David Deekes, for example, complained that he built five houses and several churches during his career in Ukaguru (1900:125). Yet requests for artisans were always rejected as too costly,[51] and local Africans were given little relevant training. Missionaries also wanted a store because it would draw many to the station:

> The Missionaries have long felt the need for a Mission store where our Native Christians would be able to buy everything they require at a reasonable rate, and not be obliged to patronize the shops which are almost entirely owned and run by Mahometans, and where they can rarely get a fair value for their money. A Mission store will tend to counteract Mahometan influence, and our Christians will not be seen (as has sometimes been the case) wearing garments with Mahometan marks and devices printed thereon.[52]

It was even hoped that the missionaries might sell frocks to the natives to get them out of pagan garb.[53] The mission did introduce the first sewing machines into Ukaguru in 1909, and some Kaguru were taught to use them.[54] The Home Committee continued to reject the idea of a store; they argued that its supervision would take too much of the missionaries' time (no such argument was raised against long hours spent constructing buildings and roads).[55] Yet such a shop was eventually established, although run by natives:

> The capital to finance this undertaking was supplied by a voluntary levy of 6 sh. from a certain number of the Christians, and the capital as well as all the profits are regarded as dedicated to the services of God. (*P.C.M.S.* 1922-23:15).

The missionaries eventually accepted the fact that African converts and staff often could not succeed without some involvement in outside secular economic affairs:

> . . . in Momboya [*sic*] there is much to contend with, there's much "going and coming" among the people over teachers as many of them gain their living by selling flour to workmen on the railway, then the cultivating and harvesting are hindrances at other times, also it is difficult to get the same people continuously, and we have to be content with slow progress.[56]

Steady work was essential for an African to be a proper Christian and maintain a respectable style of life, but this tended to involve controlled wage-labor rather than entrepreneurial trade:

> . . . the one thing most wanting [for the African] is "stability"; and where the young are committed to the missionary charge, as in the case of freed slave children, most would agree that they should be trained up in regular habits of industry, the few who show special aptitude being perhaps given a literary training, but the majority being brought up to do mechanical work, and as far as possible, apprenticed to different trades. [Pruen 1891:209–10]

The missionaries applied a double standard regarding material needs. They preached spiritual brotherhood but considered poverty a relative matter. By European standards they were poor and considered themselves altrusitic, but they appeared prosperous to Kaguru:

> In a most emphatic sense "Their God is their belly" [a quote from Krapf]. . . . They are indeed, at any rate most of them the veriest mendicants one could well meet with. I find it best to laugh at their begging propensities, telling them they ought to be ashamed to beg from a poor man like myself, when they have all their flocks and herds. Happily, the Dr. has all the cloth in his own charge, so that I am able to tell them I have nothing to give them. They then point to my boots and hat as evidence that I must be a rich man. I tell them I have riches, but they are in heaven, and I have come to show them the way to that happy place. Sometimes after asking if they have understood me, they reply, "Yes, give me some cloth, bwana."[57]

During the final years of colonial rule, mission employees such as clerks, teachers, and nurses were forbidden investment in secular business. Such separation always applied to Europeans; and as the Africans became more prosperous, the same renunciation was expected of them, even though, with an increase in wealth, their demand for profit in trade and business grew. For a small group, there were rewards of employment within the mission, which, after the government, was the largest cash employer in Ukaguru.

Unfortunately (in terms of mission ideals), the advantages of education and medical treatment appear secondary to the final goal of improved material life. Although the reasons for missionaries' success do not derive directly from those activities which the C.M.S. itself considered their primary concern, even secular authorities, who were responsible for encouraging these trends, recognized that antimaterialistic beliefs fostered by the mission shored up the colonial establishment.

Secularization of the Mission: Its Implications for Evangelism

The most observant missionaries recognized serious dangers in the growing endorsement of social services within the C.M.S. Their fears were rooted in questions about the relation between the mission and other aspects of society. Some missionaries saw the church as properly concerned only with spiritual matters;[58] others observed that all social life, from religion to agriculture, is of one piece. Ironically, nearly all heathen accepted this latter religious truth, but many C.M.S. thought that religion should exclude many other aspects of everyday life.[59]

The C.M.S. opposed development of "nonreligious" services, however practical or humanitarian, if they did not directly bear on evangelism. In 1894, Cust, one of the C.M.S.'s most influential early theorists, wrote:

> I am entirely in favour of the Lay Evangelist, the Female Evangelist, the Medical Evangelist, whenever Gospel-Preaching is the substantial work; but when it is proposed to have a pious Industrial Superintendent, or an Evangelical tile-manufacturer, or a low Church breeder of cattle or raiser of turnips, I draw my line.[60]

Medicine remained the only scientific skill readily accepted as an adjunct to evangelism, apparently on the assumption that curing still involved some element of supernatural intervention. In any case, it was never to be an end in itself.

J.H. Oldham, Secretary of the influential International Missionary Council, was the most prominent advocate of broader, more secular attitudes among C.M.S. and other missionaries.[61] His views were strongly supported in government and some mission circles through the African tours and publications sponsored by the Phelps-Stokes Fund, which was led by T. Jesse Jones, an American educator. Oldham and Jones had to convince two camps, missionaries who feared secularism in general and government interference in particular and colonial administrators who disliked mixing politics with denominationalism and who doubted the missionaries' intentions and abilities to provide education suitable to the growing secular needs of the colonies. Jones urged that government support would bring better funding and a new sense of rational organization and supervision that would raise educational standards, heighten appeal to Africans, and reduce interdenominational competition.[62] The C.M.S. welcomed Jones's emphasis on Christian education, yet feared secular taint: "How difficult this is every experienced missionary can tell. To attempt to co-operate with an evil-living official or with a rapacious trading company is indeed hard, and yet there is no other way to achieve the adjustment prescribed by such authorities" (Loram 1923:159). In Britain in 1902, similar proposals for government subsidies to and control of education, long monopolized by the church, prompted disagreement of the same sort (Norman 1976:205–209).[63]

According to Oldham, both government and missions would benefit. Yet the C.M.S. feared that more secularly educated Africans would become materialistic and dissatisfied; colonial authorities felt much the same but were willing to run the risk. Many in both camps worked on the assumption that "both Government and the Churchmen realize that a good African is a Christian" (Reid 1934:199). Training in various tasks such as gardening, carpentry, and home economics were thought to ensure the development of character (Jones 1924:12), whereas an "overeducated" African would become restless and misbehave (Cust 1889:7).

> The C.M.S. Mission in Tanganyika Territory has never attempted Higher Education for its converts. It has been thought sufficient for a Christian native to be able to read his Bible intelligently in the Vernacular, to know how to write a letter, if need be, and to be able to do simple arithmetical calculations. A rather similar standard has been accepted for junior teach-

> ers, and it is only the selected few who have passed through the Huron Training College [at Kongwa] and reached a higher level [still not in English].[64]

Opposition to collaboration between government and mission persisted among some Evangelicals and also among liberals like Leys (Cell 1976:287–90). Such opposition had a long tradition among British Evangelicals (Kitson Clark 1973:73). They were particularly concerned whether religious instruction could be part of the official curriculum, a policy hardly acceptable to a British government proposing to subsidize Catholics and Lutherans as well as Anglicans (Wright 1971:126). The C.M.S. in particular feared the closing of evangelistic bush schools which could not meet higher requirements.[65] In this the new educational policies were thought to undercut evangelism. In part, such fears were well founded. Religion was not to be taught in classrooms; bush schools were to be closed within five years; remaining schools would be upgraded at much expense; and no new schools were to be built without government permission.[66] While government subsidies supported part of the upgrading, missions became dependent upon government since they could not maintain the new level without further support (Hewitt 1971:187, 197, 332, 427). With better educated teachers, African catechists were devalued. Worse still, African pastors declined in prestige if their standard of education was below that of the new African teachers and clerks (Oliver 1952:278–79; Taylor 1958b:85). In time, even some teachers became outclassed, for by 1938 skilled cooks and third-class constables earned more than Grade-A primary teachers (Hailey 1938:1252). Some maintain the government subsidization presented another problem: Africanization of mission staffs was more difficult under government control than if it were determined unilaterally by a mission (Oliver 1952:282). Worst of all, the C.M.S. had to spend more to get more. Government funds were available only if the educational qualifications of staff were raised radically; this requirement presented new costs in training and in recruiting since such Africans expected higher salaries.[67]

The most eloquent and persuasive Anglican critic of the new secularization was Roland Allen. To him, anything that distracted missionaries from evangelism was to be dismissed.[68] The C.M.S. took Allen's views so seriously that their major historian and theoretician rebutted him in a long article (Stock 1912). The C.M.S. might not have survived in East

Africa without government subsidies—although there are people who deny that even today (Hewitt 1971:432). What the C.M.S. probably resented most was not their loss of independence but their realization that the religious beliefs which they had promoted did not correspond to the realities around them.

It is difficult to secure documents in which East African colonial administrators express their views about working with missionaries. The most useful account of official policies on mission education in Tanganyika is in Lord Hailey's magisterial survey:

> ... expenditures on staff should be the basis upon which governments calculate their grants in aid of mission schools. This policy, however, immediately encounters the difficulty, that mission teachers rarely expect to be paid the full salaries which they could command if they were not giving their services from other motives. This difficulty, it is suggested, can be overcome if the government assumes for the purpose of the grant, that the missionary body is paying a certain salary for a certain type of qualified teacher. If, then, the mission and the teacher agree on a lower salary, the balance of the grant may be used by the mission for other educational expenditures. The Commission on Education in East Africa expressed itself as extremely doubtful about the wisdom of this provision. It has not, in practice, proved possible to enforce the provision that mission staffs must possess qualifications equal to those of the government education service. As standards rise, however, this question of securing adequately qualified staff in mission schools is becoming increasingly difficult: it may be expected to present the governments with complex administrative problems, and even more to impose a great strain upon the resources of the missions in money and in personnel. [Hailey 1938:1237]

Subsidies were sometimes used for evangelistic rather than educational purposes, and government controls were often ineffective given the size of the country and shortage of inspectors. One example from Ukaguru suggests that the problem involved incompetence in all quarters, government as well as mission. When the government agreed to subsidize a Teacher Training School, the C.M.S. appointed an aged missionary with no training in education. The government education officer complained, not about academic failings, however, but that the appointee was too old to supervise football; the officer viewed that as the *sine qua non* of education.[69]

The C.M.S. felt that they merited special consideration because they provided services for altruistic reasons, and therefore more cheaply than alternative civil employees:

> . . . it is most important that all parties engaged in promoting educational co-operation should frankly acknowledge and steadily remember that technical efficiency is not the only thing, nor is it indeed the chief thing, that missionary educationists must care for. They have gone to Africa, as one of our bishops has reminded us recently, first and last to do religion's work. They regard educational work as part of that religious work, and as in many ways a means to it, but in no sense whatsoever as a substitute for it. For this they have been willing to surrender the adequate salaries they were earning in English schools, their hope of satisfactory pensions in due course, and a hundred other advantages which were none the less real because they held them lightly. [Spanton 1928:108]

The difference in salaries between Europeans employed in missions and those in government was bearable to zealous missionaries but to few Africans. Differences in the salaries of Africans employed by the C.M.S. and the salaries of those in nearby government service were a source of intense dissatisfaction, especially since transfer between the two systems was difficult and mission comity led to its near monopoly of jobs in parts of Ukaguru. Once, when African agents, led by growing inflation, sought modest raises in pay, they were rebuked for their "discourteous and avaricious spirit."[70]

Government subsidies caused soul-searching and controversy among both missionaries and administrators. Yet neither side devoted much time to considering how Africans themselves judged these arrangements. Kaguru certainly favored more secular, improved education and the expansion of schools, but it did not matter to them whether these came from missions or government provided quality and costs were equal.

Conclusion

The C.M.S. never varied in maintaining that its only goal was evangelism and that all other work, however beneficial, was only a means to that end. Medical work was not to improve Kaguru health so much as to secure attention for evangelizing. European material goods were used to attract Kaguru attention, but this was considered a cheap and degrading method. Education was admitted as necessary for religious study and to attain a minimal standard of living that would not offend European sensibilities. Beyond these considerations, medicine and education were dangers drawing attention from the "real" work. As Evangelicals, the C.M.S. were profoundly suspicious of all materialistic and secular influence from government and business. Yet as the colony developed, they were unavoidably co-opted into these sectors; indeed, that they were subsidized and encouraged at all was only because they provided cheap, readily available services to a government short of funds. The C.M.S. sold its services, compromised its ideals, and restricted its geographical expansion in exchange for funds and the guarantee of a monopoly in the areas it already occupied. Ironically, while the C.M.S. viewed these changes as, at best, inevitable compromises, and, at worst, a betrayal of their original goals, their co-optation into the broader, secular world is the main factor accounting for any success that they had in converting Kaguru. As Evangelicals committed to the primacy of religion separate from much of everyday life, they tended to ignore those very features of European life that most attracted Kaguru, economic and political power. Committed to being directed by the Holy Ghost, they were averse to pragmatic development of resources and to deliberation about evangelistic policies. The intrusion of government, first German and then British, forced them, against their own beliefs, to apply more rational and successful criteria to their work and organization.

Appendix

Curriculum, 1909, Archives, Deekes to Baylis, 29 November 1909.

To graduate from Inquirer or Probationary Agent, a Kaguru had to read a few passages from the four Gospels (in Chikaguru), write a brief passage dictated from one of the Gospels (in Chikaguru), and pass interrogation concerning Jesus' life, especially the events around his birth, baptism, and final days from Gethsemane to the ascension. He was tested in the rudiments of the Catechism but spared the complexities of the sacraments. The candidate was tested in Swahili by translating a passage from a Swahili reader into Chikaguru. He was given a few simple problems in addition and subtraction to test arithmetic. This training might take as much as a year.

A candidate passing this initial examination was promoted to Junior

Reader. Now his reading and writing were tested almost entirely in Swahili. (Even at the lowest level, texts such as those in arithmetic were available only in Swahili. Only a few religious texts were translated into Chikaguru so that a student completed religious training in Swahili.) His reading skills were tested by having him read a morning and evening prayer (from the *Book of Common Prayer*) and sections from those Gospels studied. Unlike the previous stage, his spelling, penmanship, capitalization, punctuation, and syllabization were taken into consideration. He was examined on the meaning of one Old and one New Testament book: Genesis and St. John. As a guide to instruction, missionaries consulted the Cambridge Bible for Schools and Colleges. The student's arithmetic included not only more addition and subtraction but multiplication and short and long division. He was also expected to have some notion about the outside world, being tested on general geography—the names of continents, oceans and definitions of geographical terms. He was taught the rudimentary features of the African continent, and expected to write a two page letter (about 300 words) on any subject he chose.

If the candidate passed, he became a Senior Reader. To pass that stage he had to read the evening and morning prayers, the litany, and some Scripture in Swahili. His dictation from Scripture was judged more carefully than previously. His knowledge of Scripture was demonstrated by three essays: on Exodus, Numbers and the Acts of the Apostles. He was quizzed on biblical history: the basic features of Palestine when Jesus lived, the geography of Paul's missionary journeys, and the areas through which the Israelites migrated. He was again asked to compose a two-page letter and to perform all the arithmetical texts previously required, only better, as well as reckoning amounts in German money.

In the final phase, the Catechist was directed toward refining and broadening his grasp of Christianity. He wrote essays on Deuteronomy, Joshua, the life of Jesus, and Paul's Epistles to Romans. He had to know the order of the church year and memorize short prayers for the first, second, third and fourth Sundays in Advent, for Christmas Day, the fourth Sunday after Epiphany, Quinquagesima Sunday, Ash Wednesday, the first Sunday in Lent, the three prayers for Good Friday, for Easter, the Third Sunday after Easter, Ascension Day, Whit-Sunday and Trinity Sunday, and examined on the *Book of Common Prayer* from which these come. He was questioned on the Articles of Religion and had to give two scriptural proofs from each of the principal sections. He was examined on the history of the early church as conveyed by a Swahili text. His ability in Swahili was tested by translating a page from St. Mark from Swahili to Chikaguru. He was examined in the basic geography of Europe and Asia and tested on the contents of an elementary arithmetic text. His composition was tested by writing a brief sermon on a biblical text selected by the examiner. Sometimes prizes of a few rupees were given the best examinees. After passing, the candidate would be baptized after a wait of six months when he demonstrated his new way of life. He was then a full member of a congregation.

8 Missionizing: The Image of the Native and How Best to Change Him

In this chapter I consider the ways in which the C.M.S. characterized the morality and culture of the Kaguru and their neighbors and the policies which stemmed from this. The stereotypes which the missionaries held derived from a muddled view that both over- and underestimated the capacities of Africans. Africans were judged unable to confront and control the challenging aspects of modern Western self-rule; yet they were expected to attain standards of moral conduct beyond those exhibited by the vast majority of Europeans at home or in the colony. The missionaries entertained a contemptuous view of most aspects of Kaguru life, though they made little effort to learn what that life might be. The apparent simplicity of African village life seemed to offer good grounds for developing simple, unsullied Christian communities redolent of a simpler, preindustrial age now lost to Europe; yet the mission attacked the institutions that sustained the close-knit communities.

The changes effected by the C.M.S. were not simply the results of mission policies. The mission provided ways in which the Kaguru could redirect their traditional beliefs and customs so as to secure such advantages as domination over their fellows and escape from obligations which they felt onerous. A few Kaguru customs such as polygyny, rites of initiation into adulthood, and propitiation of ancestral ghosts posed problems new to the missionaries; eventually they revealed themselves as more complex and enduring than the missionaries had anticipated.

Missionizing is based on a contradictory evaluation of others: Africans and Europeans are equal in God's eyes, all with souls worth saving and dear to God, yet Africans clearly have beliefs and customs inferior to Europeans or they would not require conversion. The Kaguru human

being merits love and respect, but the culture and society that make that person what he is do not.[1]
As Bishop Chambers observed:

> To be a friend to the African need not mean giving him your daughter in marriage, but it does mean understanding and fellow-feeling, anticipating his needs, helping him to rise, and taking trouble to enable him to enjoy the riches of his inheritance in Christ. [1931:61]

The C.M.S. saw little value in African culture:

> . . . undoubtedly the races of Africa with whom we have come into contact have been so miserably low, intellectually and morally, in the scale of humanity, apparently so dull and unimpressionable, that to persons who take no account of the generating power of the Holy Spirit, it must seem a thing incredible that any of them should become intelligent Christians. [Price 1891:22–23][2]

Less generous minds saw the Africans as inherently inferior; the proof was their weakness in resisting colonialism. As Bishop Chambers of Tanganyika put it: "Trusteeship for the child races of the world involves the watchful care of their interests. . . ." (1931:60). Missionary life fitted well within such a paternalistic view, but not all C.M.S. could comfortably resolve their egalitarian, low-church values with their colonial situation. In any case, C.M.S. understanding of European culture appears nearly as unrealistic and narrow as their understanding of Kaguru; for that reason their problems in formulating realistic policies were doubled.

Stereotypes of Kaguru

The Kaguru and neighboring Gogo were considered benighted, even by the low standards which the C.M.S. set for Africans:

> Anything like the total, persistent indifference of these people to everything bordering on the spiritual, I have never met before. We pray and have our services and classes and are translating the Scriptures; but the people seem so dead. Humanly speaking work among the adults seems hopeless. There would be more hope for the children, if we could get them away from their evil surroundings. But even the children seem to expect to be bribed to learn . . . my co-worker was lamenting the absence of any

> signs of the Holy Spirit working in the hearts of these people. If we could only see conviction of, and sorrow for, sin, it would be a great encouragement. But the native ideas of sin are most lamentable and this alas! among many who have been baptized. Were it not for the promise of God's work, we must have given up in despair long ago. At the same time I am not quite sure, and want to ask your opinion (unofficial) how far we are warranted in continuing our efforts among the same, comparatively speaking, few people, who wilfully reject and despise the Gospel, when there are so many others among whom we might itinerate with no one working amongst them. Personally I do not think it is according to Apostolic custom, nor like our Lord's words in Luke IV.43 [I must preach the Kingdom of God to other cities also: for therefore am I sent.][3]

> The people, though industrious and inoffensive, are not intelligent, but are dull witted and not in the least desirous to receive either religious or secular instruction or to improve their social position. After I had for months tried to induce young people to come and learn, a few children only were brought together, who consented to learn and to attend school; but at the end of a month they asked for wages for attendance, and refused to come again unless they were paid. It took months of patient waiting and of visiting in their homes and in the fields before I could induce them to return and get them to understand that they would benefit by instruction. Their ideas of books were amusing, they regarded them as a means of magic. On one occasion when some packages were missing from a caravan at a certain village the list of the contents was brought and was read in public. The accuracy of the list of contents created such a deep impression that the people confessed who had taken the goods. They thought that the papers which could tell what was in each case, could also tell who were the thieves and cause some calamity, should they refuse to produce them. [Roscoe 1921:29–30]

Last conceded Kaguru "dullness of intellect" and laziness but found them less cruel than their neighbors (1879:665).[4]

> Knowing the African character as I do, the strength of the animal nature and the facility for wrong-doing, the low standards of public opinion with regard to sins of immorality, the lax way the young people are brought up by the parents, the ordinarily low and degrading topics of conversation, even amongst the Christians, the low example set by the European community—I say again, it is a wonder to me, humanly speaking, that any commandments are kept. [*P.C.M.S.* 1897–98:100]

Some C.M.S. described Ukaguru as a moral nadir abounding in "slavery, witchcraft, sorcery, fetishism, devil-worship, and a hundred nameless woes and evils" (*P.C.M.S.* 1905–1906:69). Kaguru were "devoid of any sense of sin, and completely engrossed in providing for their bodily needs or in drinking and dancing" (*P.C.M.S.* 1907–1908:61); they were "simple, except in Evil," and the "worship of the Evil one" (*P.C.M.S.* 1906–1907:767; 1912–13:52), or "possessing but the faintest and crudest idea of the God and of sin."[5] Some thought Kaguru had no religion at all (*Handbook for Workers* 1905:72), yet this was because few missionaries troubled to learn Kaguru tradition. Indeed, it was sometimes thought corrupting to do so: "it is a loss not to be regretted. Can a man touch pitch, and not be himself defiled?" (Pruen 1891:106).[6] Others acknowledged that Kaguru had a crude notion of God but insisted that they had "no ceremonies, whatsoever, which could be at all designated as worship,"[7] though they were shocked by "licentious dances" and "horrible orgies."[8] There was no appreciation of Kaguru music, although I found it most appealing:

> The native minstrels with bodies besmeared with a filthy mixture of fat and red earth, going about singing songs that could be relished by none but people of utterly depraved minds. . . .[9]

For the C.M.S., no beliefs other than Christianity qualified as religion: "non-Christians, until quickened by God's Spirit through faith in Christ, are 'dead through their trespass and sins' " (*C.M.R.* 1914:658).[10] Important Kaguru ritual conducted by elders has probably never been well witnessed by missionaries; public ceremonies such as initiation, marriages, and funerals are often accompanied by dancing and drinking, which automatically condemned them as irreligious. The mission held prayer meetings against the "evil of drink and drum" (*P.C.M.S.* 1920–1921:34). Missionaries themselves tried to break up witchcraft ordeals[11] and allowed their converts to tear down religious objects put up by pagans. They even persuaded some rainmakers to destroy their medicines publicly (Westgate 1913b:155).

Drink was clearly the paramount evil in C.M.S. eyes. Perhaps this was related to their experiences at home, for Victorian Britain witnessed considerable drunken escape from misery. Drink was considered not only synonymous with pagan ritual but a sign of absorption in physical pleasure and lack of control which were repellent to the C.M.S.

> The utter indifference to the Gospel story of the majority is painful in the extreme, and this is sadly illustrated just now by the excessive pombe [beer] drinking. Night after night we hear the noise of the drum, and we know that many who attend the house of God are present at these immoral dances and drinking feasts. Their need of the Saviour is great, but oh, how little they feel that need! [*P.C.M.S.* 1896–97:108; cf. Pruen 1891:231).

> The change from famine to plenty has not produced any perceptible change in the attitude of the people at this station toward the Gospel. . . . In famine time they are too hungry to read, and in time of plenty they are too excited with dancing and drinking to think of anything beyond the grave. *(P.C.M.S.* 1896-97:109)

Yet the C.M.S. recognized that African life provided a basis for morality:

> There is a high code of morality, theft is almost unknown, and houses are never secured by day or by night except against an enemy or wild beast. [Roscoe 1921:29]

> . . . in judging the native convert, his life is all before the public. There are no doors inside his house; no rooms into which he can shut himself. All he does is known to all the world. When we do particularly sinful actions, it is usually within closed doors; and the world never knows, and the Church never guesses, and the critic continues to think well of us. Is there any man living would feel no shame if all his life were made public? To compare English and African Christians fairly, it would be necessary to compare African Christians as they evidently were with English ones as they really are, all their private life made public. . . . [Pruen 1891:271][12]

Kaguru were thought to be like children, with little control of their appetites (many Kaguru considered Whites to be more sensual and shameless than they). Kaguru were considered enfeebled mentally, due to their harsh life, or inherently sensual:

> Their main object and purpose in life is to get rich, marry as many wives as they can, and indulge their animal appetites in every possible way.[13]

> Lying is so natural to all these people that it seems almost impossible for them to tell the truth.[14]

> The principal obstacle so far is the seeming incapacity of the people to take in any ideas whatsoever above those of their daily life and wants.

> "Sometimes," writes the Rev. J. C. Price, "after I have tried to talk a little seriously to them of eternal realities, and have asked if they understood me, they reply, 'Yes, Bwana (master), give me some cloth.' " [*P.C.M.S.* 1880–81:37]

> . . . men and women who think that they have renounced forever their allegiance to the devil yield to the more subtle temptation of the "lust of the flesh."[15]

> His religious devotion is sincere and fervent, with a childlike directness and also childlike instability, yet capable of great sacrifice and loyal fidelity.

> . . . while immature in the faith he is ready to testify simply of what he knows; he is easily misled but responds to sympathetic guidance. And, under good conditions and influences, he is capable of overcoming racial defects and developing a strong Christian character. . . . [*C.M.R.* 1923:229–30]

Africans required special supervisory discipline.[16] At one time an Executive Conference resolved that no missionary should beat his erring servants without consulting other missionaries.[17]

Besides being expected to foreswear alcohol and loose sexual conduct, converts should assume a sober and serious bearing in all their actions. Restraint was a sign of true Christianity. Thus, it was pointed out that

> a man who, with his wife, was led to become a pupil by observing the quiet resignation of their daughter when she lost her little son—a resignation in marked contrast to the noisy wailing of the Heathen. [P.C.M.S. 1903–1904:95][18]

Catechists were required not only to be restrained themselves but to restrain all in their homesteads.[19] The C.M.S. were concerned about their agents' conduct when Europeans were absent, like parents testing maturing children (*P.C.M.S.* 1897–98:110). To encourage morality, agents were often sent out in pairs.[20]

Observing the Sabbath was important as a first step before "higher things"; if they recognized that day, Kaguru could begin to envision a less worldly view.

> They have no desire to be taught about God or a hereafter, but nevertheless come to worship on Sunday, which they call "dancing to God"

> (kumuvinila Mulungu)—The numbers vary, generally from two to three hundred. They used to bring their pipes, snuff-boxes, etc., and sit and smoke, chew and spit. I have gradually got them to leave off these things during service, but they often have to be called to order for laughing or talking. They are beginning to observe Sunday as a day of rest. [*P.C.M.S.* 1900–1901:120]

Since the African character was assumed to be weak, unstable, and both childlike and bestial, renunciation and restraint were essential to prevent it from succumbing not only to the temptations thought prevalent in the tropics, but also to the new dangers of modern materialism which it was unequipped to handle.

The Assault on African Custom

The C.M.S. considered Kaguru customs and beliefs the antitheses of Christianity. For them, Christianity involved a wide range of European behavior, from dress and etiquette to monogamy. Yet Kaguru were not to absorb all aspects of European life, for that would subject them to the same evils that existed both back in Britain and in the colonial establishment. Ironically, much that appealed to the missionaries, the supposed simplicity of rural tribal life, was what evangelism destroyed. The great psychologist and anthropologist, W. H. R. Rivers, pointed out in a C.M.S. journal that the missionary failed to realize that

> in destroying the religion, or rather in destroying or undermining its ritual and beliefs, he was at the same time, and unwittingly, destroying all that gave coherence and meaning to the social fabric. [1920:210–11]

Pruen is one of the few missionaries to suggest that they had applied more stringent criteria of morality to Kaguru than to fellow Europeans (1891:271). Ironically, those aspects of African life which appealed to the C.M.S.—communal life, pervasiveness of common values, and initial naiveté about European goods—were the very ones that they had to undermine if they were to make converts.

The C.M.S. was scandalized by nudity. Its Executive Council once passed a motion requiring all African employees to buy and wear knickers.[21] Traditionally Kaguru wore skins or grass or bark skirts. Women wore something about the waist but went bare-breasted. Men wore a

Maasai-type toga over one shoulder; the left side was unfastened so that, as they walked or gestured, their genitals and buttocks were exposed. Little girls wore pubic aprons, but boys often went naked.

Kaguru began changing dress even before they adopted European notions of morality. Cottons, trade beads, and other goods entered the area with the first caravans; and by the time the C.M.S. arrived, payments and wages had been standardized in cloth. Six years after the C.M.S. came, most Kaguru wore cloth.[22] Cotton was more convenient than skins, and clothing quickly became a mark of higher social status. The Arab *kanzu*, resembling a white nightshirt, was worn by men not engaged in labor. It became associated with elderhood and authority, as were Arab skullcaps. Trousers and jackets were worn with increasing frequency, though the trousers were eventually superseded by shorts. The *khanga*, a black or colored pair of cotton cloths wrapped around the body, was soon the garb of even the poorest women and remains so today, except on special occasions when the very affluent wear dresses. Even small children were now covered. Those who were converted adopted "proper" garb, and agents were given official coats with buttons bearing church insignia.[23] Besides encouraging modesty, cotton clothing would divert Africans from spending their new cash on alcohol or other material luxuries (*P.C.M.S.* 1883–84:44).

Yet the C.M.S. had ambivalent feelings about such garb. Some did not want Africans to dress just like Europeans, presumably because this might encourage aspirations beyond a Kaguru's proper station.[24] The C.M.S. at Freretown had tried to pass rules forbidding converts from wearing trousers, but the Africans so vehemently objected that they gave up (Ashe 1890:8). The C.M.S. in Ukaguru never went so far, but did discourage white skullcaps and other Arab and pagan attire.[25] Oddly, the Arab *kanzu* was never included, perhaps because it resembles the surplice worn by Anglicans during services. Of course, converts were forbidden to braid their hair African style, to stretch their earlobes and wear earrings, to knock out their lower incisors, to smear on ochre-colored fat, or to wear traditional jewelry. That men would wear jewelry at all was unthinkable, and that women should wear traditional jewelry was a sign of "decidedly heathen significance."[26]

The best way to indicate C.M.S. attitudes toward Kaguru culture is to cite the prohibitions which the Executive Committee listed for converts:[27]

(1) boring lobes of ears and wearing discs in them
(2) taking emetics from medicine men
(3) sleeping except on a bedstead[28]
(4) wearing coiled wire on arms and legs, numerous rings, and ornaments in tops of ears (women)
(5) wearing only a loincloth (women)
(6) knocking out the incisors[29]
(7) wearing numerous chains on the neck
(8) observing taboos on certain foods and animals[30]
(9) excising girls' genitals[31]
(10) allowing hair to grow long and matted[32]
(11) extracting blood from the forehead center[33]
(12) wearing charms
(13) consulting a soothsayer
(14) finding out from sacrifice to the dead what a child's name should be[34]
(15) washing in urine[35]
(16) eloping
(17) public rejoicing when a girl reaches puberty[36]
(18) living filthy and unwashed[37]
(19) practicing witchcraft[38]
(20) playing musical instruments through the night[39]
(21) making loud threats regarding friends and relatives of persons suffering from illness[40]
(22) finding the cause of death by consulting a witch doctor
(23) undergoing ordeal by drinking poison or piercing the ears[41]
(24) singing indecent songs[42]
(25) wearing coiled wire around the waist (women)[43]
(26) having professional lamentation at a death[44]
(27) intimidating someone by placing a euphorbia branch in a doorway[45]
(28) braiding men's hair with fiber[46]
(29) fasting for a long period as a suitor at a girl's home[47]
(30) washing publicly before marriage[48]
(31) shaving the head in mourning
(32) consulting a witch doctor about misfortune[49]
(33) placing charms in a house, garden, or kraal[50]
(34) consulting oracles[51]
(35) mixing native medicine with seed corn[52]

(36) sacrificing to the dead[53]
(37) making use of heathenish medical treatment
(38) dancing and singing around corn to make it grow[54]
(39) giving medicine men women's clothes after they are cured of barrenness[55]
(40) keeping the family pot of fat[56]
(41) placing prohibitions accompanied by oaths and curses

The mission found it more difficult to forbid male circumcision than to forbid other pagan ceremonies. The Old Testament supports circumcision, and even Christ was circumcised. The C.M.S. took a dim view of both male and female initiation rituals since they associated them with licentious songs, instructions, and magical practices. Male circumcision was publicly performed by Kaguru as the quintessence of their culture, although women were not allowed to attend. In contrast, labiadectomy and most of its associated ceremonies were performed indoors by women only and consequently were difficult for the missionaries to investigate; and while sexual instruction was essential to girls as well as boys, the girls' operation was never viewed as vital. The C.M.S. tried to legislate the form in which male initiation took place, although they were unable to enforce this (I again cite the previous set of rulings by the Executive Committee):

(1) a male European missionary must be in residence at all times[57]
(2) only children of Christians and catechists are to be admitted to the circumcision camps[58]
(3) public rejoicing is allowed only at the actual cutting and no dancing and singing is allowed then or later
(4) the operation must be performed by a Christian and in a European manner[59]
(5) thanksgiving for the operation can be conducted in homes only as a form of thanksgiving[60]
(6) when the wounds heal, these can be oiled and washed, but the youths are forbidden to wear masks[61]
(7) a fee of 1 rupee will be divided, half to the Medical Mission operator and half to a church fund[62]

The C.M.S. were against dancing and drinking at any celebrations, considering these sensual and lascivious (*P.C.M.S.* 1924–25:15). The

C.M.S. never recognized that alcohol and dancing were essential for completion of Kaguru ritual, much as sacramental wine and singing mark Christian services. By forbidding anyone in the church to attend activities where dancing or drinking occurred, the C.M.S. forbade participation in all traditional ceremonies. Early on, converts at Mpwapwa interfered in local religious activities if they noticed them, though truly important sacrifices were almost certainly never held anywhere near a mission. The missionaries never seem to have tolerated such activities if they could disrupt them:

> A large procession of people passed one day on their way to one of their sacred places for the purpose of building a tiny grass hut (their apology for a temple) and make offerings to the gods. The young fellows came to me (one of them the late chief's son) saying they were going off to protest this folly. I did not know exactly what they meant to do, however, they rushed the "temple" they had just erected, and scattered the offerings placed therein. Of course the people were in a great rage, and threatened all sorts of things. At last they called a meeting of the head-men, and they had to appear and give an account of themselves, the people wanted them to pay a fine, but they refused to do this, so at last they let them go, saying "Well, you worship your God as you like, only let us alone to follow our customs and worship our gods in our way." Of course the matter did not really end there. One young man (a catechumen) was told that if he got baptized they would take his wife from him, and tie him up, or drive him away. He said he would rather give up his wife than his Saviour! [*P.C.M.S.* 1892–93:46]

Missionaries disapproved of all traditional religious beliefs and required converts to renounce such notions publicly.[63] Although beliefs about a connection between the order of nature and the morality of mankind have parallels in the Old Testament, one missionary disdainfully remarked:

> Sometimes we got queer answers from our scholars. On being asked, "How one man could do another a bad turn during the cultivating season," one young fellow replied "he would hinder the rain from coming to his garden." He said it in all seriousness. [Spriggs 1910:33][64]

Kaguru and their neighbors counterargued that Christian beliefs often seemed irrational. They asked why, if God were beneficent, did he send locust which decimated the mission's crops as well as pagans'; how could any sophisticated person believe that a rotting corpse could be resurrected; or how could anyone believe that young converts knew more than their pagan elders.[65] When a missionary had a nervous breakdown, Kaguru were convinced he had been bewitched by pagans whom he had offended (*P.C.M.S.* 1905–1906:70). When the collapse of the newly built church at Mamboya killed one Kaguru and injured others, but hurt no European, some Kaguru believed that their ancestors had punished them for abandoning tradition (Briggs 1918:30). Certainly, Kaguru found it ridiculous that God favored the poor and persecuted; to them, misfortune was usually a sign of impurity and moral weakness.

The C.M.S. hoped to convert Kaguru headmen and their heirs in order to provide influential models for the populace. Yet such converts were forbidden all involvement in traditional ritual, even though leadership was integrally bound up with the rituals associated with the land and those who dwelled on it (*P.C.M.S.* 1910–11:58).

Many activities were condemned by reference to Deuteronomy 8. 10–12: "There shall not be found among you any one that maketh his son or his daughter to pass through fire, or that useth divination, or an observer of times, or an enchanter, or a witch. Or a charmer, or a consulter with familiar spirits, or a wizard, or a necromancer. For all that do these things are an abomination unto the Lord: and because of these abominations the Lord thy God doth drive them out from before thee." Yet the C.M.S. took hope that Kaguru did supplicate God *(mulungu)* for rain, even though they beseeched the ancestors as intermediaries (Roscoe 1921:27). To this day, Kaguru do not speak of witchcraft, sorcery, divination, or the ancestral dead as illusions but only as unchristian realities. The C.M.S. interfered with witch finding and protested the killing of inauspicious children such as twins and those who teethed upper teeth first.[66] Although converts were forbidden participation in pagan rituals, this was not as disruptive as it appears, for ancestral propitiation was monopolized by elders and a few young men, and no women attended, much less officiated. Furthermore, such rituals were conducted far from settlements, in the bush and on hillsides. Thus, it was possible to be converted to Christianity as an individual yet remain part of a larger, sacrificing pagan group, even if one did not always attend rituals. Many Kaguru surreptitiously made the best of both ideological worlds. The joint or communal aspect of ritual allowed Christians to receive vicarious benefits from the practices of their pagan kin, to which they would contribute goods. Usually it was difficult to reject giving aid. If both pagan and Christian kin contributed to one's bridewealth payments, one could not exclude either from celebrations. The solution would be to hold two different weddings, funerals, or naming ceremonies, one at the mission and one back in a village. Nearly all Kaguru are sympathetic to such procedures, and few such compromises are reported to the missionaries.

Even naming involved a potential clash between Kaguru and Christian ideology. Kaguru believe that one should be named for the ghosts of the dead since naming placates such spirits (Beidelman 1974a). To insist on an alien, exclusive Christian name is to antagonize the dead and endanger not only the unnamed child but other kin as well. The C.M.S. considered Christian names as an essential mark of conversion:

> East Africans are generally savage—sunk in a low estate of barbarism, low in intellect and low in morals. Their names generally are those of animals or of deities, or they bear some grotesque meaning on the face of them causing the owners to blush with shame when a European pronounces the word.[67]
>
> The names chosen are those of the early Bible days, the times of the Apostles, and the early Church. Shem, Ham, and Japheth live with Shadrach, Meschach, and Abadnego; Apollo and Timothy, Athanasius and Perpetua have their twentieth century successors in Central Tanganyika to-day. [Chambers 1931:29]

In general, Old Testament names were favored; it seems to have been an unstated rule that names associated with Roman Catholic saints were avoided as much as possible. Traditionally, every Kaguru held a number of personal names. Few would see any reason why they could not assume a number of names, pagan and Christian, each to be used in its appropriate setting. Usually a traditional pagan name, often that of one's father or father's clan, is taken as a last name.[68] Kaguru now often have such patrilineally inherited family names in imitation of Europeans, even though traditionally Kaguru names change entirely with each generation and rights and titles are ordinarily inherited matrilineally (c.f. Beidelman 1971c, 1974a).

The C.M.S. and Kaguru Marriage

The C.M.S. was unalterably opposed to polygyny:

> ... monogamy is not a mere factor of civilization; it is vital to the life of the Church and its value has been realized in its own experiences; it was taught by the Lord Himself and has scriptural authority behind it. [*P.C.M.S.* 1939–40:6][69]

Polygyny was thought to debase all involved, to promote sensuality in men and lack of respect and dignity for women. The C.M.S. recognized that at least jurally marriages were decided by men and therefore women were not considered morally responsible for polygynous unions. In 1856 Henry Venn ruled that the C.M.S. could convert such women but not their husbands (Harries 1953:1909). For a man to be received as a catechumen, he had to discard all but one of his wives.

The C.M.S. disapproved not only of polygyny but of divorce as well; however, in the case of polygynous unions, real divorce was considered to take place only with the first wife, since the other unions were not proper marriages.

> The Bishop rules that heathen first marriages be regarded as valid, but that the system of divorce which obtained amongst the heathen be not recognized.[70]

In recent times, the C.M.S. has allowed the dissolution of some marriages where a Christian husband has lapsed into polygyny:

> If the husband in a Christian couple takes a second wife and the first wife acquiesces in his polygamy, she is disciplined. She must report the matter to the Church. Then she is regarded as blameless. If the husband, in spite of warning and Church discipline persists in keeping his second wife, his first wife is permitted to leave him and obtain a legal divorce. She may then marry another man, but the marriage cannot be celebrated in Church. The Church of England does not allow a church marriage when one of the parties has an ex-partner still alive. However, the above woman after remarrying is allowed to come to communion.[71]

The C.M.S. often make judgments about marriage which seem inconsistent or perverse. Thus, although they encourage polygynists to dismiss all but one of their wives, they forbid a Christian convert to divorce a spouse who persists in being pagan, even though a convert may find a pagan spouse a source of difficulties if he or she continues to consult diviners and medicine men.[72] A converted woman often finds it particularly difficult to live with a pagan husband who has jural authority over her, yet she is not allowed to divorce in order to find a Christian spouse. In the earlier period of mission work, a woman would not, as part of a polygynous household, have proper grounds to leave her husband. Instead, the C.M.S. advised her to redouble her efforts to convert him and view her condition as a testing by God. The mission is now more flexible.

In the past a Christian was allowed to consider a pagan marriage dissolved only when he or she had been deserted by a spouse for four years. If the spouse had been driven away, no dissolution was countenanced:

> A non-Christian marriage, however little understood it may be, is a true marriage; and the Christian partner at least must regard it as such; if it is to be dissolved it can only be by the action of the non-Christian partner. Ideally, the marriage is exclusive and life-long. Whatever may be urged theoretically in favour of polygamy, the fact remains that it is only found among primitive and backward races. In every civilized nation monogamy is the rule. There is no question that polygamy can only obtain where a low view of the dignity of womanhood is held. Polygamy and home life in a true sense of the word are mutually exclusive. Wherever polygamy has obtained there has been trouble in the household. [Uganda 1921:243–44]

Even pagan monogamous marriages were considered sacred and worth preserving. Where a pagan divorce was secured, the C.M.S. allowed a spouse who protested the separation to remarry, though not in the church.

Divorce, of course, was forbidden except in the most harrowing or extraordinarily difficult situations. Some of the missionaries were aware that a polygynous pagan might use his conversion as an excuse to dismiss wives of whom he was tired. Although it was expected that he would retain his first wife, he tended to retain his youngest and prettiest.

These marital rules were imposed by the C.M.S. with little grasp of the functions of marriage in traditional Kaguru society. For example, polygyny enabled influential and prosperous men to maintain or enhance their positions. Not only did polygyny carry prestige in itself, it provided more offspring, more wealth and security (since part of each wife's labor enriched her husband), and a web of alliances with other groups. Furthermore, many Kaguru say that polygyny encourages morality. Kaguru women observe many and prolonged prohibitions against sexual relations after childbirth, and a man with several wives would not be led to have adulterous affairs even when one wife was nursing a child. The missionaries and later the colonial government forbade widow inheritance. It is true that sometimes women, especially if they were young, disliked being passed on to one of their dead husband's kin; but with the new rules a woman often found herself unprovided for anywhere, especially if she were old or had no children. In one lugubrious account, a Kaguru youth who had inherited a kinsman's elderly pagan widow had become converted and hoped to divorce her to take a younger Christian mate but was refused by the mission.[73]

The mission also disapproved of the sororate, in which a man replaced his dead wife by her sister; Kaguru favored this because it allowed certain kin groups to retain their affinal ties and keep bridewealth which may have been distributed in a manner that made repayment difficult. The mission also disapproved of various forms of cross-cousin marriage, though these almost never involved true first cousins and therefore did not fall within any religious bans. Whenever missionaries were told that Kaguru were marrying kin, they simply reacted negatively, apparently assuming that Kaguru were a depraved lot. Such marriages remain fairly common among Kaguru, perhaps 20% (Beidelman 1966:369). Given the missionaries' general ignorance of local affairs, it seems unlikely that they would know much of such matters unless a disgruntled Kaguru reported them.

Kaguru are matrilineal. I do not propose to present an anthropological exegesis of matrilineal social organization; but for Kaguru society to work, divorce must be possible. A woman's matrilineal kinsmen should be able to assert power and authority over her and her offspring even in opposition to the woman's husband. One means by which this is done is by calling the woman home and dissolving the marriage. One of the ways by which a Kaguru woman may assert her rights and influence within the system is through such threatened divorce, encouraged by her kin. The C.M.S. ban on divorce made domestic life more difficult for many women.

The C.M.S. hoped to abolish the payment of bridewealth:

> ... the system of dowry [bridewealth] in the case of Mission and Christian girls should not prevail in the Christian Church and the only form in which the members think this custom can be tolerated is that the bridegroom should settle something upon the bride at the time of marriage if such can be satisfactorily arranged.[74]

Yet a century after the C.M.S. arrived, even the most educated Christian converts were horrified at the thought of a marriage without such payments. The missionaries at first applied the term *dowry,*[75] which only further confused matters in some foreigners' minds since the functions of Kaguru bridewealth are different. Women themselves encouraged bridewealth and saw it as a measure of their esteem. The accumulation of such payments and their distribution tied together large numbers of kin over several generations through repayments and debts and thereby provided an important means of linking kin who would interact in other matters as well. As cash incomes rose, bridewealth payments increased. This alarmed missionaries, who vainly sought to persuade the Germans to set limits on bridewealth for Christians.[76] Later the Kaguru Native Authority under the British passed such rulings but to little use. Ironically, the highest payments were among mission personnel and involved educated girls, who were scarce and in demand by teachers and clerks. Because such excessive payments were illegal and not registered, there was no way they could be retrieved in case of divorce. Of course, proper Christians were not allowed to divorce, and this led parents into demanding payments in full before the wedding; traditionally payments were often by installment, and threats of taking back the girl were used to extract continued payments.

In the past, Kaguru often paid bridewealth by installments over a long period. This enabled poor young men to marry; they resided with their wife's kin and performed brideservice. Under Christian arrangements, marriage took longer to undertake and involved residence according to the husband's desires, rather than with his wife's people.

Although the C.M.S. considered themselves as innovators who bettered the rights and conditions of women, many of their rulings undermined the conditions of women. Divorce and the threat of separation were crucial weapons for women in playing off the demands of their natal kin against those of their husbands. Furthermore, although Kaguru men were admitted to the church after casting aside loyal wives of many years, Kaguru Christian women were forced to remain in polygynous households regardless of their feelings. To the best of my knowledge, no Kaguru openly argued the virtues of polygyny with the C.M.S.; however, some remarked to me that they found it difficult to understand why they were forbidden more than one wife when prominent figures in the Old Testament had several wives and were favored by God.

Christianizing Kaguru Customs

Although they reacted harshly against many aspects of traditional Kaguru life, the C.M.S. saw parallels to things they knew from home or from the Bible. Some, such as circumcision, were too much a part of biblical thought to be rejected out of hand, even though the missionaries rejected the ceremonies associated with it.[77] Other practices, such as seasonal prayers of supplication and payment of tribute (tithing), were incorporated into church life.

Kaguru circumcision takes place annually during the dry season after harvest when there is much grain for feasting and beer. Christian boys were usually absent from school for at least two or three weeks during this time. The mission hoped they might find a way of christianizing circumcision by replacing the bawdy songs and explicit sexual instructions, which are at the heart of such ceremonies, with prayers and hymns. For Kaguru, circumcision is the occasion on which the basic beliefs of their society are inculcated in youth. Such beliefs involve the proper relations between men and women and the means of procreation. With recovery, novices are feted with dancing and drink. The C.M.S. sought to separate the physical operation from its cultural context:

> Christian circumcision may be performed from infancy to eight years but in no case to synchronize with the circumcision rites of the heathen.[78]

A person undergoing circumcision after baptism was required to make a public confession before he was readmitted to the church. The C.M.S. hoped to incorporate Christian teachings at circumcision but failed in all attempts to modify the ceremony. It was advocated that

> during the boys' seclusion, instead of the usual obscene formulae, they receive teaching on truth, honour, purity, abstinence from drink, humility, love of one's neighbour, and duties toward God. [Chambers 1931:36]

The mission was accustomed to expect local support for its work, though African contributions could not sustain the missionaries' activities. Initially, Kaguru brought produce to church; they presented plantains, flour, chickens, and vegetables at the altar. Later, money was collected. The mission tried to routinize such contributions, which were then devoted to local expansion. This was termed God's Daily Portion Offering Fund *(Fungu la Mungu la Kila Siku).* Missionary employees were also encouraged to donate a few days of their time to cultivate church land; the harvest was used for church causes. None of these practices brought in much profit, but the C.M.S. emphasized them because they signified the kind of sincere local attitudes that might eventually lead to a self-sustained Kaguru church. What the missionaries never mention is that such contributions of goods and labor resemble the tribute which Kaguru previously provided any local big man *(mukulu)* who protected them from outsiders (*P.C.M.S.* 1911–12:51; 1924–25:14).[79]

The mission also sought to incorporate seasonal activities into the church ritual. The most important annual traditional Kaguru rituals involved cleansing the land and propitiating ancestral ghosts to ensure a prosperous and peaceful year. The mission avoided taking special notice of this preplanting season, perhaps because it would have been difficult to recognize any significance in the season without calling attention to the dead whose exclusive domain it was. The mission did call services to pray for rain and to ward off disasters such as locusts and epidemics; but such misfortunes, transcending the particular localities of any kin group, were always the sphere of God and not of any particular groups of ancestors.[80] Harvest was emphasized by the C.M.S. instead.

> . . . some special service and meetings at the end of the harvest—a time devoted usually to drinking and dances—led to seventeen persons standing up at closing gatherings and testifying to conviction of sin. [*P.C.M.S.* 1904–1905:86][81]

The mission viewed such ceremonies as celebrations, but they do not sound like much fun when compared to the dances, drinking, and singing of the initiation feasts which took place at the same time. The missionaries associated their harvest ceremonies with the harvest services customary in rural Anglican parishes. Christmas (Great Day, *Lidjua Ikulu*), however, was the biggest Christian celebration, though it comes at an inconvenient time, the height of the cultivation and planting season when Kaguru have little free time and scant food supplies for feasting.

The missionaries eventually recognized that Kaguru did have some notion of a supreme being. At first, the mission had found this hard to credit since traditionally Kaguru directed most ritual toward contact not with God but with ancestral ghosts who controlled the well-being of particular tracts of land and brought health, fertility, and peace to particular kin. God *(mulungu)* was generally unconcerned with such parochial affairs, although he might bring widespread misfortunes on many different areas and kin groups at one time. To make their notions of God more comprehensible to Kaguru, the C.M.S. described God as "father" *(baba)*, "chief" or "leader" *(mundewa)*, and "physician" or "diviner" *(muganga)*; Jesus was often termed "shepherd" *(mudimi)*. This last term strikes close to traditional Kaguru thought, for they compare their traditional leaders to shepherds or herdsmen and themselves to a tended flock to be guided and protected by elders.

Even in the case of pagan marriage, the mission sometimes sought a compromise with tradition. For a time missionaries performed "baraza marriages" (public audience marriages); that is, a missionary officiated but did not allow the regular services or celebration within the church when one of the couple was a Christian while the other was unbaptized but studying for conversion. This custom was later discontinued because of the unclear religious and legal status of a union which was not a true church marriage.[82] In the same unorthodox fashion, a missionary granted divorces to couples if one member was a convert and one a pagan. The Home Committee reacted angrily, pointing out that such a divorce would be irrelevant to a pagan and improper to a Christian.[83]

The C.M.S. had at first condemned all use of native medicines by converts, but later modified this stand:

> . . . until this Mission has been provided with a thorough equipped hospital . . . it should not be considered an offence for native Christians to provide medicine from the native doctors, provided the remedy sought has been generally reported as efficacious and not possessing a heathenish significance.[84]

How such distinctions could be made remains difficult to understand.

The C.M.S. preferred baptism of adults because this allowed them to expect independent and responsible behavior from converts. As they began to teach children who sometimes requested baptism, they had to decide about the relation between spiritual goals and jural realities. It was finally agreed that they could not baptize children of heathen parents since the parents could legally claim control over these converts and direct their conduct. The C.M.S. did, of course, baptize children of converts when asked. They also hesitantly baptized orphans and abandoned children, recognizing that this meant that they were assuming full economic and jural responsibilities for them until adulthood. When the C.M.S. arrived in Ukaguru, they assumed that they might baptize any and all who seemed willing to become Christians; they soon realized that they had to modify their zeal to fit local situations.[85]

In some of their actions, the missionaries appear unaware of the implications of their deeds. At times, Kaguru endowed C.M.S. acts with a significance lost on the missionaries. For example, it was missionary practice all over East Africa to give local chiefs small payments for permission to reside and build in an area. To Kaguru leaders, such payments were tribute and signified that the missionaries were placing themselves in subordinate alliance with them. A Kaguru leader saw the first missionaries as potential allies much like some Arabs,[86] whereas the C.M.S. maintained that "the missionaries' aim should be from the first to lead him to regard their presence as a privilege and blessing to him and his people, for which he ought rather to pay than be paid."[87] Of course, few leaders entertained such views after the missionaries began operating in any area, and this became a source of ill will. The chief at Mamboya, for example, welcomed the C.M.S. but was later irate to find the mission building on the site of his ancestral burial grounds.[88]

The missionaries were long perplexed as to how to assemble people for church service in a hilly and difficult area such as Ukaguru. At first a cornet was used; but since the sound resembled that of a Kaguru war-signal, it caused consternation and flight (*C.M.G.* 1904:21–22). Later missionaries signaled services by firing their rifles and finally, much to the pride of the missionaries and Kaguru, by ringing a bell which is still the subject of boasting by old Kaguru. (It was destroyed by the Germans.) A large bell would appeal especially to Kaguru with their association of bells with livestock and their analogies between herds and socially cohesive groups. At other times the mission summoned its congregation with a native drum, the same type used in ancestral propitiation and possession dances. One elderly pagan informant complained to me: "The mission has taken our *ng'oma* [meaning both drum and dance] and now uses it for itself." To him it was a desecration.

Enforcing Christian Behavior

The C.M.S. pondered ways they might best lead Kaguru to adhere to Christian morality. Two approaches were recognized for achieving this: insulation of converts from pagans and punishment of wrongdoers. In societies with established and pervasive religions, there is little escape from punishment once the status quo has branded someone as wrong. In missionized areas, the situation is more complex since there are two moralities available. A lapsed Christian could return to his pagan neighbors and kin, and even loyal converts always have kin who are still pagan. It is nearly impossible for Kaguru Christians, given their general poverty, to stand alone and deny such kin. To humor them, a Kaguru Christian often contributes money and produce to pagan ceremonies, even if he himself does not attend. Often he does attend, safe from mission criticism if the celebrations are far from the European station. Most Kaguru Christians are far more tolerant of such ambiguity than are the adamant Europeans.

Early on, the C.M.S. worried whether it was wise to build their stations too far from Kaguru settlements. It was never clear whether separation was good because it prevented moral contamination by pagans or bad because it prevented converts from putting pressure on pagans.[89] From the first, the areas around the European mission settlements were set apart for converts, and proper Christian behavior was demanded there as at "a nice Christian village."[90] By the time the Germans were well established, the mission dictated the moral conduct of all those in the immediate station area. Anyone excommunicated from the mission could no longer reside within a quarter mile of the station.[91] This situation continued more or less until after Tanganyikan independence because the mission was the landlord of the area surrounding the station. The impact of such a policy was not as great as at some other stations since the C.M.S. in Ukaguru did not own a vast tract. The controls were mainly felt by

C.M.S. employees whose ejection meant loss of income and disruption of domestic life.[92]

The C.M.S. went through considerable soul-searching regarding how it administered punishments. During its early stages, when there seemed no reasonable alternative to mission assumption of "civilized" authority in the area, the C.M.S. feared that it might be taking on too many secular powers.[93] Furthermore, the very nature of Kaguru society at that time led missionaries to doubt that nonviolent punishments would be effective. Those in the field seemed disposed toward assuming such secular punishments although the Home Committee in London repeatedly discouraged this. The C.M.S. dilemma was that order and obedience were axiomatic with their survival:

> The fact is that in cases of theft, adultery, etc. by any of the people who have joined themselves to the mission if we did not inflict punishment the offender in 9 cases out of 10 would get off scot free, or be killed by the person against whom he had transgressed. Frequently rows and bloodshed would be the result if they take the law into their own hands, and certain mission property would not be safe from those who disregard the 10th commandment.[94]

The above writer advocates "administering correction" in petty crimes and assures the Home Committee that "corporal punishment has been but seldom inflicted."[95] The Home Committee was extremely disturbed by the suggestions.[96]

The issue of punishment became prominent in 1911–12 when the missionaries undertook to fine Kaguru who broke moral rules. By then the C.M.S. oversaw a large number of converts, more than just employees who could be controlled by withholding food or wages.[97] The Home Committee even wondered whether levying fines for sins did not compare to the early Catholic practice of selling indulgences and expressed hope that punishments of a more spiritual nature might be utilized.[98] Eventually, missionaries were allowed to collect fines so long as they gave them to the injured parties and did not keep them for the mission (Hewitt 1971:182). Later the Home Committee suggested that punishments should relate to "village custom," which was to replace "tribal custom."[99] Since traditional Kaguru tribal and village life were one and the same, this seems quite muddled. The final position assumed by the Home Committee was even more contradictory. After denying to Bishop Peel that they wanted to interfere in the ecclesiastical affairs of the mission, they proceeded to do just that by the following instructions (they controlled funding):

> ... it is desirable, if possible, to avoid separating out the Christians from the common life of their neighbourhood. So that if the community can still be encouraged to treat the Christians as subject to their ordinary customs, liable to penalties for breach of them, it would be much better that the Christians should be treated just as the heathen would be, and under the same authority. Of course, we quite see that if the customs and authority are mixed up with heathenism, the thing noted here as desirable cannot be attained; for no-one would suggest that the Christians must be kept under any customs or obligations that really involve heathenism. If, therefore, they must be treated as a separate community, the one question remains: Should they be punished by the Church, as such, or can they be punished by some Christian community authority? The Sub-Committee thought that, if possible, that distinction should be made, as it was felt really undesirable that the Church, as such, should be levying and receiving fines for sins. At the same time, the point was made, and I think generally agreed to, that it will be a great thing if, under Christian influence, besides any fine and ecclesiastical discipline, there can also be a real measure of social ostracism; if, that is to say, the Christian community or a wider community can, under Christian influence, be made to really boycott, so to speak, an unworthy Christian, so far as to make him really feel the penalty of his sin.[100]

I have quoted this Home Committee letter extensively because it neatly reveals both the gulf between religious theorists in London and working missionaries, and, more important, the contradictions inherent in the Evangelicals' disassociation of secular from religious life. No religious group can enforce conformity without also exerting some domination in economic and political affairs. Kaguru employed by the mission, studying in its schools, or settled on its property would respond to threats; but problems inevitably arose once the C.M.S. tried to impose their moral order further yet disdained to enlarge their economic and political base for pressure.

Until recently, all Kaguru were either pagans or Christian converts; and each set of beliefs had its own complex relationships. The negative sanctions employed by pagans rested ultimately in the exercise of religious pronouncements by elders—curses, withholding of blessings and cleansing rituals, and invocation of the dead—which in turn rested on the elders' control of economic and political resources and the need for group cooperation. Ostracism was and is the most effective means of social control among Kaguru, but its force hardly supports mission values. Rather, the need for cooperation between kin and neighbors, regardless of religious beliefs, means that Kaguru recognize common moral needs and values that make it nearly impossible for Christians or pagans to reject one another for long. This need for cooperation has held Kaguru communities together even in the face of C.M.S. pressures that Christians denounce pagans. That the C.M.S. could enforce conformity was due to economic and political factors that they themselves abjured; that the C.M.S. did not disrupt local communities beyond Kaguru tolerance was due to factors outside C.M.S. perception, factors which forced Kaguru to cooperate and forebear with one another in the face of a harsh and undependable environment.

Conclusion

The C.M.S. defined Kaguru as childlike but sensual. Kaguru needed continued and prolonged supervision by those with a more civilized and "serious" approach to life. Ambiguously, childlikeness implied an irresponsibility which required subordination, yet it also suggested innocence. That meant that Kaguru were thought incapable of dealing with the material advantages of modern Western life, but also that they were unspoiled by the same influences which had ruined industrial Britain. The Kaguru should be shielded from the very factors that they themselves and secular colonial authorities sought and hoped the C.M.S. would give them. The C.M.S. were unwitting agents of destruction of that which they sought to preserve, a rural society of cohesive, meaningful relations that was unaware of modern secularism; the C.M.S. were agents of the worldly forces they had rejected at home and had sought to fend off abroad by building a Black New Jerusalem (cf. Sundkler 1980:46–47).

The C.M.S. remained unclear about what denoted true conversion. Were the Kaguru to take on all the external attributes of Europeans—dress, speech, education, and style of life—and therefore veer toward the supposedly discordant modern, secular authority? Or were Kaguru to remain as they were, involved in practices that reinforced paganism?

Indeed, could one possibly separate out good from bad traditional customs in meddling with a society? Perhaps, also, it was realized that were Kaguru to become like Europeans, the task of the C.M.S. would cease and they would then have to abandon those activities that had defined the missionaries' very being.

The C.M.S. defined conversion as a sudden transformation rather than as a gradual process accompanied by repeated backsliding. Conversion was gauged by radical change in behavior and aggressive denunciation of pagan neighbors and kin. Although the C.M.S. were interested in the interior moral state of Kaguru, their only means to apprehend that state was through external acts. This led to a preoccupation with appearances which sometimes led both Kaguru and outsiders to complain about the C.M.S. lack of moral generosity, flexibility, and understanding of everyday needs.

The C.M.S. expected both more and less of Kaguru than of their own society. Kaguru were to accept only some aspects of Western life while retaining the best of their own. Yet Kaguru themselves were never allowed to choose for themselves. The C.M.S. sought the impossible, a way of life that was neither Kaguru nor Western, yet one that they alone as Westerners were to define. They sought to enforce their vision while disparaging economic and political sanctions. Their Evangelical views prevented them from perceiving Kaguru as whole beings with a history and with social and environmental needs, and from using realistic means to develop a new society in which Kaguru could live meaningfully.

9 The Developing Mission: Changes in Organization and Strategies and the Problems of Success

THE INITIAL IDEAS WHICH THE C.M.S. held about the organization of their work were rooted in Evangelical attitudes against any hierarchical society, against sharp distinctions and separations between lay and clerical personnel, and against any formalized organization or program of action that undercut the spontaneity which signified animation by the Holy Spirit. The C.M.S. recruits continued to entertain romantic visions of themselves as brave and lonely evangelists preaching God's message to heathen. In fact, their real activities turned out increasingly to be supervision of African agents and provision of technical services, such as education, medicine, and administration, while actual evangelism was increasingly done by Africans. As converts increased and the mission's public, secular services increased, the European missionaries occupied an ever more apical position in a broad pyramid of workers; they became ever more distant from the Africans below, a situation paralleled in the development of other colonial enterprises. In this sense, the very factors that spelled success for the mission forced them to slip from the original sterotypes they had held of themselves.[1] Success posed still a further problem for the mission. The stated aim of the C.M.S., and indeed of most missions, was to convert and teach sufficient numbers of natives that eventually they would form their own autonomous congregations within the larger church. At that point the missionaries would be superannuated. As in all colonial situations, there were serious differences between those in authority and those beneath in determining whether the new communities were actually ready to stand on their own. The C.M.S. in Ukaguru, and in Tanganyika in general, was slow to encourage such self-determination, especially when contrasted with Roman Catholics.

In this chapter the organizational and ideological problems posed by growth in the mission are examined. With success in conversion the C.M.S. was forced to confront the inconsistencies and unworkable features within its most deeply held beliefs and aims. In reacting to the quandaries which this confrontation posed, the C.M.S. developed a series of compromises and elaborations in their original system.

Self-Image of the Missionary

In its earliest calls for volunteers to East Africa, the C.M.S. set store by health, youth, and toughness of recruits. Yet the demands of lonely and time-consuming labor at a mission station made enormous personal demands as well, demands unlikely to be met without deep religious commitment. The C.M.S. stressed religious inspiration and "seriousness" rather than practical or even theological training. "To my mind a man full of the Holy Ghost is fully qualified to do the Lord's work . . . I don't think the 'rev.' is necessary for a missionary to the heathens; we are evangelists rather than ministers."[2] Only after the Second World War did the C.M.S. require all recruits to undergo missionary training. In the earlier years all women were given a few months' training, as were men, such as Last and Stokes, who had come from lower middle class origins. Anyone who had a college degree was automatically exempted from such training (Warren 1974:35–37).

A large number of missionaries were born to the life. Because they moved in a circle where kin and friends were either missionaries or evangelicals, they took such a career for granted. Even Hewitt, the C.M.S. historian, acknowledges that the missionary life could lead to an insular, parochial perception of reality in which the world is comprehensible only in terms of evangelism (1971:408). The Evangelicals' sense of being elect led them to behave like a sect apart from other churchmen (Bradley 1976:30). Because religious seriousness counted for more than training, many C.M.S. missionaries were not clergy; therefore, at times stations found themselves with no one to administer sacraments to their converts: "Great laxity has been prevailing among the Christian population, there being no one to perform marriages. . . ." (*P.C.M.S.* 1920–21:34). Sometimes proven evangelists were sent home for theological training. Thus, missionizing could became a way by which men with few resources might eventually rise to higher status. Such practices reflect inconsistency in Evangelicals: they emphasized individual spiritual inspiration yet still subscribed to the broader, formal organization of the hierarchical Anglican church. Their emphasis on sincerity and zeal prevented them from formulating a coherent and sustained set of organizational policies consistent with that church.

Traditionally the C.M.S. saw missionizing as a spiritual activity, yet it was also expected that the missionaries would undertake the various practical needs of pioneer colonial life. As I observed earlier, the C.M.S. missionaries were so suspicious of secular forces that they preferred burdening their staff with mundane tasks rather than risk infection from nonreligious artisans. Yet although religious personnel were expected to shoulder these burdens, they were given little training to facilitate their tasks. During the early period, when they actually needed builders, labor organizers, and traders, they recruited evangelists.[3] The mission hoped for all skills combined in one paragon, such as a "trained educationist with true evangelistic fervour" (*P.C.M.S.* 1925–26:5), but it was the spiritual qualities that prevailed. The Home Committee was never able to promise sufficient sums to hire African laborers to alleviate the burden.[4]

C.M.S. missionaries saw themselves as perpetual father models for the childlike Africans and to other Europeans as well.[5] As a modern Anglican missionary wrote: "It is probably true that the British as a whole have been at their best with underdeveloped peoples when they have been able to practice paternalism" (Welbourn 1961:179).

The C.M.S. was always a "greedy" institution, for even on home leave or when retired, missionaries were expected to tour congregations to propagandize for recruits and donations (Stock III:34). The missionaries' days in the field were consumed with labor from dawn to dark. On Sundays, as many as three services were held: different forms for prospective converts and the African congregation, hospital patients, staff, and heathen far from the station:

> The work at Mamboya calls forth so much effort in climbing hills to reach people that on returning home at night after a day's visiting I find I have very little energy left for reading anything beyond one's own private devotional reading and Bible study.[6]

After cataloging his many tasks, Wood laments: "I feel very very tired at the end of the Day and Sunday is very heavy. Pray for us."[7] If missionaries had any free time, they felt compelled to missionize the outlying areas, so that for the conscientious and zealous there was limitless scope for labor.

Despite their relatively low salaries, missionaries frequently donated their own funds for medicine, building, and other work. The unfortunate Stokes provides a dramatic example. Although he had been thrown out of the C.M.S. and had an orphaned European daughter and African son to provide for, Stokes made a will leaving three-quarters of his considerable estate (amassed in the ivory trade) to the C.M.S. and U.M.C.A. (Luck 1892:170–72).

Many missionaries set out for Africa with romantic notions about evangelism in the bush only to find that everyday work mainly involved uninspiring, grinding toil. Increasingly, "the work of its [the C.M.S.] leaders became more and more supervisory in emphasis and the Church itself began to resemble a bureaucracy in which every official has to be answerable to the man above him" (Taylor 1958b:13). One Executive Secretary lamented to the missionaries in Ukaguru: "From time to time one hears how in earlier days the correspondence with a Mission Secretary used to be of so much more free or familiar nature that one dreads to see the correspondence of today hardening into pure business communication."[8] As administrative needs increased, there was an ever-widening gap between Africans at the grassroots and the Europeans at the head (Taylor 1958a:90–93; 1958b:13–14). This made sense organizationally but was distasteful to those keen on active evangelism, who had entered the work because of an enthusiasm which they found difficult to subordinate to routine. During this period, even those at home began altering their criteria for recruitment to favor selection of fewer people who were more highly trained, not only theologically but technologically (Warren 1974:130).

Evangelicals were fond of viewing their individual lives as series of tests whereby the devoted could prove their faith. Hardships were welcome means for such testing. To ensure that those in the field could meet the challenges, all recruits were given rigorous health examinations and interviewed by the Home committee. Few errors in selection were made, but those few created considerable difficulty given the close-knit relations at a mission station. To monitor the suitability of a newly arrived worker, each station had a Probationary Committee of senior staff, who assigned the newcomers duties and examined their progress in Swahili and Chikaguru. Language learning consumed the greater part of their first year. If linguistic progress was slow, the committee could decide whether other abilities compensated to allow the end of probation. There was danger that probationary missionaries might succumb to frustration and boredom during this tedious period (cf. Pipes 1895), yet they were expected to display steadfast devotion, the highest moral character, and Christian humility. Given the individualistic character of Evangelicals, it was a special danger that newcomers might allow their zeal to lead them beyond their capacities. Welbourn has described missionaries as combining sublimated guilt and humility with a sense of personal superiority (1971:315–17). The C.M.S. also combined a sense of altruistic subordination to orders with intense, even rebellious individualism. The desire to work on their own was the main difficulty exhibited by recruits, and they were repeatedly cautioned to show a "spiritual sense of deference to those who have laboured before." Probationers were expected to write annual reports of their activities, recounting not only their accomplishments but also their spiritual state. Their mentors on the Probationary Committee also wrote to the Home Committee. If the candidate had inquiries or complaints, he or she could not write directly to the Home Committee but had to write through the senior missionaries at the station.[9]

The Home Committee repeatedly urged the missionaries to try to work together rather than overextend themselves to many stations since it was not always possible to replace everyone on leave. Too many stations were abandoned for months or years. This perennial shortage of staff led to frequent shiftings of missionaries from station to station.[10] Since Mpwapwa (Kongwa-Kisokwe) had primary claims for maintenance, other stations were temporarily abandoned if that was necessary for Mpwapwa to be staffed. A missionary with several years' rapport in one area might go to another. Thus after many years at Mamboya, where he became the first European to master Chikaguru, Wood was transferred in 1889 to Kisokwe where he had to learn Cigogo. Such transfers were wasteful of skills and demoralized both missionaries and natives.[11] Kaguru were mystified by the inconsistency between the urgency with which the missionaries preached the necessity of conversion and their repeated failure to provide teachers or evangelists regularly.

> You came here nine years ago and preached to us and told us that your way is the only way to salvation. Now you have come again and you tell us the same story. How can you expect us to believe that the matter is as

> important as you say when you wait nine years before paying us a second visit?[12]

Even where mission work was successful, Kaguru were hurt or shocked when a station was closed or a missionary who had stayed for many years left. The C.M.S. archives contain only one letter written by Kaguru themselves and this concerns their dismay at losing the Reverend Wood, their first competent and sympathetic missionary who knew the local language.[13] While Catholic missionaries spent long periods continuously in the field, the C.M.S. set a policy that workers could not serve up-country for more than five years without taking a mandatory year's leave home.[14] After missionaries brought their families to the field, the need for leaves became even more frequent.

With renewed success at Mamboya and with the increase in European staff, each missionary sought work on his own.[15] Three outlying stations were founded in 1900—at Berega, Nyangala, and Itumba. Each was only eight to ten miles from Mamboya, but the latter two were deep in the mountains and therefore required over twice as long to reach as Berega. This expansion stemmed from quests for independence rather than any practical policy of development.

Victorian attitudes about women deeply influenced mission thought. As I noted earlier, the C.M.S. was hesitant to send women into an area which had proved fatal to the first three resident wives. Yet women were considered essential, both because wives would keep men from straying into sin as Last and Stokes had done and because a "ladies sphere" was recognized. It was believed that people of the same sex best understood and converted one another. It was hoped that lady missionaries would be emulated by their African sisters. Women were also needed to cook, sew, and keep house: "To do such work out here with no nurse, no reliable cook or assistant of any kind is beyond the physical capabilities of any man."[16] The C.M.S. frowned on employing Kaguru women for household tasks; the implication was that, at the least, it would give a bad impression to outsiders and that, at the worst, it would lead to temptations. Besides, Kaguru women were untrained in even the simplest European skills. Kaguru men could not easily be hired for many chores associated with women, such as drawing water and fetching firewood. In the early period, the only solution was to hire a Kaguru married couple, doubling the missionaries' responsibilities.[17] By 1894 there were three missionary households in the Mamboya area, two married couples and a pair of unmarried ladies residing together, the first such single women in Ukaguru (*P.C.M.S.* 1894–95:86). From then onward the C.M.S. often had one or more single female missionaries in residence; some even ran a station single-handedly.

In general the C.M.S. Home Committee held advanced, liberal views regarding women in the field. It was especially concerned that male missionaries not seek to dominate females, for sometimes male clergymen expected deference from senior female missionaries with many more years' experience in an area. The Home Committee singled out Ukaguru as among the areas especially meriting criticism for such abuses.[18]

It was believed that lady missionaries required better housing than men; nor were they expected to travel as freely or as far. At first, women were not allowed to travel at all without the permission of the senior man at the station and then usually in a hammock carried by porters.[19] Despite the added difficulties and expenses posed by women, Bradley claims that by the end of the nineteenth century women considerably outnumbered men as missionaries among the British Evangelicals (1976:91). They sometimes outnumbered men at stations in Ukaguru.

Station Life

Station life in colonial Africa has been the subject of much reflection in memoirs and novels. Few situations at home are comparable other than those of religious or military establishments and prisons. At a station, a small group had to live together intensively for a prolonged period, sharing not only work but all other activities as well. Cooperation was imperative; every action was supposed to be geared toward "the work" and was subject to intense scrutiny by colleagues. In this, a mission is a "greedy" institution which demands devotion and conformity far beyond that which we ordinarily encounter. McGavran rightly describes the station as the quintessence of mission life (1955:9); it also embodies its greatest difficulties.

In the early phase of mission work, volunteers were sometimes accepted when not of the same class as most of the missionaries; sometimes non-C.M.S., or even non-British, persons were chosen. This could lead to problems. For example, Stokes and Watt were regarded uneasily because they were Irish. In one situation this led to fears that Stokes might be sympathetic to "popery," and the stereotype of Irish violence was confirmed when Watt beat a porter to death.[20] As a middle or lower middle class institution, the C.M.S. in Ukaguru was reluctant to admit artisans because they were of a lower social level. In one of the unhappiest letters in the archives, a clergyman writes of a miserable six weeks' trek with a blacksmith volunteer whom he describes as selfish, uncouth, dirty, and too Evangelical even for his tastes:

> . . . if any more artisans are sent out the committee should be most careful to select men who have tolerable manners and are at least cleanly in their habits as this is absolutely essential to the health of the man himself and of his companions [the blacksmith urinated and spat within their tent].
>
> . . . if possible they should be members of the Church of England. We have already had some little difficulty with the members of our party who are not so and we shall I foresee have a good deal more, and I, or course, will have to bear the brunt of all objections etc. The use of the surplice and our communion service have both been objected to but of course I shall not yield to any such objections. It will too, if the mission is established, be far pleasanter for me to work with men who are one with me on this point and not perpetually objecting first to this thing and then to that.[21]

In another case, where a missionary failed his language examinations, he could flout his seniors because of his needed ties with the Canadian branch of the mission.[22]

Of course, it was hoped that members of each station would form a smooth-working, joyful team:

> . . . naturally each will be a kind of authority in his own line—but it is most essential that you should all work together, allowing nothing to separate you one from another, but prepared to make any sacrifice, so that union of heart and action, which is strength, may be secured.[23]

Yet there was sometimes serious bickering between staff. When mutual criticisms were reported to London, the Home Secretary was not obliged to indicate the source of denunciation; therefore, one could not confront an accuser:

> . . . I did anticipate many hardships in the mission field, and was quite prepared for them, and heartily willing to bear them, but I did not expect

> any of *this nature,* nor did I ever dream that such secret defamation could exist in any Christian Mission.[24]

And when a visiting colleague criticized the slow rate of conversion in Ukaguru, a worker wrote:

> We all I am sure feel that there ought to have been more results for the time we have been here, and God knows we are humbled by the fact, but to say there are no results is withholding from God the praise due to *Him.*[25]

A headstrong and quarrelsome missionary might be shifted from station to station, disrupting life all around. Even a single difficult person could do enormous damage. In one unusual case, a missionary became radically critical. He was terminated and sent home, judged "unequal to handling men." His problem was said to be "mainly due to climatic conditions acting upon a naturally nervous disposition, which make it undesirable that he should return to any tropical climate."[26] His badgering letters and worrisome allegations pursued the staff for years, even after he returned to England.[27] Sometimes the problem was simply "an earnest worker but an impossible fellow-worker."[28] Sometimes it was found that women would serve under a male missionary but refuse to be subordinate to another woman.[29] At other times, there was tension when a woman resided in a building with a married couple.[30]

It is difficult to determine whether the arrival of European women aggravated these tensions. Unmarried missionaries could reside together; although a single male could not reside with a married couple, oddly an unmarried woman sometimes did. A single woman attached to a married couple often lost much time nursing the wife; previously such a woman would simply have had to cope by herself when sick. When women complained that they found hiking in the precipitous Kaguru hills beyond their endurance, it was thought they should reside near men who could bear many of the chores. Some complained that women required more expensive housing.[31] Rotberg contends that married Protestant missionaries tend to become more readily insulated within a station than unmarried Catholic priests (1965:53). Certainly sexual considerations required a new sense of territoriality within a station:

> . . . I would again refer to Europeans living too near: when at home I spoke to you about it, and obtained your permission to have the houses about 10

> minutes walk apart from each other. Mr. Wood has, however, established himself in the same little compound: the result is neither of us have any privacy: my wife is unable to move out to attend to her housekeeping or fowls without being overlooked by Wood or his servants: Mr. Wood likes to stroll about in the morning before completing his dress, and in the evening to go about in his dressing gown. We are so situated as to be unable to shut out such sights. Then there are petty trials about servants, gardens, fowls, etc. which after a time become most annoying: it would be an excellent rule not to allow the missionaries to live in our small compound. We are literally not more than forty yards apart.[32]

One solution to such tensions was for the fractious member to find reason either to go evangelizing or caravaning, or to found a new station. A prickly missionary might volunteer to go off into the bush to seek food or to lead trips to the coast for supplies or laborers.[33] Last, one of the more difficult local men, was keen on maintaining the support of his own African following and pressed his fellows to allow him to found a new station at Mamboya. As Strayer writes of the C.M.S. in Kenya:

> Expansion was, for example, often a means of social promotion for individuals within a small and very status-conscious missionary community, numbering over fifty missionaries in 1900, concerned with ecclesiastical status. Clerical missionaries engaged in "spiritual" work were much more highly regarded than lay missionaries who participated in secular activities such as teaching. This led to a persistent desire for ordination on the part of lay missionaries, especially since ordination exams given abroad by the local bishop were believed to be less rigorous than those required at home. Another indication of status within the C.M.S. involved having sole control over a particular mission station, and individuals' desires to create or defend their own outposts further contributed to the process of mission expansion. [1973b:231]

One C.M.S. Executive Secretary tried to discourage the proliferation of new stations by suggesting that workers should be based at a single station and itinerate to spread the word.[34] Once stations spread, those at the older and larger station at Mpwapwa tried to control those distant from them; such a tactic was resisted by their subordinates and by the bishop who observed: "Only those upon the spot can possibly know the needs and peculiarities of the work."[35] With missionaries spread thinly over many stations, any illness, death, or home leave set work back devastatingly in any area.[36]

Dependency and Autonomy of the Mission Church

A mission is by definition a dependent group. The European missionaries in Ukaguru were dependent for funds and staff upon the parent mission in London. As a consequence, they had to adhere to judgments on policy dictated from abroad, even when they felt that such decisions had been made in ignorance of local realities. Furthermore, within the mission in Ukaguru, the overwhelming number of members were Africans dependent upon the European minority for funds and skills. If these benefits were to continue, the superiority of Europeans in determining policy had to be accepted. Thus, neither European nor African Christians in Ukaguru were masters of their own affairs.

From the start, all mission funds came from the Home or Parent Committee, so it was they who determined where a missionary was posted and how long he remained. They even decided whether he married.[37] The sanctions they employed were considerable. Termination involved a legal obligation to refund money for travel and other benefits received. Furthermore, as missionaries invested ever more years in the field, they became fit for no other work and needed their positions to support themselves and receive their pensions. Besides, one cannot usually switch employment in missions as one would transfer from one business to another.

Other complications arose from the local organization of the mission. Technically, the local mission was headed by an Anglican bishop responsible to the Archbishop of Canterbury, not the Home Committee. He need not even have been a member of the C.M.S. In practice, when conflicts between the Home Committee and the bishop occurred, the Committee exerted its economic leverage (cf. Strayer 1978:10).

Within Ukaguru-Ugogo the C.M.S. had considerable difficulty maintaining control of its members. The senior missionary was theoretically the final local authority. All of the senior members at Mpwapwa (Kongwa) met four times annually at an Executive Conference, but the missionaries from distant stations such as Mamboya and Berega attended only biannually. These conferences were never held in Ukaguru proper but always at the western border. It was very difficult even to maintain communication in the huge area of over 6,000 square miles. It was 110 miles from Berega in the east to the western station at Mvumi in Ugogo. Until after the First World War, transportation was mainly by foot and took many days from one station to another. Through the years a number of local committees were formed in order to integrate mission activities, but the most important remained the Executive Committee. In recent years a few Africans were allowed to sit on it, but it remained dominated by Europeans.

European Paternalism and the Prospect for an African Church

In 1854, Henry Venn, one of the founders of the C.M.S., stated his conviction that the proper aim of missions was to establish an autonomous native church and then move on. He did add that African clergy should be less educated and paid less than Europeans (Curtin 1964 II:425–26). Antonomy was attempted with disastrous results in West Africa; because of that experience the missionaries in East Africa were exceedingly dubious about pressing such development.[38]

In East Africa the less developed C.M.S. areas such as Ukaguru watched closely Buganda, the most sophisticated and developed mission area, for a clue to the kinds of problems they too would eventually face. Quite early, Bishop Tucker advocated that in Buganda the missionaries subordinate themselves to local Africans:

> In training native Christians in the art of self-government it is a tremendous mistake to hold aloof from their organization, and this from the simple reason that if the work of the European Missionaries is carried on outside the limits of the native Church, there must be an outside organization. In that case the native Christians will not be slow to realize that the outside organization is under discussion in the Church and that their own organization is more or less a sham.[39]

Yet even Tucker acknowledged that he found it difficult to stand by and watch Africans do work that he felt Europeans could do better (Bolt 1971:126).

Tucker's stand was opposed, even though he was later proved right.

> The principle of tutelage was projected into the African church itself. Its presence is betrayed in the fact that the work of its leaders became more and more supervisory in emphasis, and the Church itself began to resemble

> a bureaucracy in which every official has to be answerable to the man above him. [Taylor 1958b:13]

As a way of side-stepping Tucker's admonitions, local councils with African churchmen were established. But the foreign missionaries continued to control education, the distribution of foreign funds, the higher levels of accounting, and the salaries and appointments of the European staff. The annual preparation of a local mission's budget invariably reminded everyone of how dependent they all were on the home body.[40] As Tucker himself observed:

> It must always be remembered that where European money is used, there will, sooner or later, follow European control. The power of the purse in hindering the development of Native Churches is truly appalling. [1889:100]

In 1900 the C.M.S. in Ukaguru proposed forming a constitution for an African church, but were told that few Kaguru and Gogo could read or write and they were therefore not ready to manage their own affairs.[41] Strayer appears correct in noting that the C.M.S. was keener on evangelizing than actually training and constructing a native church (1978:69).

When in 1911 the Home Committee was asked to allow Kaguru and Gogo to be made deacons and possibly eventually pastors, it rejected the proposal. The Committee noted that at the time the mission had only 800 baptized members and therefore was hardly ready to support deacons, much less clergy. It suggested that native catechists might, at this stage, serve just as well as deacons. It also questioned whether local Africans were sufficiently educated to be even deacons. Finally, it warned that it did not intend to provide salaries for such personnel, but that they must be supported locally. Only when the number of prosperous Kaguru was sufficient to support deacons and clergy should these be created.[42] As late as 1922 the C.M.S. General Secretary still refused ordination of Kaguru deacons since he felt there were insufficient converts to support them.[43]

In a sense, an independent church was further thwarted in the 1920s when the C.M.S. set up local councils under what the mission termed "diocenization."[44] This impeded autonomy by relegating only lesser issues to such councils while leaving more important decisions regarding funding and policies in the hands of the higher level missionaries and the

Home Committee. Diocenate councils met too infrequently to run things. Their constant preoccupation with setting up rules about the morality required of staff, their careful balancing of European and African members, and their lack of Africans with suitable educational background or access to the necessary information to review financial accounts deflected Kaguru attention from the real work of running a mission. This may well not have been the intended aim of those who set the councils up but it was the outcome nonetheless. Even where decisions were reached on matters important to Africans, with Europeans controlling the major purse strings, including the salaries of most of the African members of the council, few were likely to press for any radical changes.

In 1922 the C.M.S. devised a plan for local pastorates in East Africa. Each was to be run by a committee composed of an African pastor or quasi-pastor, four baptized African church members elected from among local African subscribers to Church funds, and a supervising European missionary. This pastoral committee was to meet every three weeks, distribute local church funds (not mission funds), prepare estimates of the local church budget, and elect two delegates to a Central Church Committee (Hewitt 1971:186). On paper this appears to have afforded a training ground for Africans; but in practice the committee had no influence on educational services and could not instruct European missionaries. Its African members were usually poorer and less educated than most of the African staff employed in secular tasks by the mission. As late as 1943 the General Secretary of the C.M.S. repeated the earlier economic arguments for the continuation of certain dependent relations between the parent mission and the African branches (Warren 1943:69–75). So long as the C.M.S. was involved in costly technical services subsidized by government, it was indissolubly wed to the parent body.[45]

Funding and the Control of Africans

Pervading C.M.S. publications and correspondence is a constant plaint about lack of funds. From the beginning, the C.M.S. in East Africa showed little caution in balancing resources with its ambitions for expansion. This was termed the "policy of faith," under the assumption that God would provide.[46] Yet funds for mission work are always among the first to dry up during economic difficulties back home. The C.M.S.

followed a policy of insisting on individualistic bases for contributions and rejecting pressure on those back home, at least when compared to some other mission groups. Its income therefore was far less predictable and assured than that, say, of Catholics. While the C.M.S. failed to improve its fiscal policies, operational costs steadily rose with no comparable rise in mission income.[47] Never did native contributions provide a meaningful amount, so the work invariably depended on British goodwill. Initially the main expenses were for construction of buildings at new stations, and for missionaries' travel and salaries. Missionary salaries were always paid from overseas; once government subsidized education, African teachers were paid by the colonial administration. Mission employees were expected to contribute a portion of their salaries to the mission. For the most part, the Home Committee advised the missionaries to rely upon contributions of labor by local Africans.[48] But as one worker noted: "True, the chiefs and people are ready to promise much but when they have worked for two or three days they tire."[49] Periodic shortages of funds sometimes crippled even the most important work; when no medical supplies were sent to Ukaguru for over six months, all medical work had to cease even though a doctor was present.[50]

At first, supplies and labor were cheap, but the range of available goods was small and the only willing workers were coastal Africans or those passing through in caravans. Caravaners worked only a few days and then took off for more lucrative trade. Coastal Africans proved even less dependable, often deserting because of the difficulties of up-country life:

> Many of them would claim sickness for days when there was nothing the matter with them, and yet we gave them their food all the same, for Mr. Last was always strongly against stopping the food of those who refused to work when they were able. We have however a few slaves who have joined us from passing caravans, and with them as well as with any others who come to us, we shall adopt the plan of "no work no food."[51]

Workers sometimes even brawled and drank and had to be constantly supervised by Europeans:

> An overseer of their own nationality has very little influence over them as they despise him and he in turn is afraid to incur their displeasure by informing on them. Their powers of endurance are very great seeing they can work the greater part of the day without food . . . they seldom care

> to remain in constant employment but prefer to have periodical rests, when they spend all they earned and then look for another job.[52]

There was no money economy at this time, and most payments were in cloth *(merikani)*. In 1879 men received yards of cloth for food and wages. The task of bringing in bales of cloth for payments was itself considerable burden. A continuing rise in costs put considerable strain on the missionaries. After 1900, the missionaries sought to convert all their payments into cash; they depended upon the Germans at the fort at Mpwapwa for coins in exchange for letters of credit. Within four or five years the C.M.S. had converted almost entirely to cash. This led to repeated disputes with their African agents who wanted to continue being paid in the old terms of cloth, which had increased in value. Furthermore, converts repeatedly asked why they should not be paid more than pagans; ironically, the C.M.S. thought that the reverse should be true and that converts should be willing to give some labor out of love for God.[53] Throughout its stay in Ukaguru, the C.M.S. expected mission employees to work for less pay than those comparably employed outside the church.

At first, Kaguru had been described as hopelessly uninterested in working for cash. Later, when Germans required taxes in cash and European goods flowed into local markets, Kaguru began to demand higher raises. They were condemned for their "discourteousness and avarious spirit" and some were fired, to be rehired after publicly recanting their sin of greed.[54] Local C.M.S. repeatedly called for rallies to secure donations from Kaguru, but a self-supporting church remained a myth. Indeed, the need for more equipment and better trained staff drove costs up with every year.[55]

What the C.M.S. hoped for was a growing band of Kaguru converts willing to work at low salaries and under a moral code far stricter than what was expected by ordinary colonialists. Of course, the missionaries themselves worked under difficult conditions and with low salaries, but Kaguru were expected to have even simpler needs. The missionaries' wide demands of their African workers resemble the awesome demands which many Victorians made upon their household servants (cf. Horn 1975:32–34, 113–15). For example:

> Tofiki, *alias* Samson, renders invaluable assistance in various ways. Every morning about 6 A.M. he goes (voluntarily) to the chief's house, about

> three-quarters of a mile off, talks to the chief about his soul, then collects his children and brings them here to be taught, and takes them home about four o'clock in the afternoon, and again at night, besides performing the duties of cook, washerman, etc., etc. I ought to mention that in addition to the above he preaches occasionally, both in Swahili and Cigogo. His wife who is also a Christian, cooks gratis for the chief's children, who are living here, and scarcely a day passes, but that some one is fed from their table for Christ's sake and the Gospel's. [*P.C.M.S.* 1886–87:43]

Kaguru were to be motivated by spiritual factors, not material ones: "A servant of servants shall he be unto his brethren" (Genesis 9.25). As a result the C.M.S. repeatedly objected to any training, even religious, that would take their charges out of Ukaguru and into areas of greater sophistication, such as the coast.[56] The missionaries eventually agreed to provide more secular education, but believed that this had to be accompanied by increased religious instruction and greater moral surveillance so that Kaguru employees did not degenerate.

> . . . .The great danger of secular education divorced from moral and religious instruction, is that it tends to break down the native beliefs, which we often regard as absurdly superstitious, but which do take the place of a religious or moral law, and keep the Native more or less straight without replacing such beliefs by anything else to take their place. The Native requires something more than an abstract moral code in place of his primitive moral law, and a definite religious belief is necessary if he is to become an honest and respectable member of society.[57]

Eventually, some C.M.S. bitterly regretted the changes which secular education brought:

> . . . the subtle modern forces of materialism and a bitter nationalism impose a new kind of bondage on the heart and mind of the African. As another missionary put it: "Our battle to-day is not with the bad old things but with the bad new things." [*P.C.M.S.* 1947–48:11]

Yet education was admitted to be the best means of securing future missionary employees:

> Schools appear to be the most important evangelistic agency in this district, for although there is much monotony about the teaching, yet from

> them eventually spring the New Testament readers, and those who, after due training, become native agents. [*P.C.M.S.* 1902–1903:102]

In 1906 the local C.M.S. bishop advocated encouraging African church workers if they manifest "spiritual fitness," but expected little from them in any academic examination.[58] As late as the 1930s the typical C.M.S. catechist was thus described:

> Usually he was recently baptized and could read and write only a little: but he attracted people and won converts by sheer force of character. [Hewitt 1971:192]

Local clergy and evangelists were also poorly educated (*ibid.*: 199). Better educated men sought better paying posts in education and other secular tasks. Certainly, an added drawback to mission employment was the rigid morality demanded of all employees. This was exacted not only from teachers and clerks but from cooks, messengers, handymen, and dispensers. Since the mission could fire those who lapsed from its standards, a semblance of morality appeared in the vicinity of the station itself.

Conclusion

As Evangelicals, the C.M.S. were inclined not to foster the kinds of organizational skills, routine, or careful fiscal policies that led to a rational, stable mission. It was believed that the Holy Ghost intervened both to inspire decisions and to bail the mission out of seemingly imprudent (but inspired) policies. Evangelizing remained far more attractive to the missionaries than the dogged, everyday tasks more essential to building a local church.

The C.M.S. held a paternalistic, denigrating view of Kaguru that made it very difficult for them to foster the establishment of an independent African church. In any case, since the C.M.S. sought to underplay secular achievements, in its educational policies but more importantly in its training of Kaguru religious agents, they failed to produce a sufficient body of sophisticated Kaguru to provide leadership for any local church. Because they separated religious life from materialism , and advocated a sternly altruistic regimen, the C.M.S. could not produce or maintain an

African religious staff with sufficient capabilities or prestige to command respect or emulation from prospective Kaguru converts. Most of these shortcomings are well reflected in microcosm in the next chapter, in which I describe the everyday life of one C.M.S. mission station and its surroundings in 1957–58. There we can readily see why C.M.S. Evangelical ideals impeded many aspects of mission organization and the development of an African church.

10 The Local Mission: A Portrait From 1957-58

THIS CHAPTER SKETCHES THE C.M.S. IN Ukaguru during my initial fieldwork (1957–58).[1] It illustrates in microcosm and in more organic detail many of the features described separately in preceding chapters. While I concentrate on the main station, I touch upon other areas to portray a fuller range of C.M.S. activities, not just those involving Europeans. The ethnographic present refers to this period unless stated otherwise.

Competing Religious Groups

The C.M.S. persistently oriented activities in terms of a Catholic threat, yet the Holy Ghost Fathers (today predominantly Dutch) have only two stations in Ukaguru: a permanent one at Ijafa just outside the district on the northeast border between Ukaguru and Ungulu and a less permanent one on the southern borders. In 1957–58 the latter had no priest although a large Catholic station ten miles south in Usagara provided services. The Ijafa station is manned by two African priests who conduct mass and religious instruction. Their repeated requests for permission to build a school or dispensary were refused by government. Kaguru are impressed by the education of the African fathers in contrast to the lower attainments of African C.M.S. pastors. Unlike the pastors, however, the priests are tribal outsiders unfamiliar with local languages and customs. Their transferral every few years prevents rapport. Catholic conversion has been impeded because Kaguru must attend C.M.S. schools. The only areas where a sizable Catholic congregation exists are the northeast and southeast, where stations are accessible. There are only five or six hundred Catholics in the chiefdom.

Despite C.M.S. fear of Islam, less than one percent of the population is Muslim (in contrast to 27 percent of the nation). These are restricted to the eastern borders and trading centers where a few Kaguru converted under encouragement from Muslim shopowners who employ them.

C.M.S. Stations and Buildings

The layout of a station—its size, the roads and grounds, the scale, the number and condition of its buildings—contribute to a mission's prestige and attract adherents.[2] The C.M.S. headquarters at Berega is a cluster of buldings in the Berega-Mgugu area of north-central Ukaguru. These appear impressive and modern when compared with Kaguru settlements nearby; but in comparison with government buildings at the district headquarters in Kilosa, they are simple and shabby. Unfavorable comparisons have been made by visiting Europeans and Kaguru.

Most Kaguru have visited Berega, many several times a year. The station is the residence of all European missionaries and many African personnel. The center of local higher education, it is the site of a clinic and the only surgery in the chiefdom, as well as the only postal agency.

Berega station lies about three miles off the main east-west road of Tanganyika. It is considered all-weather, although it is unpaved and, during the rains, is often reduced to a morass where vehicles are mired for hours. From the main road the mission station is reached by a rough track crossing two riverbeds which are sometimes flooded. The mission is cut off for days at a time during the rains and often can be reached only by trucks or four-wheel-drive vehicles.

Half a mile in from the main road is Mgugu market; surrounded by half a dozen mud-brick shops and twenty houses is a space where government-supervised purchases of produce are made. Half a mile further is the C.M.S. Middle School for boys, the only one in the chiefdom. There is only one other in the district and none in the district to the west. The school has a large building for classrooms, a workshop, three dormitories, a kitchen and mess, and three houses for staff; all are of cement blocks, with iron corrugated roofs and cement floors. Buildings are grouped around a sports field. The complex is surrounded by extensive gardens cultivated by students. The school's 104 acres of valuable valley land represent the largest local holding under African control.

Across the river and atop a steep hill about a mile eastward lies Berega.

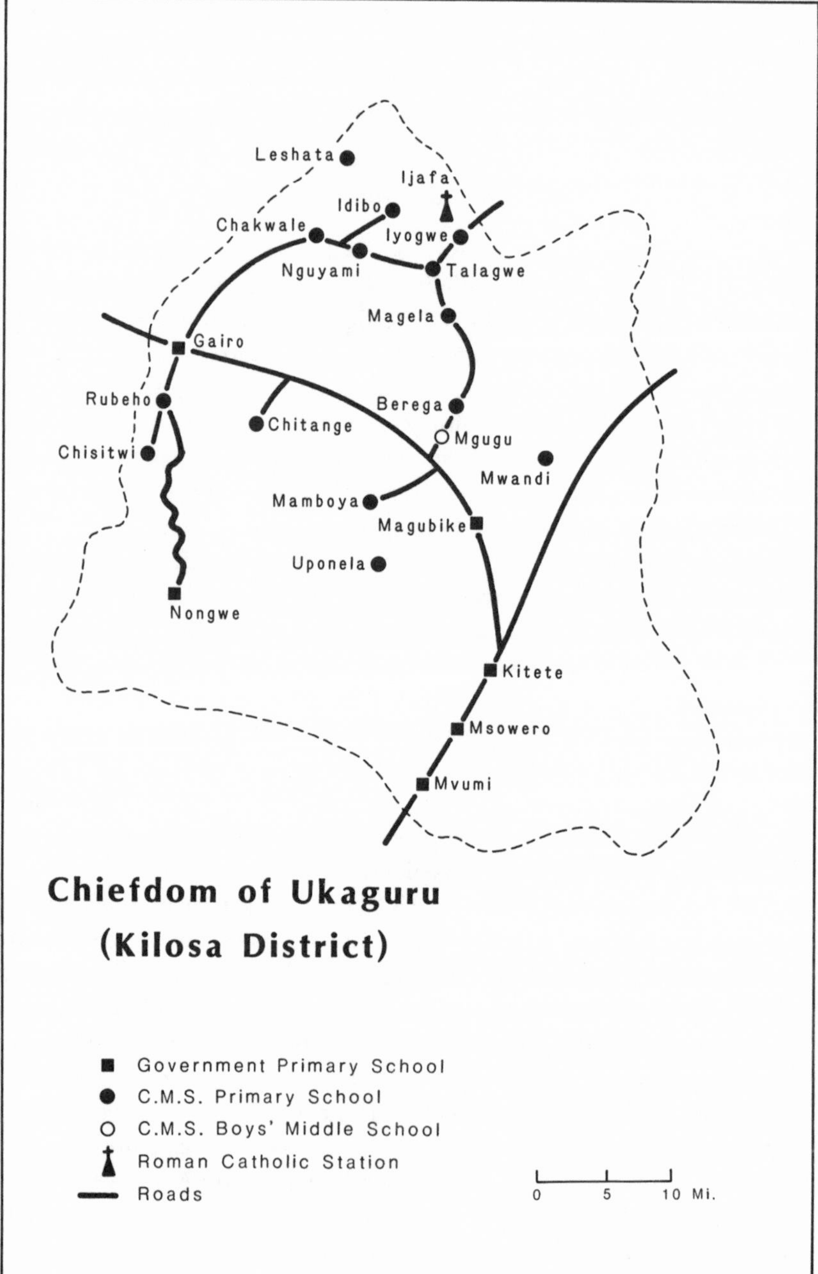
Leshata
Ijafa
Idibo
Chakwale
Iyogwe
Nguyami
Talagwe
Magela
Gairo
Rubeho
Berega
Chitange
Mgugu
Chisitwi
Mwandi
Mamboya
Magubike
Uponela
Nongwe
Kitete
Msowero
Mvumi
Chiefdom of Ukaguru
(Kilosa District)
Government Primary School
C.M.S. Primary School
C.M.S. Boys' Middle School
Roman Catholic Station
Roads
0
5
10 Mi.
CLL

It falls in three parts, two religious and one secular. At the peak stands the residence of the senior missionary, pharmacy, clinic, children's ward, and two separate wards for men and women. Lower is a house for African nurses (for a time occupied by me) and a house for female missionaries working in the hospital. All are of cement blocks with cement floors and metal roofs, except the nurses' house, which has cement floors but a thatched roof and mud walls. Residences of missionaries contrast with those of the African staff, for though all are built similarly, the missionaries' houses are separated from one another by considerable grounds, often landscaped. The houses for African staff are close together, and there is much visiting between wives cooking in the kitchens behind.

Further down the hill are the church; the mission shop which sells foodstuffs, household items, and school supplies; the mission primary school; and residences of lower level staff. Four houses have cement walls and floors and metal roofs, those for the African Archdeacon and three teachers. Three other houses of mud brick with metal roofs and cement floors are for another teacher, a dispenser, and a catechist. The primary school is of mud brick with a cement floor and metal roof. Its condition has drawn criticism from the government because it is below standards. In November 1958, the mission began construction of a new school and a cement brick church. The old church held about 150 people; the school served 150 students, 75 in each of two shifts.

At the lowest edge of the hill, below the plaza facing the school and extending down the hillside, is Mlingoti, the largest Kaguru settlement in the chiefdom. Its inhabitants are Christian and pagan, many employed by the mission as lower staff and servants. Mlingoti forms a contiguous though outwardly more indigenous section of Berega. Most houses are traditional, but a few have metal roofs. Mlingoti is not on mission land, and its residents do not depend on the mission for house plots or gardens. The area owned by the Berega mission is about fifteen acres, little in comparison to that held by the Middle School.

Outlying C.M.S. stations are more modest. In 1957–58 the mission maintained fourteen primary schools in the chiefdom and even more churches.

C.M.S. facilities vary widely. Three examples from Idibo subchiefdom illustrate this: (1) The Idibo mission station lies near the chief's court and contains a school with two classrooms and two nearby houses for teachers, surrounded by school gardens. The church is of mud and thatch and the pastor's house no different from other Kaguru's. Nearby are many buildings as modern as the school, including a courthouse, market, clinic, government staff houses, and commercial shops and housing. (2) At Diola, five miles to the east, there is a church of mud and thatch, which stands apart from the settlement and is tended by a catechist who lives in the village. (3) At Mbili, two miles further east, there are no special facilities, only a catechist working out of his home.

Number of Converts

Formal membership in the C.M.S. through baptism or regular church attendance is relatively small. C.M.S. records at Berega give District membership as 8,024. This includes a small number in adjoining Ungulu. It represents about 15 percent of the total population of the chiefdom (about 70,000, of which 50,000 are Kaguru).[3] A sample government census indicates the area's wide variation in religious adherence:[4]

Headmanship	*Percent CMS*	*Percent RC*	*Percent Muslim*	*Percent Pagan*
Iyogwe	69	10	2	19
Chilama	51	13	—	33
Chisitwi	3	—	—	96
Ikwamba	44	—	—	55
Lihulwi	—	6	—	93
Kitange I	5	—	—	94

Iyogwe is typical of areas which have had long and intensive contact with missions and whose inhabitants are subject to inducements to modernize. It is the only one with a market visited by many traders. In contrast, Chisitwi is typical of remote areas with a C.M.S. primary school but no market and few visitors. The sample is unrepresentative in that half the areas (Lihulwi, Iyogwe, Chilama) are near the two Catholic border stations.

Organization of the Mission

The C.M.S. in Ukaguru is administered by a Ruri-decanal Committee which meets at Berega.[5] This committee is responsible for church funds raised in the area, and it formulates and enforces rules concerning organization and conduct of the staff and congregation. Its members are drawn from ecclesiastical and secular staffs of the mission as well as from the congregation. The committee's activities are better considered after examining the groups with which it is concerned and from which its members come.

Just as political activities of the Kaguru chiefdom are regulated by the Kilosa District administration with its headquarters outside Ukaguru, so the local C.M.S. is regulated from outside, by an Australian Bishop whose cathedral is at Dodoma one hundred miles west of Ukaguru. Head of the Diocese of Central Tanganyika, the Bishop supervises C.M.S. in two-thirds of the country (about 240,000 square miles). He formulates and interprets religious practices and evaluates and appoints pastors. He also heads a secular administration; it manages dozens of schools, hundreds of teachers, several hospitals and their staffs, and bush and town shops which sell a wide variety of items from dried fish, matches, school uniforms, vegetables, paraffin, and hoes, to optical goods, cameras, cosmetics, books, souvenirs, and pharmaceutical supplies. The Bishop visits Ukaguru only once or twice a year, but his authority is felt constantly in local affairs since all appointments, transfers, and promotions pass through his office. He receives regular reports from local stations, coordinates their work, and represents them in serious disputes with government or rival missions. The Bishop is aided by an African Assistant Bishop of modest education who does not attend to the complexities of secular administration but confines himself chiefly to evangelism and conferences with African pastors and congregations.[6] Until November 1958, he resided at Mpwapwa; he then moved to Morogoro, the provincial headquarters sixty miles east of Ukaguru.

The most important secular activities of the mission concern education. Its program in Ukaguru is supervised by a Mission Education Secretary stationed at Morogoro. He is responsible for teachers, school facilities, and course standards. The Education Secretary spends more time in the chiefdom and has more direct impact upon staff than any other mission official outside Ukaguru.

Ecclesiastical Staff

There are six active African pastors *(pasta)* in the chiefdom, five regular and an Archdeacon; another four or five are retired. They serve the ritual needs of their parishioners, advise on spiritual and moral affairs, and mediate between their parishes and Berega through attendance at the Ruri-decanal Committee. With the exception of the Archdeacon (see later) all the pastors are Kaguru, many born in the parishes they serve:

1957 Parish	*Number of Pastors*	*Catechists Assigned to Local Pastors Directly*	*Catechists in Outlying Areas*
Berega	1 (archdeacon)	2	9
Geiro	1	1	4
Idibo	1	1	9
Uponela	1	1	8
Nongwe	1	1	5
Mamboya	1	1	4
	6	46	

Kaguru pastors have modest education; although literate, none has formal education comparable to clerks, teachers, or dispensers. No pastor speaks or reads English or has knowledge of much beyond Swahili translations of the Bible, the *Book of Common Prayer*, and other religious tracts.[7] Their average income is under 350 sh *per annum* except for the Archdeacon, who makes 1600 sh. In contrast, in 1956 the standard government wage for unskilled rural laborers was 1/30 sh *per diem* or about 400 sh *per annum* for a six-day week.[8] All pastors, even the Archdeacon, must secure supplementary income as cultivators.

For the mission, a local pastor has preeminence among his congregation since he knows parish affairs. This does not mean that pastors have great control over parishioners since many Kaguru appear indifferent to formal church activities. Still, missionaries at Berega consult pastors before making decisions likely to affect a parish. Teachers sometimes exert more local influence since they have superior education and income (elementary teachers make more in a month than pastors in an entire year). Teachers are emulated in style of life and consulted where English and other sophisticated skills are required, as in dealing with government. If pastors hold any advantage over teachers and clerks as powerbrokers toward the mission, it is because they possess long experience and diffuse social ties due to extended residence in a parish; teachers are more subject to transfer.

The ultimate sanction exercised by a pastor is his authority to deny religious rites and report immoral conduct to Berega. Such sanctions carry little weight with those who set low store by formal rites or missionary approval. Africans concerned with prestige as reflected by mission approval are teachers and clerks with higher education, who value material wealth. As a consequence, the Africans most open to Christian ideological sanctions are ironically also secularly oriented and therefore more responsive to economic sanctions exerted from Berega. Since a pastor's pay is as low as that of unskilled laborers, he works many hours cultivating his gardens to make ends meet. He therefore has limited time for pastoral duties, especially during cultivation and harvest. Furthermore, pastors do not receive regular pensions or retirement compensations such as those received by some government employees. They are also discouraged from engaging in supplementary business such as trade. The missionaries caution against materialism and requests for high wages; pastors, above all others, should appreciate that true rewards are given in the next world, not this, and serve as models of Christian altruism for Kaguru to emulate. Unfortunately, Kaguru seem more concerned with emulating those who have education, material possessions, and greater acquaintance with European life. The missionaries are short-sighted in discounting the importance of power and prestige in Ukaguru, perhaps because they themselves forego salaries comparable to other Europeans'.

Although pastors are poor, they should be prodigal in hospitality and time, visiting the sick, giving advice, and entertaining traveling Christians. Such demands are generally met with goodwill, but they impose financial strain. The burden of educating their children is heavy for pastors since their annual salaries do not equal the tuition for one year of secondary school and barely cover fees for middle school. Nor are opportunities for advancement within the clergy as encouraging as in secular branches of the mission. The post of Archdeacon may soon fall open to a local pastor, but otherwise the rank is a dead-end. A pastor may attain prestige by revival, but this requires talents not all possess and is considered unbecoming by some. Furthermore, revival is not reserved to pastors; other ambitious Kaguru compete. A decline in the prestige of African pastors in the face of increasing competition for influence from secular fields appears a common problem in East African Protestant missions (cf. Oliver 1952:282–83, 292).

Beneath pastors are senior and regular catechists *(katikisto)* and evangelists *(evanjelisto)*. There are about fifty catechists in Ukaguru; of those, less than a dozen are senior. The number varies year to year. I cannot determine the number of evangelists, but they are fewer than catechists. Each pastor has a senior catechist to assist with services and religious instruction, but only the one who assists the Archdeacon receives a regular salary as well as housing. Catechists are chosen by pastors and tend to be yes-men (cf. Sundkler 1960:170–71). Catechists pursue their duties, which are never full time, because they are "moved" by the Holy Ghost. Evangelists are to catechists as catechists are to pastors; they preach and teach but have more zeal than training. The economic insecurity and vague nature of these posts discourage regularity and perseverance (cf. Sundkler 1960:157–58).

Catechists and evangelists are "religious laymen" respected for their religious conviction. Those who are zealous nurse hopes of receiving subsequent employment and training, but today such expectations seem unrealistic. Some recall the most famous Kaguru evangelist, named Boto, who in 1932 appeared to suffer a catatonic seizure and seemed dead. Indeed, Boto claimed he had died, toured hell, and was resurrected. The mission encouraged Boto to envangelize, and he secured considerable attention by preaching. Evangelists and catechists feel emotional satisfaction at the attention preaching affords, although they may also gain hospitality and gifts.

The Archdeacon

The Archdeacon at Berega is the senior African clergyman in Ukaguru and the most powerful African in the local mission. He was ordained in 1929 and has spent most of the past thirty years at Berega. From 1942 to 1945 he served in the army in Palestine, a source of prestige to some Christian Kaguru. His discharge money provided capital far beyond that amassed by most Kaguru and was employed to enhance his style of life and promote his children's education and business. After returning from service, he was made canon and more recently Archdeacon. Like the Assistant Bishop, the Archdeacon is a Ngulu and former Muslim. Although ordained nine years before the Assistant Bishop, the Archdeacon has not advanced so far, nor has he been encouraged in English. He has not exhibited enthusiasm for revival or junketing about the country.

The Archdeacon is the oldest active clergyman in Ukaguru, a man of striking appearance and manner. He has written works in Swahili, chiefly on local customs. Some have been published, and others are on file with the mission and government. His duties resemble other pastors'. However, because his parish contains the main station and has the largest attending congregation, the Archdeacon communicates directly with the Bishop at Dodoma without recourse to intermediaries.

As Chairman of the Ruri-decanal Committee, the Archdeacon exerts considerable influence on local mission policy; yet his power stems from qualities not entirely explained by his office. Although aliens are often at disadvantage in Ukaguru, that the Archdeacon is Ngulu has not impeded him. Kaguru sometimes explain his assertive, independent character by his ethnicity.[9] Although an outsider, he has been very successful with marital alliances in Ukaguru. One daughter is married to the son of the government headman of Mgugu where the Middle School is located; a kinswoman in his matrilineage is married to the headmaster; his son married a daughter of the local headman's deputy at Mlingoti; and other female kin are married to members of the local staff.

The Archdeacon has devoted many years to studying Kaguru custom and has prepared a long manuscript on the subject. His hobby, along with his residence at Berega, qualifies him as the obvious expert to whom missionaries turn for advice upon traditional Kaguru practices. In this, the Archdeacon has an advantage over Kaguru teachers, for though he is an outsider and has less education than they, his age, status, long local residence, and many affinal ties provide a more credible reputation than many younger men possess. Besides, only someone of unquestionable Christian eminence could afford to take interest in pagan tradition.

The Archdeacon provides information important in determining whether particular marriages should be allowed among Christians,[10] whether a particular rite is classified as harmless or idolatrous, and whether there are grounds for separation or divorce. Although younger, educated Kaguru may seek to compete with the Archdeacon, their education has cut them off from traditional affairs and sympathies. The Archdeacon enjoys as many modern conveniences as teachers and clerks, but he dresses in conservative African gown and cap and often goes barefoot or wears sandals. Teachers and clerks wear shoes, shirts, and trousers. Some Kaguru like the Archdeacon's mixture of prosperity and conservatism. They can aspire to his favor and interest without feeling threatened or embarrassed. Since the missionaries have so little knowledge of everyday African life and custom, some interpreter is essential, and complaints by some Kaguru that the Archdeacon's ethnicity prevents his knowing proper Kaguru tradition are viewed as jealous carping.

Aside from the Assistant Bishop, the Archdeacon is the only African clergyman whose wealth enables him to lead a life consistent with the prestige of his post. His home is in semi-European style and furnished with goods similar to those possessed by wealthier schoolteachers. Although his salary is five times greater than other pastors', it is less than some teachers'. Yet his actual income appears to be greater since he has invested some of his military pay in buildings and other capital. Also, while still a pastor, he dabbled in trade. When reprimanded, he transferred his business activities to his sons. One is employed outside the chiefdom; another is a C.M.S. teacher in Ukaguru; two others are in business at Mgugu market, presumably with their father's support. The Archdeacon resides at the mission station, but owns three (and possibly four) shop buildings at Mgugu.

In 1958 one of the Archdeacon's shops housed the first commercial flour mill in the chiefdom. This was registered in the names of two former government employees; but since one of the Archdeacon's sons worked there and since the building was his, Kaguru suspected that the clergyman was involved. He also may have backed a lorry scheme advanced by the Kaguru teachers' association (Beidelman 1961b); earlier he did back another lorry venture. One of the Archdeacon's shops has been used by two opposing political parties (TANU and UTP) at different times, as well as for a tribalistic union (USA) whose General Secretary is his affine. The Archdeacon has kept in the background of these ventures; but when any proves successful, he accepts some credit. If activities, such as commerce or politics, are forbidden by the mission, these are publicly shouldered by his sons and kin. Since the missionaries have little informed contact with Kaguru and never casually visit neighboring settlements, their criticisms are easily avoided. Within the premises of Berega station, the Archdeacon fulfils the mission ideal of an African clergyman uncorrupted by secular interests; through his kin across the river, he meets the Kaguru conception of an effective man involved in the economic and political activities essential for patronage and prestige. Because he has not conformed to the missionary ideal, he is an effective and valuable member of the church.

There are still other bases for the Archdeacon's power within the community. The African secular staff enjoy none of the religious prestige which would add moral weight to claims they might make; and because of their poor education and meager economic state, African pastors have little influence with subordinates. The Archdeacon has neither set of disabilities; he enjoys both religious authority and secular power and prestige. Thus, he is sought as mediator in most complex difficulties between Africans and Europeans within the mission; he is influential far beyond his rank.

Educational Staff

In 1957–58 the C.M.S. maintained fourteen primary schools (Standards I–IV) in the chiefdom.[11] Each school served about 150 students, and most were staffed by two (rarely three or one) teachers. One teacher (temporary, at Berega) was a woman. Since 1953 the C.M.S. has maintained a boy's Middle School (Standards V–VIII) at Mgugu; it is staffed by five or six teachers and serves about 150 youths. The C.M.S. also maintains a girls' Middle School and a boys' Secondary School (Standards IX–X) over a hundred miles to the west.

Within each primary school teachers hold equal rank, but their income depends upon their education and years of service. Most are Grade II class. Their salaries range from 250 to 500 shillings per month, though the Headmaster of the Middle School and the African School Inspector receive over 500 shillings.[12] Teachers are thus the economic elite of Ukaguru; yet they have few legitimate means of investing cash other than postal savings or bridewealth for their own or their sons' marriages. Government forbids teachers' involvement in business. A large portion of a teacher's income is spent on food since few have much time to cultivate; also, they do not usually live near their homelands where they might have access to land. Some purchase consumer goods which add comfort and prestige but no economic advantage. Others feel thwarted and speak of quitting for better paying posts in business or government.

The twenty-five to thirty primary school teachers in the chiefdom are supervised by one African and one European. In 1957 both spent much time at Berega. The African Inspector is an elderly Kaguru Grade II teacher who has not taught for some years and knows no English. He travels about the chiefdom (by bicycle or receiving lifts from lorries) collecting reports and complaints regarding attendance, equipment, funds, and housing. He mediates between the scattered village teachers and the missionaries at Berega. Unfortunately, his ignorance of English and his Grade II status do not encourage respect from subordinates; nearly all of them speak some English, and some have Grade I status. Some African teachers call the African Inspector a yes-man of the missionaries; he lives at Berega on the mission station and is very mild-mannered.

The Middle School at Mgugu was headed by an African headmaster in 1957–58. He teaches, draws up schedules, and reports school matters to the European Education Secretary. His routine is open to only minor alteration since the government syllabus outlines the courses taught. The Headmaster is also in charge of accounts (although they are checked by the missionaries and the Education Secretary); they involve school fees, cost of food and equipment for students, and income from sale of crops in the school garden.

In 1957–58 the Headmaster pressed for better working conditions for mission teachers, both at the Middle School and elsewhere. The teachers requested terms equal to those at government schools and accused the mission of stinginess. They complained about too close supervision by the Education Secretary. Complaints had been voiced before, but this time the teachers tried to form a union (UTA, Ukaguru Teachers' Association)[13] and pressed for association with the larger government teachers' union (TUAT, Tanganyika Union of African Teachers). The changes were not made; and the Headmaster, who persisted in his criticisms, was privately reprimanded for his aggressive behavior. In 1959 he was transferred to a lower post outside Ukaguru, replaced by the less qualified African Inspector. The Headmaster sought to resign and secure employment in government schools, but his resignation was not accepted and he returned to the mission.[14]

Although teachers have personal prestige as educated and prosperous Africans, they are dependent upon the missionaries for tenure, promotions, and placement. The C.M.S. hires teachers trained within the mission who profess church standards. Any defection is considered a moral betrayal, not a mere change of jobs. A teacher may legally transfer while on good terms with the mission, but this appears rare. Teachers usually seek to leave only after difficulties with other staff or because the mission disapproves of their conduct. Despite a shortage of teachers, defectors require approval from their former superiors before being hired at another mission or government school. The mission could hardly be expected to recommend a teacher with whom it quarreled so severely that he disregarded his obligations and sought posting elsewhere. Consequently, the threat of quitting is somewhat hollow; dissident teachers who quit must choose between returning chastened or giving up teaching.

The teachers' education and prosperity sometimes cause envy. They live far beyond their neighbors since they receive more cash in one month than most Kaguru secure in a year. Some are tribal outsiders, and even Kaguru teachers are often stationed outside their home areas. Free from most local constraints but expecting respect out of proportion to his age or the favors he provides, a teacher may become a victim of back-biting to the missionaries.

Medical and Shop Staff

Although most secular personnel within the mission are concerned with education, a few at Berega are otherwise employed. One works in the mission shop; two others are mail couriers; and about a dozen work in the hospital as nurses, aides, dispensers, cleaners, and builders. The missionaries also employ several houseboys, gardeners, and cooks. All must go to church to retain their posts.

The African nurses at the hospital are quartered far from other employees and seem to be discouraged from mingling freely, presumably because they are unmarried, apart from their families, and on short-call never far from the hospital. Other employees reside in Mlingoti and Mgugu. All receive far lower salaries than teachers. The mission also employs a few grounds keepers; in 1958 these struck for pay equal to that of workers in town. Their demands were not met.

The Missionaries

When I arrived, a pastor, his wife, a female doctor, and a nurse resided at Berega. Shortly before I left in 1958, a second nurse was added. All were trained to conduct religious services as well as to perform secular tasks. The doctor and pastor held comparable rank and rarely contacted one another in their daily routine. In 1958 the doctor also oversaw the shop and postal service. In 1957 the pastor also served as School Inspector. When he was on leave or traveling, the entire staff was female; that hindered some facets of the work since African men dislike discussing some matters with women.

The pastor held church services at Berega and enthusiastically supported revival. He was in charge of the mission accounts and dispensed monthly salaries through the office attached to his house. He was assisted by the African School Inspector, who exerted considerable influence through reports and recommendations but could not authorize changes himself. These could be made only through the Education Secretary at Morogoro. In 1958 the Pastor-School Inspector went on leave and was replaced by another married missionary who was not a pastor. The new inspector confined himself to education. Religious activities were assumed by the Archdeacon, and financial duties were split between the new inspector and the mission medical staff.

The medical staff is absorbed in the routine of running the hospital and make few visits outside the station. They encounter a wider range of Africans than do their colleagues, who are almost wholly engaged in administration. The medical staff conduct compulsory religious services for their patients: hymns are sung, Bible verses read, and religious exhortations made (cf. Harding 1920?:15–16); but most working hours involve actual medical work.[15] At night, they do perform supplementary chores. One does accounts, draws up shipment lists for the shop, and supervises the postal service. Another sews much of the bedding, curtains, and clothing used in the hospital. The medical staff's Land-Rover is occasionally used to visit emergency cases and rarely to distribute religious tracts and medicine. The medical workers receive little or no government funds and therefore, unlike those in education, have almost no contact with government officials. White writes of the pressure on such personnel:

> The strain of hospital life is tremendous for European nurses. On them falls the supervision of the staff, training girls whose background is completely African, battling with relatives, and frequently having to deal with problems that would worry a doctor. Add to this the rigours of the climate, frequent night calls, continuous warfare against the thousands of insects and you will understand how it is that nurse after nurse cracks on the job. [1952:118][16]

Certainly a medical staff that is exclusively female feels especially insulted:

> Hitherto one result of the inferior position of women in the hierarchy of the overseas diocese has been that hospitals have had very little place in the thinking of church leaders. For indigenous medical personnel is largely made up of women nurses and a few male nursing orderlies. [Anderson 1956:10]

The missionaries define Christian morality for local Kaguru and provide the model for them to emulate. All, including the wives, are vastly better educated than any Africans in the chiefdom. Most are better versed in religious matters than the Archdeacon himself, even though he is their ecclesiastic superior. Most come from missionary families which provided them with intensive religious indoctrination in childhood. The missionaries attend some African religious services (the medical staff are often too busy) and revivals at Berega and confer with the Archdeacon and other pastors regarding religious policy. They also hold regular prayer meetings by themselves.

Judging from their styles of life, the missionaries receive salaries many times higher than those of the most highly paid African teachers, not to mention pastors and clerks. Although their salaries are low in comparison to those of other Europeans in the Territory, they appear enormous to Kaguru. The missionaries maintain a vehicle and modest but proper European-type homes. They can afford bread, tinned goods, European clothing, books, and newspapers. They employ servants and entertain government officials as equals on the rare occasions when they visit the station.

Mission Kaguru presume that common cultural and linguistic ties override any possible differences among Europeans and mistakenly assume that interests of government and mission are nearly identical. Within the mission, such cultural solidarity exists that when the Bishop, Education Secretary, and others visit, they dine and sleep at the homes of missionaries and never at those of Africans, not even at the Archdeacon's.

The missionaries rarely associate with Africans in informal, nonhierarchical situations, nor do they visit the African settlements adjoining the station. Tours off mission property are confined chiefly to trips by motorcar to inspect personnel and collect supplies; rarely, they make emergency medical calls for which expenses are collected. Even at Berega I know of no visits or meetings between African and European personnel outside business or worship. The Europeans' heavy burden of administrative and medical work fosters isolation (cf. Pauw 1960:69; Taylor 1957:11), and their distance from Kaguru is increased by the fact that few spend repeated tours at Berega. The C.M.S. lacks sufficient funds or staff to keep as many missionaries in Ukaguru as it wants, and more important stations are given priority in staffing. Furthermore, Berega's remoteness leads some to prefer assignment elsewhere. Finally, the smallness of the European staff means that personal relations become more intense and difficult than at larger stations and transfers are sometimes sought.

Missionary power is based on control of the reports sent to superiors, closer cultural and personal ties to superiors, and higher incomes and education. Only the first of these is endorsed by C.M.S. ideology. Missionaries see themselves as more responsible and better tested in their faith than Kaguru while Kaguru resent their claims and term this *kalaba* (color bar).

Materialism, Altruism, and Prestige

Since arriving in Ukaguru, the C.M.S. has presented Christian belief as inextricably linked with the material and technical superiority of Europeans. The mission's near monopoly on education within the chiefdom has made such an association plausible to many Kaguru even though such notions are rejected by many elsewhere (cf. Wilson 1969:188).

Missionaries recommend some forms of behavior even though they are not essentially Christian. European-type clothing is considered more modest and proper than traditional undress. Tea is encouraged in place of beer, which is thought to lead to violence and debauchery. Drinking tea from a china cup and saucer is considered more civilized than using a tin cup or, worse yet, a calabash. Wearing shoes, at least to church, is considered more proper than going barefoot; and many Christians now buy shoes for Sundays and other special occasions. I do not mean that the missionaries explicitly represent such articles as Christian, but Kaguru who resemble Europeans in manners and dress are given more notice by missionaries and Kaguru interpret this accordingly.[17] Inevitably, Kaguru associate material advantages with worthiness in the church. Material wealth is cited by Kaguru as proof that they are enlightened. Despite C.M.S. disclaimers of materialism, requisite clothing and education represent enormous expenses to Kaguru. In 1957, an ensemble of shorts and shirt cost at least 20 shillings; trousers about 40 shillings; a boy's tuition in primary school 10 shillings, a girl's 5, shillings;[18] a boy's annual tuition in Middle School over 200 shillings (not to mention uniforms and utensils) and in Secondary School over 350 shillings. To Kaguru these expenses represent luxury; in 1957 the average Kaguru family received less than 300 shillings ($45) in cash per year, and the average man among the fifty top elite in the chiefdom had income of no more than about 3,600 shillings.

Few, if any, Kaguru Christians comprehend the niceties of Christian ideology, and few, if any, missionaries have the ability, interest, or time to learn how Kaguru reinterpret Christian doctrine. While the two groups cannot easily communicate with one another concerning their religious views, they can define Christian status by external conduct. It is difficult to enforce common religious beliefs in such a situation; but conduct, especially abstention from things thought to be enjoyed by unenlightened pagans, is checked and enforced.

The missionaries encourage education and press government to maintain their near monopoly in local education because they believe that it is the most effective means of conversion. Yet this same education leads Kaguru to value material well-being. While missionaries see themselves living in altruistic poverty when compared to other Europeans, to Kaguru their houses, autos, furniture, clothing, and education represent a standard of living infinitely beyond that of Africans. Kaguru demand this as their right as well, as brothers and sisters in one church (cf. Beidelman and Winter 1967:185–86; Oliver 1962:242). To the C.M.S., African demands for higher pay and threats of resignation or strikes are at odds with the spirit of Christianity and sacrifice which has maintained the mission. This is of little importance to the Kaguru when compared to obligations to educate, clothe, and feed their families according to their growing aspirations. Kaguru believe that the mission owes them special economic considerations as part of their religious affiliation. Thus, some expect extended credit at the mission shop even though this nearly ruined the shop. A sharp note was prominently posted stating that parishioners had over 1,200 shillings in unpaid debts and no more credit was available.

The very poverty of the missionaries forces them to adopt procedures reinforcing the negative stereotypes which Kaguru have of them as money-minded and hypocritical in their denunciation of materialism. In contrast to most colonial Europeans, missionaries charge for services and goods that others give away. Missionaries charged small fees to patients at the dispensary and small fees to primary students during a period when government dispensaries were free and (prior to 1958) boys and girls in government primary schools paid less than at missions. The missionaries post advertisements of charges to African riders of mission vehicles. Kaguru expect Europeans either to allow Africans to ride free or to refuse everyone. Missionaries collect costs for petrol used in special visits. They sell vegetables and fruits grown in their gardens and sometimes sell used clothing and furnishings. They even post rates for using the mission typewriter. While these charges are far below the actual worth of goods and services, Kaguru see this as penny-pinching. The bitterness felt by some Kaguru creeps into a letter written to me in 1960 by an educated Kaguru member of the church:

> You wanted to know from me about the C.M.S. Some of them regard themselves as they are always right, they don't respect the African; they regard the African of today as the same as the one of yesterday. They are not frank. They use the African as a non-living tool. They like to be called bwana [master], and the African to run to him when he is called by one of them. Few of them show by their life what they teach. If the doctrine they teach originated in Europe, I would not be a Christian. But to be a Christian as the name suggests is a very difficult life. I think if the world was full of good Christians there would be permanent peace. Jesus Christ foresaw what would happen afterward. People will come in his name to deceive people.

Christian Conduct

In 1957 the C.M.S. in Ukaguru expected Christian conduct from both staff and congregation, although in the latter case this was difficult to enforce.[19] Emphasis was upon abstinence from traditional pagan rites, regular attendance at church, and acquisition of Christian names through baptism.

Most parishes hold one service on Sunday morning, but Berega holds two, a brief 10:00 service for Middle School students and staff and a longer one at 11:00 for others. Sunday service lasts one to two hours with men and women seated separately and few children attending. Ritual is spoken in Swahili, but sermons are delivered in a mixture of Swahili and Chikaguru. Services begin with a hymn; it is followed by a short prayer which ends with the Lord's Prayer spoken in unison. Then there are announcements and comments on local events. A sermon is preceded by selections from scripture and a hymn and followed by a collection of donations, another hymn, and a benediction. Communion is given to those who desire it, and their names are listed by the pastor. Donations are taken only on Sundays. On Fridays parishioners are expected also to attend a 2:00 Bible class taught by the local pastor.

Young, aspiring Christians are urged to attend classes taught by the pastor and catechist. Most "learners" (*wanafunzi*) are between ten and eighteen years old, and more girls than boys attend. Learner classes meet twice a week (2:00–3:30). At Berega about thirty attend. Selections from the Bible and *Book of Common Prayer* are read and discussed, and students are instructed about baptism and communion. After 20–40 days of instruction, the candidates are examined by the pastor and catechist; they are usually passed and baptized. They should then attend further Bible classes every Friday. In Berega about one hundred, over half women, attend such classes.

The missionaries remain ignorant of Kaguru traditions and express revulsion about them. This seems little different from elsewhere in Africa (cf. Sundkler 1960:90). The Archdeacon shows interest in recording local tradition; in contrast, some African teachers and students are more vigorously opposed than some missionaries.

Many traditional practices condemned by the C.M.S. are also condemned by other missions: polygyny, premarital sexual intercourse, concubinage, female genital excision, rainmaking, witchfinding, ancestral propitiation, and divination. The mission is adamant against divorce, however much this fits Kaguru social organization. It also is cool toward male initiation, blood brotherhood covenants, and cross-cousin marriage, although it would be difficult to provide scriptural support for such condemnation. Kaguru were horrified when in 1958 the mission's female doctor demanded that boys be sent to her for circumcision.

Some Kaguru make the best of both ideological worlds; they abstain from actual rites themselves but contribute funds through their kin to local experts who carry these out. Sometimes odd compromises offend everyone: I once attended a "Christian" female initiation near the mission where most dancing took place indoors. The initiate appeared fully dressed but, as ritual required, mimed sexual congress. The missionaries would have been horrified by the dancing; pagan Kaguru were horrified that ritual was performed for all to see, supposedly because there was no nakedness and therefore no reason to hide.

The C.M.S. denounces alcohol, tobacco, drumming, and dancing, all popular pastimes easily observed and reported:

> In some quarters heathenism is still strongly entrenched and licentious dances are indulged in by all the youth of the district, even young lads and girls frequent these horrible orgies. In such places there is no desire for the gospel message. [*P.C.M.S.* 1922–23:15]

One evening shortly after arriving in Ukaguru, I was excited to hear drums celebrating initiation (that sort of thing excites an anthropologist). I asked one missionary what this signified. She told me that it was "a blinkin' orgy" with "dancing and fornication." If any mission staff is found guilty of attending such celebrations, he is threatened with discharge or temporary suspension. The most common grounds for such punishment are, in order of frequency, adultery and fornication, drinking and dancing, and participation in pagan rites. Besides being the main available recreations, dancing and drinking are essential to traditional rites —including marriage, initiation, and funerals—in which Christians are expected to participate with their pagan kin and neighbors. Selling tobacco and beer is, of course, forbidden, but is among the few means by which Kaguru can obtain extra cash without leaving the chiefdom.

At Berega, Kaguru celebrate even Christian festivals in a pagan manner. At Christmas, houses are decked with flowers and green boughs, everyone tries to purchase new European-type clothing, and there is continuous dancing, drumming, and drinking. People consider both the 25th and 26th of December holidays. Drinking, drumming, and dancing continue late into each night. In 1958 the Archdeacon broke up some dances held at the boundaries of the station grounds. The annoyed celebrants merely moved a few yards onto public land and continued all the louder. Christmas is appreciated since it is the last break before the heaviest work of the agricultural year.

Since the missionaries have little informal contact with Kaguru and rarely visit Kaguru settlements, they depend upon their staff for reports of infractions against the moral code. Consequently, selective enforcement of Christian behavior has become an important means by which Africans exert pressure on one another; they expel persons from mission service because of quarrels or because they seek posts for themselves or relatives. The process by which this is accomplished is complex, for not all persons' word would be taken seriously. Denunciation within the mission functions similarly to earlier social control through accusations of witchcraft. Gossip and suspicions may be rife, but successful accusations fall against those unable or unwilling to come to terms with prevailing and working social relations.

Here are four examples:

(1) Alfred was a teacher who worked over five years at the mission and attended church regularly. He frequented the local beer clubs and was a notorious philanderer, yet paid little attention to gossip about himself. Alfred made fun of his superiors behind their backs. His unfaithfulness was not openly criticized by his wife since he supported his family comfortably and would probably lose his job if his misconduct became an issue. Alfred began an affair with a married woman living near the station. She was also having an affair with a local headman. It was rumored that this headman complained to a relative prominent in the church. A year later Alfred was dismissed for fornication and drinking and forced to take a job as clerk with an Asian shopkeeper in a distant area. His new post provided less than half his former pay and kept him far from his kin. Later, Alfred was "saved" and again employed by the mission. When I returned to Ukaguru in 1962, the mission schools were under more direct control by government and Alfred had resumed open drinking, confident that he could not be fired.

(2) Kenneth was also a teacher. He had been employed by the mission for less than a year. Shortly after he arrived, he began an affair with Anna, the runaway wife of an elder of the church and half-brother to a local headman. Anna had given up most connections with the church when she had deserted her husband. At that time she was having a notorious affair with Noah, a member of the church who had also lapsed. Noah was married but kept Anna as his lover. On account of this, Noah quarreled violently with both the headman and his half-brother, and moved his homestead to just outside the headman's area. He gave up active membership in the church yet attended services occasionally. Anna lived by herself under the protection of her mother's kin (she was illegitimate and did not know her

father) earning money by brewing beer and prostitution. She occasionally attended church. In 1958 she became pregnant. Most Kaguru believed the child was Noah's although it could have been by one of her clients. Since Noah was only a cultivator and had shown himself stout-hearted under pressure, Anna did not trouble him for support of her pregnancy. Instead, she went to Kenneth, a "rich schoolteacher." She is said to have told him that it was his child and that he should pay expenses. If he refused, she threatened to denounce him in church. She reminded Kenneth that she had little to lose but that he would lose his job. Kenneth complied and Anna has not spoken since of him as the father. The child is under the control of Anna's matrikin which pleased them.

(3) Ruben, son of a prominent church elder, was divorced and known as a rake. He impregnated the daughter of Esau, another elder. Ruben was willing to marry her, but Esau refused and instead requested 70 sh or he would go to court. Although the court would have awarded only 30 sh, Ruben paid 70 sh instead. It was rumored the fathers wanted to avoid publicity for both church families.

(4) Brighton was a mission teacher. His wife visited outside Ukaguru and asked her sister to cook for him while she was away [an unorthodox request]. Brighton seduced his wife's sister who is rumored to have slept regularly with him. The women's kinsmen brought the case to court but failed to win due to insufficient evidence. The kin were not concerned about adultery but with the breaking of traditional prohibitions against sleeping with affines, an offence believed to pollute and supernaturally endanger matrikin. Brighton's father put pressure on kin including a chief in the Native Authority. These men forced the couple to separate and go through a pagan cleansing ceremony (*nhemera*, see Beidelman 1966a) involving animal sacrifice, ritual nudity, and invocation of ancestral ghosts. Christian neighbors reported this and Brighton lost his job. This was ironic since he had tried to hide his escapade but had properly submitted to demands for the good of his kin.

At Berega the mission has created a theocratic enclave within a secular chiefdom (cf. Sundkler 1960:98–99).[20]

Revival

Although Kaguru convicted of immorality may lose their mission posts, they may regain them through revival. Public confession of sin has always been a feature of the C.M.S. (cf. Chapter 8) and appears to have been encouraged as a means of obtaining evangelists during the financially difficult years of the depression. Revivals were first led by Africans from Kenya, Uganda, and the Lake Provinces of Tanzania.

In 1957–58 the C.M.S. organized a series of revivals in the chiefdom. They were led by the African Assistant Bishop who toured Ukaguru between opening and closing rallies at Berega. He was aided by evangelists from outside Ukaguru as well as a few locals. The Archdeacon attended but did not take an active part. To many Kaguru, the Assistant Bishop is living proof of the socioeconomic advantages of confession since he owes his advancement to his revivalistic skill.

The meetings themselves last most of the day. They are attended by as many as two or three hundred people. Visiting evangelists are feasted with sheep, fowls, and other good foods contributed locally. Hymn singing, informal prayer meetings, and conversational interrogation extend into the night after the rally ends. Sometimes the missionaries attend and speak, but the major attraction is the African evangelists and those who, seized by the Holy Spirit, publicly confess their sins and repent. This is described as receiving manna from Heaven. Confession affirms a speaker's superior moral status in two ways: his own sins are confessed and repented, and the sins of others who have not repented are described and condemned. In speeches, everyday comments, and conduct, revivalists stress their own superior morality and grace and demean their neighbors.

Some evangelists began their careers as "saved" confessors. These are usually persons whose sordid deeds and eloquence as speakers attract a large crowd. One wag describes such rallies as the Kaguru substitute for the cinemas in town, and indeed some of the details and emotionalism of the disclosures are dramatic and sleazy. Sometimes onlookers implicated in the sins confess, in violent reaction. The chief sins confessed are adultery and fornication, drinking, dancing, irreverence, covetousness, theft, and materialism. Rarely (more frequently in the past), some confess practicing magic and sorcery and destroy medicines before a crowd. Such entertainment draws both pagans and Christians. A few cynical Kaguru observe that missionaries watch Kaguru revivals but conduct their own confessions in private because they would not want to disclose their misdeeds to subordinates.

To convicted sinners dismissed from mission posts, revivals provide convenient means whereby they can reinstate themselves; in this sense they allow the mission to reabsorb lost but essential personnel. Confessed sinners can not only resume their old posts but become part-time evangelists as well. The following cases illustrate these processes:

(1) Mateya was a teacher whose love affair with a local woman came to the attention of his superiors. He was dismissed but after a few months confessed his sins at a revival and was taken back. He was not allowed to teach at his old post but given employment outside the chiefdom. He hoped that in time he would be allowed home.

(2) Marki was a teacher who took a girl to his bachelor's quarters at night. He was caught by the girl's kin who complained to the mission. He was dismissed, but six months later confessed at a revival and was taken back in another district.

(2) Luka was a teacher who attracted attention by abusing people when drunk. He was admonished by the mission but not fired. He was transferred to a station four hundred miles to the west. Two years later, he attended a revival and confessed his sins, protesting that he had not drunk a drop since his transfer. He was allowed to return to a post in Ukaguru.

(4) Yohanna was a teacher brought to court for adultery. He was an excellent teacher needed by the mission. Apparently for that reason he was told that, although dismissed, he might reapply for employment after six months provided he demonstrated true contrition. A few weeks later, he attended a revival, declared himself saved, and was rehired before the six months' probation expired.

A celebrated revivalist might receive evangelistic training or be given a job as a cook, houseboy, or gardener. At the least, he could expect money for itinerant preaching, food, and lodging. The revivals which the missionaries attended at Berega were among the few means by which Kaguru could demonstrate moral superiority and leadership to those in power without relying upon the intermediary control of the Archdeacon. This may account for the Archdeacon's lack of enthusiasm for such rallies.

Those who subscribe to revival and its stricter interpretation of conduct call themselves *wangofu* ("the broken-down") or, if they speak English, the "saved" or "straight and narrowers." Those who do not emphasize such rectitude ironically refer to themselves merely as *wakristo* ("Christians"). The former group disdain the latter, but they regard with more contempt those who were saved and then sin again. Those offend both camps. Proponents of revival include not only the Assistant Bishop and missionaries but some teachers and young men who hope for advancement or employment. Nonrevivalists include the Archdeacon, a few teachers, those headmen who profess Christianity, and the more established, elderly members of congregations. Revivalism seems favored by those ambitious for higher status, while those already in power see such goings-on as threats to their positions. Since they occur only a few weeks a year, revivals may be cyclical "rituals of rebellion" where ambitions and resentments which have accumulated over the year may be worked out.

Revivalists who vehemently reject pagan neighbors and kin are eventually forced into more tolerant attitudes, since few Kaguru have sufficient economic security to be independent of others. Those few who assume some independence are mission employees, and they have only exchanged one type of dependence for another, which in some ways is even riskier. Emilia provides a dramatic example of someone who denounced the traditional code and failed:

> Emilia was the wife of Senyagwa and was saved at a revival. She criticized Senyagwa for his pagan beliefs and encouraged her children to do the same. Senyagwa did not divorce Emilia but took a second, younger wife. Senyagwa was a very prominent and influential Kaguru who for many years had been a senior member of the Native Authority. Despite this, Emilia and her children refused to associate with him and moved to Berega. After being saved, Emilia secured a job at the mission. This kept her from housework so she hired Maria, a local girl. Emilia's eldest son, Julius, completed Secondary School through his father's support and secured a clerical post outside Ukaguru. Emilia remained at Berega with her younger son, Nahum, and her daughter, Yudia. Yudia went to visit Julius and became pregnant. When she returned from the town with this news, Emilia told her that she was no good and refused to help. Yudia sought help from Senyagwa, who reminded her of her ingratitude.
>
> Julius became a leader in a local political movement and sought support from prominent Kaguru; therefore, he became reconciled with his influential father. In the meantime, Nahum took advantage of Maria, the housekeeper, who became pregnant. He sought reconciliation with Senyagwa to secure bridewealth to make Maria an honest woman.
>
> In the midst of these difficulties, Emilia became seriously ill and lost her job. She did not recover after several weeks at the hospital and left Berega to live invalided halfway between Berega and Senyagwa's. She had spent all her savings on medical bills and sought reconciliation with Senyagwa.

In another case, a Kaguru was saved by his neighbors, who then helped cut down his profitable tobacco crop. Later his wife became ill, and he lamented his crop's loss since it would have paid her bills. His neighbors refused him loans, and he regretted being saved.

Education

Missionaries and laymen agree that mission schools are the most important means by which the mission attracts converts and promotes its message. In 1957 mission schools conformed to the general format of a government syllabus, and students took examinations set by government authorities. I cannot provide a detailed account of local Kaguru education, but a few general facts illustrate the situation. One is the low level of education, although there is no reason to assume it is much better with other mission or government schools.

The schedules at the mission primary school at Idibo give a dejecting impression. The classes—Standards I, II, III, and IV—are on two overlapping shifts due to shortage of facilities and staff. In 1957, such double shifts were also followed in local government schools. Formal classes were separated into grades; but play, work, and religious instruction were often pooled. Class sessions were brief: the shortest for Standards I and II was half an hour; the longest for Standards III and IV, forty-five minutes. Much time was spent cleaning rooms, working gardens, and puttering around. Time was thus allocated: Standards I and II, 45 percent secular classes, 13 percent religious instruction, 8 percent breaks, 34 percent work and games; Standards III and IV, 56 percent secular classes, 10 percent religious instruction, 10 percent breaks, 28 percent work and games. The primary classes were taught mainly in Swahili although a little English was introduced in the final year. Students learned reading and writing Swahili, simple arithmetic, elements of health and physiology, and basic geography and history of East Africa. Crafts included basket-making, tool-making, carpentry, and agriculture.[21] Boys were taught football and girls games such as tag.

In Middle School (Standards V–VII) considerable time was spent working in gardens; cleaning grounds, classrooms, and mess; cutting firewood; and drawing water. Most students worked about one and a half hours each morning and another two and a half hours in the evening on school chores.

After the first year of Middle School, class instruction was almost entirely in English. Classes met from 8:15–4:15 with a noon lunch break. Since Middle School was residential, teachers had considerable control over everyday life and enforced strict work and study hours. Boys attended meals promptly, helped in mess and kitchen duties, and obeyed curfew. Middle School classes continued in advanced Swahili, English, agriculture, biology, arithmetic, religion, and African and world geography and history. Students were given courses in general science and access to a workshop for carpentry. Students in Middle School, unlike Primary students, considered themselves a fortunate elite likely to secure better jobs than others. They were considerably older than students generally are in our own eighth grade since many delayed entry until kin saved up fees. Ages ranged from eleven to nineteen; the average age of a graduate from Standard VII was seventeen. Because of their age and because of constant nagging by kin and teachers, who reminded them how extraordinarily lucky they were to be in school at all, such students were soberer and more industrious than Primary students in America or Britain. Most were painfully aware that much was expected of them due to their families' sacrifices. Education represented an immense capital investment, not only in funds for tuition but because students were absent from productive labor at home.

C.M.S. education is inextricably related to Christianity. Bible readings, religious instruction, and church attendance are required of all Middle School students. What is written is absorbed uncritically, and the Bible is presented as the book among books. I once overheard a conversation between a sophisticated African political agitator and a Kaguru teacher which neatly illustrates the veneration of literacy:

> Teacher: The Bible is written proof of what God wants.
>
> Agitator: How do you know that a book like Revelations was not written by a madman? It sounds like my dreams when I have a fever.
>
> Teacher: Don't be foolish! How could a madman write a book?

Those who do poorly in Middle School resign themselves to jobs as clerks or shop attendants; most hope to pass to Secondary School, though less than a quarter do. Those lucky ones usually want to be teachers since few other good posts are open in the chiefdom.[22]

The Kaguru Congregation

The most striking feature of local congregations is the absence of important group activities apart from common worship. It is not membership in a congregation but in a kin group, headmanship, or neighborhood which binds Kaguru. There are congregational committees established by the mission, but these have few members and are unsuccessful. A pastor's wife presides over a woman's group *(mama chama)* which teaches householdry at Saturday meetings in a school. An education committee composed of laymen selected by the pastor and local teachers discusses collection of school fees, prevention of truancy, and donation of labor for maintaining schoolhouses. A hospital committee composed of the medical staff and laymen meets at Berega each October to discuss community support. These groups have no formal powers but diffuse limited information about mission policies and local needs. Membership in such groups is not prestigious but an onerous obligation to superiors within the church or to prominent men who have nominated one.

The mission staff exercise power over a congregation in order to secure two ends: (1) conversion of Africans and enforcement of Christian conduct; and (2) material support of personnel through donation of labor, goods, and cash. The congregation seeks the benefit of religious rites, employment, and education. It achieves some control of African mission staff through the threat of reporting unchristian conduct to Berega; but its chief means of exerting influence in the mission are through representatives to the Ruri-decanal Committee, through withholding cooperation and contributions, and through not attending services.

African laymen provide only a small portion of the funds by which the mission runs. I have attended church services where African pastors pled for donations from each member of the congregation and were met with silence rather than refusal. When an individual was asked directly, he claimed poverty.[23] The only parishioners whose incomes are actually known by the mission are mission employees. The mission controls their payments by deducting a voluntary contribution from monthly earnings. It is the fifty or sixty employees who provide over half the local contributed income. Besides making contributions, employees are expected to evangelize. Students are also expected to contribute labor to mission needs, e.g., while I was at Berega and Idibo, students helped construct the local church and provided free labor to local teachers.

Aside from the sanctions applied to employees and students, the mission is mostly ineffective in controlling its congregations. Mission leaders can bring legal sanctions to bear in two sectors, education and marriage.

Children of school age are required by law to attend schools, and parents are required to pay school fees when asked. It is allowed for a Kaguru to send a child to a cheaper, more distant government school, but this poses so many economic problems regarding food and residence that it is impractical. Parents of truant children and those who are delinquent in paying fees are prosecuted in court. The law, therefore, guarantees that most Kaguru receive at least four years of C.M.S. proselytization in primary school if they live in an area of C.M.S. comity.[24] Although this is not wholly effective, a sample census reveals that in 1957 no Kaguru educated beyond Standard IV reported as pagan and few completing primary school did so.[25]

In the colonial period, government did not allow courts to dissolve marriages made through a church. In Ukaguru such cases could be heard only through the Archdeacon. To circumvent control by the C.M.S., some Christians contracted marriage outside the church. Others contracted first marriages in the church but subsequent ones outside. A Christian man could become a polygynist without violating secular law but could not easily divorce his first wife. The initiative lay with the Christian wife who might eventually be granted divorce and her husband expelled from church. Thus, the law does not prevent divorce or polygyny; but it does support the mission insofar as most cases involving Christians eventually come before the Archdeacon, local pastors, and missionaries, and Christians are impeded in securing divorces. This works more to the disadvantage of women than men, even though the C.M.S. insist their values have brought women new freedom and dignity.

Mission authorities can prevent disobedient members from enjoying communion and other rites; but they cannot prevent anyone calling himself Christian and, because of their own beliefs find it difficult to forbid any sinner to church attendance or revival. Condemnation by the mission seems tempered in cases of men who hold political authority. Some headmen and the Paramount Chief were baptized but now ignore the rules of the church (the Paramount Chief drinks heavily and has three wives). These backsliders are still treated courteously on their rare visits to Berega and sit as adjunct members on committees.

Among various rites and services which missionaries and pastors withhold from backsliders are the following:

(1) Church services: While the C.M.S. estimates that there are about 8,000 members in the chiefdom, less than five or six hundred attend weekly instructions. In some areas pastors record attendance and question those who are irregular. I know of no case of persons refused entry to a church.

(2) Communion: This does not appear to be valued highly by most Kaguru; they seem hostile to confessing sins and avoid communion because missionaries and some pastors request periodic confession before communion is given.

(3) Baptism: Kaguru attach importance to the official bestowal of a Christian name. Adult converts are baptized only after passing catechism, but children of Christians are baptized as infants. A small fee of a few shillings is requested.[26] Kaguru refer to this as "buying a name." There is nothing to prevent Kaguru from adopting Christian names without baptism.

(4) Marriage: Church weddings are prized by many, especially people who are educated. To carry prestige, a marriage should be performed by the Archdeacon at the main church at Berega. Such weddings occasion conspicuous consumption and imitation of European behavior: bedsheets may be used as bridal trains (one bride wore argyle socks); guns may be shot off; and a truck may be rented to convey the party and guests to and from the service.

(5) Funerals: Burials are not important rites among Kaguru. Traditionally such tasks were considered so polluting that they were assigned to "joking relations." Kaguru do hold elaborate mourning and funerals to settle the affairs of the deceased. The C.M.S. has no rituals for death apart from those of interment or memorial rites in church. As a result, pagan ceremonies such as wakes and estate settlements are held outside the mission. Interment in consecrated ground is important to some Christians. In Berega and Mamboya there are distinct burial zones: an area for Christians in good standing, outlying areas for backsliders, and scattered bush for those outside the church. A few Christians left the church because mission leaders would not allow burial of pagan kin in consecrated ground.

Although these rites are important to Kaguru Christians, each has a pagan counterpart which in most cases is performed as well; no one is without pagan kin, who demand such rites be performed before they lend their support.

Ruri-decanal Committee

Local mission business is regulated by a thirty-person Ruri-decanal Committee which meets at Berega at least twice a year.[27] This is the only local mission group in which ecclesiastical and secular members formulate a common policy and in which African laymen formally voice opinions directly to missionaries. The Bishop and Assistant Bishop are ex officio members; they do not attend but receive its proceedings. The chairman is appointed by the Bishop. He invariably selects the senior local clergyman, and in 1957–58 this was the Archdeacon. All active ordained African pastors (five or six) are members, as well as their senior catechists. All four Europeans are members.[28] The African secular staff is represented by the Headmaster of the Middle School and a committee treasurer chosen by the Bishop (in 1957, the African School Superintendent). Of the African laymen, one is elected from each parish (usually following the local pastor) and three are selected by the Committee Chairman (Archdeacon); the secretaries of the current mission committees, such as the hospital, education, and women's are included. The Paramount Chief and other elders are invited to attend some of the meetings; because the elders are illiterate, they make little of the proceedings.

The committee controls about 5,000 sh at any time: it receives 200 sh biannually from teachers and somewhat less from other members, and it has about 1,000 to 1,500 sh in reserve from preceding years. Major expenditures consist of the salaries of the Archdeacon and pastors, small sums to repair mission buildings and equipment, and travel funds for pastors and revivalists including the Assistant Bishop. Small sums are also available as loans to parishes. These funds are small indeed, and the mission can hardly maintain itself by these alone; yet they provide all support for parish work and bush evangelism. The budget for the committee does not equal the annual salary of one European missionary and barely surpasses that of the headmaster. Still, to Kaguru, the budget is large and worth deliberation. Allotment of a few hundred shillings to one rather than another parish can be important. The African pastors are dependent upon these funds although they contribute little; teachers provide half, yet have little vote or benefit from their provision.

The committee is expected to formulate the local Christian code of behavior and discuss whether staff or congregation meets standards. In serious breaches, the committee invites those involved to confess or risk dismissal. Laymen risk public reprimand in church and denial of communion.

Such policies have characterized the mission for decades:

> The Berega district church council, for example, passed resolutions warning against intemperance, and inviting total abstinence on the part of the teachers and elders of the Church; prohibiting the use of native medicines which are in any way associated with heathen superstitions; and forbidding participation by Christians and other adherents in heathen dances. [*P.C.M.S.* 1924–25:15]

These resolutions were still in effect in 1957–58, and further controls were suggested from time to time. In 1958 the committee discussed the advisability of forcing Christian unwed mothers to divulge the names of lovers before being allowed rites in church. This was rejected although it was likely to be passed later. "Saved" members favored it, and cynics suggested that more traditionally minded members might support it because it facilitated suits for fines.

The structure of the committee and the behavior of its members outside the meetings suggest the following pattern of control. The Bishop and his staff are outside the committee but have final control. The largest bloc of votes in the committee is controlled by the Archdeacon; he holds six votes and can usually count on nine more. He is the key member within the committee as chairman, nominator, and mediator.

External Relations with Other Groups

In preceding sections I described past hostilities between the C.M.S. and Roman Catholics.[29] Such conflict has continued unabated up to the present and has had considerable effect upon relations between missions and government, which is responsible for all education within the district. The District Commissioner at Kilosa has ultimate control for locating schools; his decision is made in conjunction with Provincial Headquarters. Up to 1958 the District Administration prevented the establishment of Roman Catholic schools in the chiefdom since it was a C.M.S. sphere of comity. Conversely, the administration perpetuated Catholic comity in the chiefdoms to the south. The Kilosa District Book refers to serious C.M.S.-Catholic conflicts in 1954, 1955, and 1956, when Catholics made unauthorized attempts to establish schools in northeastern Ukaguru. Catholic missionaries (mainly Dutch) allege that the C.M.S. uses its monopoly to put undue pressure on Catholic children to become Protestant. They claim that this contravenes the principles of religious freedom guaranteed in the Territory's U.N. trusteeship. Protesting parents who withdrew children from school were taken to court and fined, and their children were returned to school. These disputes reached the higher levels of government. From 1955–61 local officials often expressed dismay about the friction.

Roman Catholics and C.M.S. do agree to oppose expansion of government schools (the administration's solution to choosing between denominations). Interreligious guerilla warfare is viewed as a special burden by an already overworked administration. Even worse, it sometimes draws attention to a district which administrators prefer to run without outside interference. The strain such squabbles put on government-mission relations is not eased by the usual *camaraderie* found among Europeans elsewhere. The C.M.S.'s low incomes (which discourage entertainment and travel), their isolation, and their condemnation of drinking, dancing, smoking, and card playing (the ubiquitous palliatives to colonial life) cut them off from the social life which joins other Europeans. One missionary writes:

> How often on the mission field is heard the voice of perplexity: "We cannot keep pace with station entertaining"; "We cannot afford club subscriptions"; "We haven't time for social life"; "We cannot entertain as they expect to be entertained." [Breed 1930:29]

It would be difficult to accept the Kaguru assertion that the C.M.S. and government work together. The mission cannot invariably count on government support. Some missionaries see the government as a competitor or irksome inspector. Certainly the C.M.S. has to modify activities to retain government subsidies. It must subdue its aggressive attitudes toward Catholics and adapt religious education to more secular terms. It has repeated disputes with administration over funding, housing, and use of transportation. Misunderstandings between government and mission encourage some Africans in the Native Authority to feel more free to ignore the mission. Unlike the German and Arab period, in 1957–58 the C.M.S. were unable to offer African leaders any economic or political advantage not already afforded through the Native administration. Mission requests for land, labor, or other benefits no longer met compliance from such leaders.

Relations between the C.M.S. and government (both the district administration and Native Authority) are aggravated by the activities of a tribalistic organization established by young, disgruntled, educated Kaguru. This group (USA, Ukaguru Students' Association) repeatedly criticizes Native and District administrations and advocates an aggressive tribalism which causes friction in this ethnically diverse chiefdom (Beidelman 1961b). USA's meetings are often held on mission premises, and the Archdeacon and other staff and congregation play prominent parts at meetings. Though the missionaries appear ignorant of most of these activities, in the eyes of many officials the C.M.S. is associated with them.

In 1957–58 African nationalism exerted little impact in the chiefdom. TANU (the nationalist party) sporadically sent agents to tour Ukaguru, but little came of the visits. TANU concentrated its attention on more politicized lowland areas with a large proletariat. Educated Kaguru, especially teachers, were keenly interested in the nationalist movement. None was openly a member, for admission of membership would mean loss of jobs. Government employees were forbidden membership in political parties, and teachers were categorized as government servants. At this same time, to the east, Roman Catholics appeared to encourage African politicians. The contrast was not lost on the few educated Kaguru.[30]

Summary

Within the C.M.S. in Ukaguru, individuals exercise what power they may have to attain two sets of goals: (1) missionaries want establishment of a society where everyone lives according to Christian principles; (2) Kaguru feel a new sense of individualism and egalitarianism and want to acquire education and the prestige and material benefits derived from schools and cash employment. Differences in aspiration sharply divide Australian and African mission members. Missionary incomes and positions are determined entirely outside Ukaguru so that their goals and actions need not respond to local pressures. Christian indoctrination rests on the mission's near-monopoly of education, an advantage maintained through government. Enforcement of Christian conduct is limited to those over whom the mission has economic and educational control.

The missionaries claim moral and ideological bases for their power, but their effective control of subordinates is based largely upon factors which they themselves publicly disparage—an inconsistency they do not seem to feel.

The C.M.S. recognizes that ideal missionaries should mingle with converts, inform themselves of local affairs, learn native languages, and inspect local conditions; yet they are inhibited by their heavy burden of administration, a shortage of staff, and the size of the area, as well as by their apparent discomfort at personal intimacy with supposed cultural inferiors. Between the few missionaries who bestow benefits and the mass of Africans who seek them is a small group of African intermediaries who derive power from such exchange. These intermediaries modify mission policies by providing key information to both groups and combining attributes attractive to each. The Archdeacon meets these attributes best of all; his pivotal role combines endorsed missionary qualities with those traditional and materialistic ones required by Kaguru. His power depends on the failure of the formal mission organization and ideology to fulfill local needs and upon his own assumption of activities contrary to his formal, endorsed position.

The local mission resembles the Kaguru Native Authority: the missionaries correspond to European district administrators, the Archdeacon to a chief, and the pastors to headmen. Like the Kaguru court-holders (cf. Beidelman 1966b, 1967b), the Archdeacon exercises power because he is able to act in a manner not entirely authorized by either his superiors or his subordinates.

11 Postscript and Conclusions

Postscript: After 1958

My understanding of the C.M.S. in Ukaguru derives mainly from my stay with them in 1957-58 and my subsequent study of the historical record. Today the story of the mission continues, although presumably under conditions far different from those I knew. In 1962-63 I resided in Idibo and other areas of northern Ukaguru, and in 1965 I briefly visited the chiefdom again. These stays were after Tanzanian independence and profound alteration in what had once seemed a settled manner of life. By 1965 most of the European administrators had gone and new, African leaders were dramatically altering all aspects of society.

By 1965 the government had completed a new east-west road to the north of the old one, and Berega was now a further two or three miles off the main route. The government had begun closing out private entrepreneurs in favor of government-supervised buyers of produce. When the new government disbanded the tradition-oriented Native Authority, the replaced local government was staffed with different personnel, including outsiders, selected either for their political affiliations or technical skills rather than for membership in local Kaguru groups. It had also begun to integrate the mission schools into a more uniform body of teachers and administrators. This affected salary, pensions, and other benefits and gave mission teachers new personal freedom. No longer could they be easily dismissed for their conduct outside the station. When I visited the beer clubs in the Berega-Mgugu area, I found mission teachers drinking and smoking in a carefree manner unknown before.

The new government opened Ukaguru to increased Roman Catholic activity. By 1965 the Catholics had erected a handsome church (excellently built of cement with simulated stained glass) about fifteen miles from Berega and were talking about setting up a dispensary and school. Clearly the old rules of comity would not go unquestioned. Nor was it clear how long the new government might tolerate a church still staffed by many aliens. As Welbourn states: "the new nationalism which desired to be both African and technological at the same time . . . had at least the suspicion that Christianity was an enemy of both" (1975:422). There were few familiar faces at Berega by 1965. Both the African Archdeacon and Assistant Bishop have now died, and I do not know who has assumed their functions. The Australian Bishop has gone home and been replaced by an African who has reorganized the diocese.

Recently the African government embarked upon a vast, far-reaching plan of mass socialism: compulsory villagization of the countryside; stricter economic controls to prevent the rise of privileged economic groups, especially entrepreneurs; a drive to discourage "unnecessary" consumer goods; and the creation of compulsory work groups for "nation building." Of course, all this is outside the limits of my study. My purpose in mentioning these changes here is to indicate some of the many forces at work to change still further the world described in the preceding chapters. The new policies mean further undermining of the mission's influence as it once existed. Yet ironically, they embody features of the Evangelical tradition: an emphasis upon work, anti-intellectualism, denial of materialistic and supposedly frivolus pleasures, and distrust of disagreement and deviancy. There are new kinds of missionaries afoot in Ukaguru. Some of the sermons now preached by socialist bureaucrats may appear new, but their tactics and aims are not that different from what has passed away.

One of the misfortunes of the Kaguru is that for over a century powerful and aggressive strangers have tried to inflict supposedly useful and progressive changes upon them. Few if any of these supposedly well-intentioned outsiders paused to listen to what Kaguru themselves might want. In an earlier period, the proffered goal was a new, Christian Kaguru society alien both to the world the European missionaries and administrators knew at home and to that of Kaguru tradition. Now the goal takes the form of enforced sociability and communality founded on an altruism harshly pressed upon Kaguru by a self-righteous, schoolmasterish, bureaucratic elite. Empire building has been replaced by nation building, and Europeanization by African nationalization; but the forced benevolence remains the same. Like the imperialistic past, the present has judged Kaguru society backward and in need of change; tribalism is denounced. Some of the keys to fathoming new and disturbing developments lie in considering the mission as it functioned in the past.

Conclusions

In the preceding chapters I described the workings of one obscure Protestant mission in East Africa. The greater part of the study is social history; the final section gives a sketch of the station in the last years before independence. I have tried to provide material to support the basic issues and theories which the narrow, intensive focus of my study raises; I have avoided the broader, extensive approach of most mission studies.

Were one to choose a mission station for anthropological study, it is unlikely that the one considered here would be a first choice. Not only is it a relatively unsuccessful station in terms of converts, but it is small and not as richly documented as stations elsewhere, even among the C.M.S. The study is a by-product of my wider study of Kaguru society rather than a choice on its sociohistorical merits. In this sense, it should be contrasted with future studies of larger, richer C.M.S. stations such as those in Kenya and Uganda. The Evangelical persuasion of the C.M.S. is an interesting social feature, but its significance cannot be determined until we compare this group with nonevangelical Protestants. Even more important, an intensive study of a comparable Roman Catholic mission is essential to secure a better idea of the implications that sacerdotal celibacy, more hierarchical organization, and more formalistic theology and ritual may have on mission work.

The ethnicity, class, religious beliefs, and finances of the C.M.S. influenced personal conduct and policy as well as attitudes toward other imperialists. The religious beliefs of the C.M.S. affected a wide range of attitudes on sex and marriage, as well as the definitions of pleasure and work. The ideal missionary was defined in complex, contradictory terms which led to muddled policies and ambiguous conduct. Were the C.M.S. to be committed to a frugal and spartan male celibacy, or were they to present a model of Christian home life? Were Africans to be literate in their native languages but not in English? Should Africans be required to read the Bible but discouraged from secular literature? C.M.S. views on secularism and materialism reveal grave misapprehension of both their own and African societies and of the means and results of their labors. Sectors that should have formed integral wholes were fractured into unworkable segments. It is difficult to see how the missionaries were to use the attractions and advantages of Western technology as inducements to conversion when the techniques would eventually backfire to create a new materialism similar to what it had rejected at home. C.M.S. dilemmas were rooted in its ambivalence toward primitive culture: an attraction to the supposed simplicity and antimaterialism, yet an ethnocentric conviction that English life and culture were superior expressions of the human condition.

We have seen complex interplay between religious and secular aspects of C.M.S. mission life. This led to contradictions necessary to the missionary's vision of self-identity, his definition of both the ideal world and his work. The success of the mission depended on contradictions: it denied worldly values while at the same time maintained a wide range of practical, ruthlessly secular skills; later, it denied the material implications of education even while capitalizing upon them to draw in converts and secure government support.

The missionaries liked to think of themselves as different from neighboring administrators and traders whom they disdained, but it became increasingly difficult for them to sustain such a self-stereotype. Early on, some C.M.S. could entertain idealized illusions about themselves because their ethnicity differed from that of the prevailing economic and political powers; this became far harder in a British colony, though it would have been difficult in any colony once it was sufficiently developed.

Evangelical belief led to curiously uncommunal and impractical views of Christianity. Religion was set apart from many other sectors of life. In this, C.M.S. antisecularism represents a position opposed not only to many other forms of Christianity, including Catholicism, but to pagan Kaguru society as well.

C.M.S. Evangelical beliefs also had profound implications for organization and staffing: they recruited diversely trained staff, married pastors alongside workers with no formal religious qualifications; Evangelical individualism mitigated rational hierarchical organization; and zeal to convert, as supported by claims based on the Holy Spirit, led to understaffed, underfinanced, and overextended stations. C.M.S. attitudes about conversion and revival also differed sharply from those of some other Protestants and Catholics. The full implications of their beliefs were never worked out by the C.M.S., and because of this they had limited ability to foresee the outcome of policies. One must ask whether Evangelical belief itself inhibits rational, sustained policies and actions.

The C.M.S. are actors in an intercultural exchange, medial and mediating figures between two alien societies. Because the missionaries made few concessions to Kaguru culture, their ability to utilize it was limited. The true medial figures in this situation are those acculturated Africans who stand astride both cultural spheres without conforming to either. These figures convey and obstruct information and instructions between the two orders. C.M.S. missionaries retained economic control, but in terms of strategic perception and manipulation of the system, certain African staff emerged as equally, or even more significant. Their powers, as in the case of the Kaguru Native Authority, were all the greater because they were either unrecognized or poorly understood by those above.

The *raison d'etre* of mission work is the undermining of a traditional way of life. In this the missionary represents the most extreme, thoroughgoing, and self-conscious protagonist of cultural innovation and change. How the C.M.S. resolved this role as destroyer with a desire to preserve an idyllic, rural community is a tangled story. The missionary, at least in the past, was unashamedly ethnocentric, though he saw the struggle to impose his values as loving and altruistic. He was cruel to be kind. His ethnocentrism and proselytization represent a blend of exclusion and inclusion, domination and brotherhood, and exploitation and sacrifice. Most curious of all, he exalted modern Western life but loathed many of its features; he felt a parallel fascination and contempt for simpler societies.

Historical material has been particularly useful in illustrating the developmental pattern of complex organization, including imperialistic or colonial groups. Such organization and the values behind it may be divided into three broad developmental phases, each illustrated by mission history: (1) The mission was founded in romantic zeal, and the initial phase exhibits a loose organization highly responsive to individualistic, egalitarian behavior. In the case of missions, this characterization seems more consistent with Protestant than Catholic beliefs and organization. (2) The second developmental phase reveals a growing routinization in tasks and the development of a staff of semieducated, partially acculturated Africans utilized by the missionaries in order to control and minister to an ever-increasing mass. Now begins the problem of success, for with increased numbers the task of the missionaries alters to become administrative and technical rather than evangelistic. Many later difficulties experienced by the C.M.S. involved their inability to accept and recognize departure from their initial stereotypes of themselves as heroic, crusading evangelists. With increased organizational size and a growing body of staff culturally different from those at the top, missionaries found it more difficult to understand and directly control their following. The power and influence of African staff consequently grew, but the full significance of increased development was found among other specialists and professionals, whose success eventually led them to become administrators and overseers rather than practitioners of their crafts. (3) Finally, the success of the imperialistic enterprise, of which missionaries were only a part, led to even greater organizational problems and co-optation of the mission by other sectors of society. The mission began as a nearly autonomous group within an incipient colony. At that phase it was fairly successful in conforming to its antisecular ideal because there was no working colonial society with which it had to interact. The missionaries' unrealistic stereotypes of themselves could be acted out since there was no coherent social backdrop to contradict their illusions. With a firm and persuasive colonial society involved in developing economic, political, and other aspects of life, the mission found itself again embedded in a world it had either rejected at home or had at the least misunderstood from the start. Later, when the realities of that social life encroached on them, the missionaries were under considerable pressure to secularize their activities. Not only had success brought routinization and organizational problems of control and communication, it had also led to decreasing insulation of separate institutions and their growing integration into a single colonial enterprise.

In the long run the mission was no more self-destructive than other institutions in the broader colonial endeavor; as the task of converting an alien world to one's own values succeeds, these values exert powerful influences to reduce differences between teacher and taught, alien and native, administrator and administered. With that, the bases for colonial rule are undermined. The C.M.S. formally recognized this end and claimed to anticipate the day when the mission would be replaced by an indigenous church; yet this was in actual practice resisted, for the missionary without dependent converts or believers is a person without purpose much as is a teacher without students or a doctor without sick people.

Missionary resistance to this stated goal parallels the secular sphere where administrators, who claim to be training Africans for self-government, persist in arguing that their apprentices remain unready for self-rule.

I have presented these developmental processes in terms of the Christian mission and colonial experience, but it is not difficult to discern parallels even beyond. The social universe of the Third World today resembles the colonial world which preceded it. A few highly educated and privileged people continue to attempt to dictate to the public the proper beliefs and ways of life which they must follow. Culturally, that elite is often as different from the masses as were the Europeans before them. We have little reason to assume that such a developing world is truly the reflection of the will and desires of the mass of its population. Much is still imposed though economic and political force, sometimes with brutality, by elements outside and beyond the grassroots. It is in this sense that I suggest in the opening chapter that the study of defunct institutions of colonialism would provide insights into social features still evident in contemporary situations. Studying such aspects of contemporary societies is often discouraged although little opposition is met today in studying the colonial past.

This study should indicate the theoretical and practical value of anthropological research in colonial studies. Anthropologists' traditional concern with the actual workings of societies at the grassroots adds a much needed dimension to a field unfortunately dominated so far by overgeneralized studies. Any anthropological account should reveal that the colonial situation necessarily exhibits contradictory values and motives. Anthropology with its attempted alienation from prevailing values would seem an especially useful discipline for uncovering the countervailing characteristics which have up to now often been taken for granted or considered self-explanatory. It should be clear from this study and the works cited how little has been so far achieved in this topic. We must be on guard that research of life in colonial societies is not reduced to the dubious task of social criticism; for then we could hope for little but moralistic harangues. It is easy to criticize colonial rule in terms of exploitation, injustice, and ethnocentrism, such accounts are common and have led to cheap and easy judgments. Rather than this, what is required is analysis and review that allow us to perceive the colonial world as a system, both in terms of its thought and values and in terms of the ways it was organized. We must see colonial rulers as acted upon by those they attempted to rule, quite as much as the reverse and more conventional approach.

The history and sociology of the Third World must be more than a supplemental comment about imperialistic expansion or a cataloging of curious social artifacts and practices of some exotic, aboriginal peoples; it must also be a statement of the complex ways the West reorganized and rethought its nature within that overseas context. Assuming, perhaps wrongly, that we fully comprehend our own culture, we have still tended to overlook the fact that colonial life itself requires a further effort at cultural understanding on our part. This has seldom been achieved. That understanding may be as demanding and difficult as understanding more exotic and seemingly alien peoples is because apparent similarities with life at home obscure what is in fact a profoundly different social experience and set of beliefs.

Notes

Preface

1. My initial research was conducted under the sponsorship of the University of Illinois, Urbana, from a Ford Foundation research grant issued to J. H. Steward.

2. After the First World War, however, missionaries in Ukaguru appeared less ready to submit their views to public scrutiny. Not only did they publish far less, but even in those archival sources open under the fifty-year rule, post-1918 reports are far less extensive and certainly less frank and detailed than earlier ones.

3. E.g., "Will you kindly excuse this scrawl as I am unable to get to my pens and have to write with a quill from the wing of an owl," Archives, Baxter to Wright, 4 March 1878.

4. There are a few superlative accounts of colonial careers, though each is cast in terms of a particular colonial personality rather than a group (e.g., Crowder 1973; Rutherford 1971; Winter 1979).

1: Anthropology, Culture, and Colonialism

1. This was eloquently noted by Balandier (1966). Scholars of colonialism such as Furnivall (1956) and Maunier (1949) influenced some anthropologists, but less than one would hope.

2. Kuper (1957, 1971) is one of the few anthropologists working in Africa to discuss Europeans, though not in detail. Jahoda (1961) published a fascinating study of Ghanaian stereotypes of Europeans, but this does not directly relate to present issues. Malinowski advocated such research, but his prolegomenon for it is so ethnocentric and pontificating that one may be relieved that little came of it (1945). Balandier advocates theoretical analysis of colonialism but fails to relate this to a coherent set of theories (1970:21–56). Works by Fanon, Memmi, and Mannoni take us far from social theory and into sloppy psychologizing and Gallic rhetoric. Perhaps the situation is changing, for recently (1972) O'Brien published a perceptive social study of the French in Senegal.

3. The political scientist Heussler (1963, 1968, 1971) exhibits little appreciation of the sociological aspects of class, authority, or power; but the historian Crowder has written perceptively on such issues (1970, 1973). A few administrators such as Temple (1918) and Leys (1926, 1941) produced studies of remarkable insight. There are general surveys, some of considerable value for placing colonial material within a broader perspective: Delavignette (1950, 1971), Buell (1928), Symonds (1956), Gann and Duignan (1967, 1977), Cohen (1971), and Berque (1967) write perceptively on colonial social life but aim to picture society as a whole rather than a detailed aspect of it.

4. For example, Bayley (1976), Bendix (1945), Crozier (1964, 1973), Dahrendorf (1969), Dore (1973), Nakane (1970), and Rohlen (1974). Perhaps the first to per-

ceive these issues, though dimly, was Veblen (1939, 1943; both first published, 1915).

5. The adjectives *colonial* and *neocolonial* are often used loosely in African studies with little contrast to *imperialistic.* We must not allow these terms to lose significance for indicating differences in the nature of overseas societies, nor should we be misled into preoccupation with typologies so that we confuse labeling with understanding. In the strictest sense, a colony is a group of settlers attempting to replicate the society of the original metropolitan power. It approaches this only to the extent that conditions abroad are identical to those at home, one condition being the absence of an alien subject race. British society in North America or Australia approached this. In contrast, no European society in Africa comes close. In most of sub-Saharan Africa Europeans dominated and exploited lands and peoples to their advantages but never saw themselves as permanently part of that world, even though they spent most of their working lives in it.

6. Consider Maunier's insight that colonialism is not mere contact between races but "a contact of social types" providing some "source of relationships between human groups" (1949 I:xii, 5). It involves complex interplay of both differences and commonalities in beliefs and values out of which social action stems. It is a social and therefore an ideological and moral phenomenon.

7. Davies (1973) is one of the few recent writers to observe such parallels.

8. These issues are complex. Reference to one example suggests some of the permutations involved. In past research on prisons, Cressy (1961), Sykes (1958), and others put forward a concept of "prison culture," viz., that beliefs, values, organization, and language in prison formed a subculture requiring study similar to that applied to any alien society. They argued that though prisons exist within our society, they are in some ways apart from it. More recently, Giallombardo (1966) points out the limitations and distortions which this approach involves. Despite common features, women's prisons differ strikingly from men's. No concept of prison culture accounts for this, but reference to broader cultural notions about men and women and the different offences they commit does. Analysis comes full circle with the finding that there is value in the concept of subculture yet that subculture needs to be fitted into a broader cultural matrix. The features shared by both types of prisons derive not only from common cultural notions about criminals and punishment but also from common organizational features of all repressive total institutions.

Incidentally, Giallombardo raises a further point pertinent to my concerns here. She found that since a prison consists of opposed subcultures of prisoners and staff, it was impossible for her to study both with equal access. Those involved in fieldwork in colonialistic societies confront similar situations (cf. Whyte 1959:100–106, 254–55).

9. My interpretation of missions in terms of bureaucratic theory was criticized by a historian who believes this may apply to political but not religious institutions (Etherington 1977).

10. Until recently, studies of mission theory have often conveyed an impression of ethnocentrism and denigration of alien beliefs, cf. Bavinck (1960).

11. The International African Institute symposium volume edited by Baëta (1968) is disappointingly superficial. Few studies specially of missionaries seem in progress judging from *African Religious Research,* African Studies Center, Univer-

sity of California, Los Angeles. *The International Review of Missions* (since 1970 *International Review of Mission*) contains a bibliography in each issue which is essential for those interested in missions and which indicates the staggering amount published on the topic. Despite this, little reflects any grasp of sociological principles. Prior to 1900, missionaries did not provide coherent analysis of their own methods, even insofar as it would facilitate their labors (Harries 1953:371). Other relevant journals are *The Bulletin of the Society for African Church History*, the *Journal of Religion in Africa*, and *Practical Anthropology* (now *Missiology*), which encourage publication on missionary problems; but nothing has appeared of sociological import. Other useful bibliographical sources for Christianity in Africa are *Colonialism in Africa 1870–1960*, edited by D. Duignan and L. H. Gann (Cambridge: Cambridge University Press, 1973), 5:151–58; *Select Annotated Bibliography of Tropical Africa*, D. Forde (director) (New York: The Twentieth Century Fund, 1956, Section V: Education, Section VI: Missions); R. C. Mitchell and H. W. Turner, *A Bibliography of Modern African Religious Movements* (Evanston: Northwestern University Press, 1966), updated as H. W. Turner, *Bibliography of New Religious Movements*, Vol. I: Black Africa (Boston: Hall, 1977). In America, the best library for mission research is the Mission Research Library in New York City.

An issue of the *American Journal of Sociology* (1944) was largely devoted to missions. The leading papers (Park, Stuntz) are sententious and glib. Heise (1967) published a position paper advocating the sociological study of missions; he too comments on the lack of useful sociological analyses. His paper is followed by a muddled critique (Carleton).

Most papers on missions which appear in anthropological journals are unhelpful in dealing with the questions posed here, e.g., Duignan (1958), Jeffreys (1956), Rapoport (1954). Malinowski had extensive correspondence with Oldham, Secretary of *The International Review of Missions* and architect of modern policies in Africa; but little came of this (Cell 1976:74).

12. E.g., Taylor (1958a, 1958b), Taylor and Lehman (1961), Tippett (1969), Welbourn (1961).

13. E.g., Allen (1912, 1919, 1927a, 1927b, 1968), Allen and Cochrane (1920), Beyerhause and Hallencreutz (1969), Luzbetak (1970), McGavran (1955, 1959, 1970), Mylne (1908), Neill (1964, 1966), Nida (1954), Sundkler (1960), Warren (1951, 1960, 1964, 1965, 1967).

14. E.g., Achebe (1958), Beti (1971a, 1971b), Echewa (1976).

15. Oliver (1952), Sundkler (1948, 1960, 1976).

16. Ajayi (1965), Ayandele (1967), Crummy (1972), Ekechi (1971a, 1971b), Linden (1974, 1977), McCracken (1977), Markowitz (1970, 1973), Murphree (1969), Rotberg (1964, 1965), Slade (1959), Taylor (1958), Taylor and Lehman (1961), Temu (1972), Welbourn (1961), Wishlade (1965), Wright (1971), Wyllie (1976), Johnson (1977), Strayer (1978), Tasie (1978), Pirouet (1978), Bhebe (1979). Ranger has sought to encourage historical research on the interaction between traditional African religions and Christianity, but this bears only indirectly on missions, Ranger and Kimambo (1972), Ranger and Weller (1975).

17. I am informed that East German scholars have published highly critical Marxist analyses of mission endeavor in Africa: Loth (1963) and Mohr (1965).

18. Directly inspired by Sundkler are Andersson (1968), Beyerhause and Hallencreutz (1969), Hellberg (1965), and von Sicard (1970). Other Protestants have

also written usefully, Mobley (1970), as have Roman Catholics, Shorter and Kataza (1972).

19. Among recent useful works of this type: Bartels (1965), Rubingh (1969), Smith (1969a), Webster (1971).

20. We have standard works by Grove (1948–58) and Latourette (1955), as well as Stock's official history of the C.M.S. (1899), brought up to date by Hewitt (1971), Cole (1971), Guillebaud (n.d.); for discussion of current problems in mission historiography we have Ajayi and Ayandele (1969), Gray (1968, 1969).

21. From the East African C.M.S. alone we have biographies and autobiographies in Ahse (1894), Briggs (1918), Chambers (1931), Harford-Battersby (1898), Luck (1972), Mackay (1890), Roscoe (1921), Tucker (1911), Warren (1974), Watt (n.d.), and White (1942, 1977), though unfortunately for my purposes, most emphasize work in Uganda rather than Tanzania. An outstanding exception, written from an anthropological perspective, is Winter (1979). Rutherford's account of Shirley Baker of Tonga is also remarkable (1971), though not about Africa.

22. Johnson's (1977) excellent study of an American Black church's branch in Zambia especially emphasizes organizational principles over ideology.

23. C.M.S. were critical of many government and settler policies in neighboring Kenya (Strayer 1978:103–108; Rosberg and Nottingham 1966:110–11).

24. When an anticlerical Belgian colonial minister moved against Catholic privileges just prior to Congolese independence, the Church did a *volte face* and supported Africans against the regime (Markowitz 1970).

25. An anthropological colleague used to quip, "What mission station did you prefer visiting? Did you go for drinks (Catholic, Europeans) or baths (Protestants, Americans)?"

26. The C.M.S. Evangelicals were an important source of policies for contending groups within the Anglican community (Rosberg and Nottingham 1966:110–11).

27. Since Sundkler's study (1960), Wyllie (1974) and Johnson (1977) are among the few sociological considerations of African pastors. Johnson in particular points out that such studies have emphasized ideological factors to the detriment of group organization (1977:133–34). Welbourn briefly but perceptively contrasts pastors and priests (1975:403–404).

28. All Catholic priests may not be so well educated, cf. Lee (1968).

29. Nida suggests that Protestants are potentially more racially prejudiced and class conscious than Catholics since Protestant laity are members of the church and thus allow features of society to affect church policies more directly. This holds only if one assumes that theological training necessarily inhibits racism or class consciousness (1957:35–36).

30. During field work I never heard Africans complain that educated persons received higher pay than illiterates. Rather, they complained that they had been denied access to higher education and received less pay for doing the same as or more than Europeans. Any assumption that increased education merits increased financial compensation is not a universal notion even in Western culture. The modern Africans' assumption reflects their entry into the bureaucratized modern masses.

31. See Nzekwu (1962) for a provocative novel on this theme.

32. Whatever the reasons for this stereotype of benign Capuchins in the

Congo, it cannot derive from Capuchin beliefs and organization since one of the most horrendous accounts of missionary cruelty and rapaciousness involves Capuchins in South America (Bonilla 1972).

33. Schapera (1958:1–10) studied Tswana conversion but paid little attention to missionaries. More recently, Horton reconsidered conversion in West Africa (1970, 1971), was criticized by Fisher (1973), and answered these criticisms (1975); yet none of these writers displays interest in the converters, much less in their notions about conversion. Discussion is confined to the intellectualist or ideological aspects of conversion whereas it seems difficult to separate conversion from political and economic dominance and strategy. Recently, more modest but useful considerations of West African conversion, grounded in ethnographic fact, have appeared by Salamone (1972, 1975, 1976), Isichei (1970), Peel (1977), and Ifeka-Moller who makes telling criticisms of Horton (1974:59). Jarrett-Kerr (1972) discusses conversion through brief accounts of converts from Third World countries but is superficial, cf. also Tippett (1977), Etherington (1976), and Doornbos (1976).

34. To pursue the comparison, just as missionaries presume to teach converts a way of life, so, conversely, anthropologists are, like children, taught a new way of life by those with whom they live and whose culture they record.

35. Lest I be accused of exaggerating the durability and pervasiveness of such attitudes, consider three often cited though now, one hopes, discredited sources: J. C. Carothers, *The African Mind in Health and Disease,* World Health Organization Monograph (Geneva: United Nations Organization, 1953); L. S. B. Leakey, *The Progress and Evolution of Man in Africa* (London: Oxford University Press, 1961); O. Mannoni, *Prospero and Caliban* (1950) (New York: Praeger, 1964). All three seem to be presenting what they honestly consider to be objective, well-supported arguments, although their ethnocentrism, sloppy use of data, and distorted reasoning should be apparent. Ironically, these reactionary and repulsive views were presented by men who appear to consider themselves liberal.

36. Such a view is also presented in the main missionary review, Fullani (1919:162).

37. Jesus is quoted from Matt. 24.13 and 28.19 and St. Paul from Rom. 10.14, 15.

38. Phillips describes the dogged persistence of American missionaries in Morocco despite almost no success and little encouragement even from local Europeans (1975).

39. The most famous example of such ideological compromise involved the sinecization of Jesuits in China (Rowbotham 1942). For a striking recent example, see Haule 1969.

40. The C.M.S. chronicler Stock put it less sympathetically, remarking that Catholics seek only numbers while Protestants seek individual souls (1899 I:412).

41. In his study of nineteenth-century German Roman Catholic missionary attitudes in East Africa, Kiernan suggests that Africans were described as depraved and debased and therefore requiring chastisement (1969).

42. For an anthropologist's criticism of Gurtmann's view as wrong, not theologically but sociologically, see Wagner (1936); cf. also Winter (1979).

43. Berkhofer notes that when American Indians reject Christianity, they often resume traditional garb to symbolize their apostasy (1972:111–12).

44. It is difficult to understand Ajayi and Ayandele's failure to understand why

missionaries emphasize individual rather than group conversion (1969:96–97) since most of the missions studied by them are Protestant.

45. Stations such as Freretown (Kenya), Bagamoyo (Tanzania), and Livingstonia (Malawi) were mainly composed of freed or escaped slaves and therefore automatically alien to the indigenous population.

46. I do not mean that Europeans serving as advisers in Africa demand salaries beyond what is reasonable in terms of their experience and beliefs. Some, such as missionaries, are paid by overseas funds, but expatriates cost more than natives because they do not remain and do not invest wealth or progeny in these lands.

47. This may explain the failure of missions in India and the Far East, which led missions later to see Africa as their last hope to prove the evangelistic dream; cf. also Dodds 1970.

48. Government support of any education may have seemed adventurous since even in Britain no government supported national education until 1902 (Neill 1966:100–102). While missionary theorists such as Allen and social liberals such as Leys opposed this from the start, recent writers continue to attack such policies as subverting proper evangelical spirit (McGavran 1955:53–58; 1970:60–62, 114–15). Even moderates such as Taylor (1956:155–68) and Sundkler (1960:64, 95) express serious misgivings.

49. J. H. Oldham, editor of *The International Review of Missions* and Secretary of the International Missionary Council, was the main advocate of such involvement in secular services; Allen was the most eloquent critic (Oldham 1927; Allen 1927:18–19; 1929:14–21). Recent C.M.S. policies support Oldham (Warren 1967:109–114; cf. Thompson 1976:31–34).

50. Deng (1971:230) contradicts this: " . . . missionary education itself was designed to make the child remain in his traditional set-up, lest he become 'materialistic.' "

51. Missions parallel other colonial structures even in what is now termed neocolonialism. Young churches cannot provide publications, educators, technicians, and supplies and equipment. While some supervisory controls were withdrawn locally by Europeans, control was maintained through financial and technical means (Smalley 1958; Taylor 1958a:88–89).

2: Before the Missionaries Arrived

1. This sketch can be expanded by consulting other publications in Kaguru ethnography (see Beidelman 1971b, bibliographies in Beidelman 1967, 1969, 1974a, 1981). Much that I state may seem simplistic to an anthropologist, but I have tried to meet the needs of historians, theologians, and sociologists.

2. As Christie's survey shows (1876) epidemics sometimes were spread by indirect contact from the caravan routes until they affected peoples hundred of miles away.

3: C.M.S. Background and Early History in Ukaguru, 1876–91

1. For a summary of John Venn's principles of mission, see *The Centenary Volume of the C.M.S.* (1902); see also Shenk 1977. The early history of the C.M.S. and arrival of C.M.S. missionaries to East Africa are described in Stock 1899; Oliver 1952.

2. Elliott-Binns 1936:398. Several surveys were conducted regarding C.M.S. support, Stock 1883; Anonymous *C.M.I.* 1893; Flynn, 1904.

3. The C.M.S. and other Evangelicals call themselves "parties."

4. Neill notes that Anglicans are less theologically inclined than continental Europeans (and Evangelicals weakest of all) and that Evangelicals seem the branch which provides strongest support for missions (1965:128, 238f, 242–43, 401). C.M.S. writers emphasize their moral superiority over other Anglicans (Editor, "The C.M.S. Missionaries as Evangelical Churchmen," *C.M.I.* 1890:283–89; cf. "The C.M.S. and the Board of Missions," *C.M.I.* 1894:88–95; for more negative views, cf. Bradley 1976:17–33).

5. For accounts of Victorian Evangelicals, see Kitson Clark 1972:1–3; Davies 1961:210–40; Chadwick 1966:440–55; Bradley 1976; cf. also Kitson Clark 1962:147–205, and Norman 1976.

6. The Victorian Anglican church advocated a laissez-faire attitude toward social reform, despite considerable involvement in parish social work (Norman 1976:122–48).

7. Although Livingstone began his travels associated with the London Missionary Society, he was a free-lance explorer from 1856 on; for this reason he could inspire all British mission groups. For Livingstone's impact on C.M.S. missionaries, see the Rev. Roscoe's opening statement in his autobiography (1921:1) and Elliott-Binns (1936:387), as well as the exhortation of C.M.S. volunteers (*Special Appeal on Behalf of the Victoria Nyanza Mission* privately printed London: C.M.S., 1878).

8. *Report of the Sub-Committee on Proposed Mission to the Victoria Niyanza* [sic] *Region*, C.M.S. House, 1 December 1875. Since the southern route was safer, it was also less than half as expensive in porters' fees, *C.M.I.* 1877:396. The Rev. Price of the London Missionary Society published a pamphlet urging mission work near Mpwapwa (1976); he maintained that it was a fertile area favorable to Europeans, a baseless judgment which the C.M.S. accepted, *C.M.I.* 1879:530. Hutchinson also exhorted missions to work in the area (1876). The C.M.S. published an elaborate fold-out map in its journal, presumably to encourage subscribers' interest, *C.M.I.* 1877.

9. The activities of the C.M.S. in Buganda and Kikuyuland offer fields for historical research. The drawback is the richness and complexity of the materials. The smaller scale of Ukaguru allows us to develop initial models for analysis without the inhibition we feel if confronted with the greater task in these other areas.

10. *The Victoria Nyanza Mission, Instructions* (C.M.S. pamphlet, 1876).

11. Archives, Mackey to Wright, 18 September, 14 October 1876.

12. *P.C.M.S.* 1876–77:44; cf. *Instructions of the Committee* (1879):146, C.M.S. pamphlet; cf. also Tucker 1911:3–5.

13. Ages and other information are not always available from the *C.M.S. Register of Missionaries* (1895). The ages cited refer to the time when the person is first mentioned in my account.

14. Archives, Last to Wright, 6 June 1879. There were 33 men and boys and 16 women; Baxter to Wright, 26 November 1879.

15. *C.M.I.* 1879:532; Archives, Last to Wright, 25 November 1878; 20 January 1879.

16. Archives, Baxter to Wright, 26 November 1879; *P.C.M.S.* 1879–80:27.

17. Archives, Last to Wright, 18 May 1878.

18. Archives, Last to Wright, 22 January 1880. Another missionary, Stokes, was later to marry the Nyamwezi's daughter.

19. Luck 1972:63–64; this provides a moving biography of Stokes, a much maligned and attractive personality; cf. Archives, Lang to Baxter, 26 March 1886.
20. *P.C.M.S.* 1882–83:51; 1883–84:47; Archives, Lang to Price, 28 January 1886.
21. *P.C.M.S.* 1884–85:46; 1885–86:42–43; 1886–87:41–42.
22. Archives, Wood to Lang, 25 October 1889; Rees, *History*, 1902, ms.
23. See Walker (1914) for a biography of Tucker.
24. *P.C.M.S.* 1890–91:52; 1891–92:53; Archives, Price to Lang, 15 August 1891.

4: Contradictions in the Sacred and Secular Life

1. Archives, Instructions Delivered to the Missionaries Proceeding to the Field, autumn 1897.
2. Stock 1916 IV:31; Archives, Price to Wright, 14 May 1880.
3. I am publishing a more detailed account of C.M.S. caravans than what appears in my recent article (1981); n.d.
4. Oliver 1952:83, Archives, Watt to Long, 19 July 1886, Luck 1972:31–33, 50–52.
5. Archives, Long to Watt, 4 November 1886; Baylis to Watt, 9 October 1896.
6. Archives, Instructions of the Committee to the Mission, 1878.
7. Archives, Doulton to Manley, 23 February 1924; cf. Archives, Baxter to Baylis, 29 January 1895.
8. Archives, Baxter to Lang, 12 February 1883; Price to Lang, 2 November 1889; Baxter to Wright, 18 May 1878.
9. Elliott-Binns 1936:382; Archives, Instructions of the Committee, 23 July 1896; cf. Stock 1899 I:191).
10. Archives, Price to Lang, 2 November 1889.
11. Archives, Wood to Lang, 13 February 1890; cf. Archives, Price to Lang, 2 November 1889; Price to Wright, 14 May 1880; cf. also Edwards to Lang, received 11 November 1882; Watt n.d.:42. Shortly after denouncing materialism, one writer requested more books and a new typewriter.
12. Archives, Price to Wright, 14 May 1880.
13. Archives, Instructions Delivered to Dr. E. and Mrs. Baxter, 31 July 1888.
14. C.M.S., *Special Appeal on Behalf of the Victoria Nyanza Mission*, January 1878.
15. Archives, General Instructions to Missionaries, 4 February 1896. Cust, one of the C.M.S.'s publicists, characterizes missionizing as a rejection of "guilty leisure" (1886:1). For accounts of Evangelical assumptions about man's depravity, see Bradley 1976; Kitson Clark 1962:149–205; 1973:71–73; Norman 1976.
16. Cf. similar, more recent observations: Murray 1967:71, Loewen and Loewen 1967:194–95.
17. Archives, Roscoe to Lang, 19 July 1885.
18. Archives, Executive Conference, 14 August 1890; cf. *C.M.S. Centenary Volume* 1902:46; Archives, Doulton to Baylis, 1 December 1909; Lang to Roscoe, 13 August 1886.
19. See Cust, quoted as representative by Oliver 1952:25; cf. also Mackay 1890:58; Fullani, 1919:159–60.
20. Archives, Baylis to Doulton, 25 August 1909; 27 January 1910.
21. Archives, Baylis to Doulton, 27 January 1910.

22. Archives, Last to Lang, 22 May 1882; cf. Wood to Baylis, 30 August 1895.
23. Archives, Wood to Lang, 1 April 1888; cf. Wood to Baylis, 24 September 1894.
24. Archives, Deekes to Baylis, 16 April 1895.
25. Cf. Archives, Wood to Lang, 1 April 1888; Wood to Baylis, 24 September 1894; Pruen 1891:293; *P.C.M.S.* 1903–1904:98.
26. Archives, Doulton to Manley, 14 April 1924; cf. Beidelman 1971:120.
27. Oliver 1952:242; for similar, more recent conditions, cf. Beidelman 1971:120; Beidelman and Winter 1967:184–86.
28. Archives, Copplestone to Wright, 16 February 1878.
29. Cust went so far as to advocate ten years' celibacy for C.M.S. missionaries (1891:12); cf. also Cust 1892:14–15.
30. Archives, Instructions Delivered to Missionaries at Meeting of Committee, 5 July 1898; Archives, White to Last, 30 June 1881.
31. Archives, Baylis to Beverley, 4 December 1896; cf. also Tucker to Baylis, 8 July 1894. A large proportion of mission marriages were among missionary families.
32. Archives, Lang to Baxter, 28 January 1886; Baxter to Wright, 13 June 1879; Reports of Nyanza Sub-Committee, 22 January 1880. For examples of such petitions and replies, see Archives, Doulton to Baylis, 12 October 1896; Hutchinson to Baxter, 6 May 1881; Manley to Green, 28 February 1913; Manley to Barling, 22 June 1921.
33. Archives, Instructions to Missionaries, 5 July 1898.
34. *C.M.S. Centenary Volume* 1902:47; Archives, Pruen to Lang, 24 February 1897; Executive Conference, received 12 January 1909; *P.C.M.S.* 1880–81:37.
35. Archives, Doulton to Spriggs, 15 November 1909. For a C.M.S. idealization of female missionaries, see Cust 1895:105–106.
36. Archives, Baxter to Lang, 29 January 1886; cf. also Roscoe to Wigram, 1 June 1885. Stokes's union was thought to compromise European authority. As proof, missionaries noted that Stokes's African father-in-law began acting high-handedly, Archives, Wood to Lang, 17 March 1892. It was also noted that Stokes's African wife was unfaithful. Stokes speculated: "I suppose God wishes to punish me in this way," Archives, Price to Lang, 31 March 1890.
37. Archives, Baxter to Lang, 27 February 1886.
38. Archives, Lang to Baxter, 21 April 1886.
39. Archives, Lang to Pruen, 10 May 1886.
40. Archives, Instructions of the Committee to Missionaries, 1879.

5: Colonial History

1. During this period the size and scope of C.M.S. activities increased although the European staff was as few as in the pioneer period. As the routine of work and policies became well established, the personalities of the staff left less mark than had those of colorful characters such as Last, Stokes, Roscoe, and Watt. Missionaries now moved so frequently from station to station that recitation of names and places could only be confusing. I provide names and related information only as they relate closely to my later arguments. For a useful summary of the broader picture leading up to this period, see Flint 1963.
2. Anonymous *C.M.I.* 1906:111; for an authoritative appraisal of German rule,

see Iliffe 1969; 1979:88–239; see also *P.C.M.S.* 1905–1906:66–68; 1906–1907:74–75; Archives, Peel to Capt. von Hirsch, 15 November 1906.

3. Yet only rarely did a missionary complain about secular tasks; and when they did, they were soundly rebuked. See Archives, Lang to Roscoe, 13 August 1886.

4. For a biography of Peel, see Stock 1919.

5. Archives, Baylis to Staff of Ussagara, 20 October 1897; Peel to Baylis, 10 February 1904; Baylis to Rees, 30 July 1907; *P.C.M.S.* 1908–1909:56.

6. Missionaries received full pensions only after laboring for thirty years, cf. Archives, Manley to Rees, 26 July 1927.

7. The missionaries had translated St. Matthew, St. Luke, and St. John into Chikaguru, as well as 109 hymns. This was probably done by Wood with help from Rees and Deekes, but publication was anonymous: *Nzachilo Nswamu kwa Mattayo nonga ya Kaguru* [St. Matthew] 1894; and *Zinyimbo* [hymns] 1894. I can find no record of whether the translations of St. Luke and St. John were published. Some years earlier (1886) Last published *Grammar of the Kagúru Language*, but this was too poor to be a useful tool for later work.

8. *P.C.M.S.* 1888–89:49; 1894–95:868; 1895–96:108; 1899–1900:110; Archives, Price to Baylis, 17 March 1893; Baxter to Baylis, 15 November 1894; 29 January 1895; Wood to Baylis, 29 January 1895; Roscoe 1911:149–52; *P.C.M.S.* 1908–1909:56.

9. Just before a severe famine, a visiting German published an essay extolling the lush prosperity of Mamboya mission station (Sixdorf 1894).

10. *P.C.M.S.* 1889–90:110–12; Briggs 1918:30.

11. Archives, Baylis to Ussagara-Ugogo Mission, 12 November 1900; Baylis to Peel, 8 January 1903; 29 March 1911; 2 June 1908; 27 November 1908; Baylis to Beverley, 18 June 1897.

12. Archives, Baylis to Doulton, 8 January 1909; Baylis to Peel, 27 November 1908; 9 January 1909; Baylis to Doulton, 8 January 1909.

13. In 1905 there were 5 clergy, 1 doctor, 3 laymen, 9 wives, 6 single ladies; in 1908, 2 clergy, 1 doctor, 3 laymen, 6 wives, 5 single ladies, Archives, C.M.S. Memorandum, 16 October 1908.

14. Ekechi describes comparable C.M.S. policies in Nigeria (1971:429–30).

15. *P.C.M.S.* 1900–1901:120; Briggs 1918:32. These official figures are less than those provided by Rees, *History*, 1902, ms.

16. Briggs 1918:23–32; Archives, Beverley to Baylis, 29 December 1896.

17. Archives, Deekes to Baylis, 26 October 1898.

18. Archives, Minutes of Conference of Ussagara Mission, 16 July 1894; Price to Baylis, 15 December 1894; Tucker to Baylis, 8 July 1894; Cole to Baylis, 23 January 1896.

19. Archives, Report of Ussagara-Ugogo Mission, 1909, ms.

20. *P.C.M.S.* 1908–1909:56–57; 1910–11:57; Briggs 1918:41–44; von Sicard 1971:202; Archives, Executive Conference, 28 February 1912; Rees and Baxter 1918:41–44.

21. *P.C.M.S.* 1913–14:59; students were nearly evenly divided between the two sexes.

22. *P.C.M.S.* 1915–16:52; 1916–17:34–36; Anonymous 1916; 1917; 1919; Archives, Doulton to Manley, 19 September 1917.

23. They had received some training from the Huron Training College,

founded in 1913 at Kongwa in order to train missionary agents and clergy. The odd name derives from the Canadian donors who funded the school, *P.C.M.S.* 1913–14:57.

24. Archives, Doulton to Lankester, 4 July 1923; Oldham to Manley, 15 December 1924; Executive Conference 24, 25 April 1925; Briggs to Manley, 24 August 1925; Doulton to Manley, 5 April 1924; Briggs to Manley, 16 October 1925; *P.C.M.S.* 1925–26; Hewitt 1971:408, 423.

25. *P.C.M.S.* 1927–28:xxvi; 1928–29:7; for a biography of Chambers, see Sibtain 1968.

26. Cole 1971:45–62; *P.C.M.S.* 1932–33:7; 1934–35:5; Warren 1967:147–48; Hewitt 1971:1, Austen 1968:167.

6: The C.M.S. and Its Sacred and Secular Competitors

1. For example, K.1885, 1888, C.C.F. 1888; Mackay 1889; Manley 1913; Westgate 1918. For a survey of the C.M.S.'s persistent fear of Islam in East Africa, see Holway (1972). This fear of Islam continued even into recent times, Thompson 1976:41.

2. *Pamphlet of Instructions to the Missionaries,* Sydney, New South Wales, 24 October 1893, sent to E. W. Doulton bound for Ukaguru.

3. Ashe 1971:249; the frontispiece to Ashe's autobiography shows him, a C.M.S. clergyman, dressed in full Arab costume including a sword; cf. also Ashe 1890:39–40; Mackay 1889:19–21.

4. Archives, Journal of Bertha V. Briggs (9 March 1909).

5. *C.M.I.* 1878:534–35; cf. Archives, Rees, History, 1902, ms.

6. Archives, Hutchinson to Kirk, 19 November 1880; the C.M.S. Parent Committee even required the C.M.S. at Freretown to apologize formally to the Sultan for persistent interference in local domestic slavery, Archives, Hutchinson to Sultan of Zanzibar, 7 November 1881.

7. Archives, Reeves to Baylis, 16 April 1900.

8. Pruen 1891:254–55; Archives, Baxter to Wright, 13 June 1878; 10 July 1878; 18 April 1879; Oliver 1952:83–85.

9. Archives, Baxter to Wright, 21 March 1880; *P.C.M.S.* 1883–84:59. At this time it was the custom for all European caravans to fly a flag at their head. Such flags came to signify not only European authority but nonslaving expeditions.

10. Archives, Price to Lang, 5 August 1884; Baxter to Wright, 10 July 1878.

11. Archives, Baxter to Wright, 3 August 1880.

12. Archives, Edwards to Lang, received 11 November 1882; *C.M.I.* 1882:294.

13. Pruen 1891:95–96; Roscoe 1921:36–41.

14. Cohen also reports that French priests in West Africa especially favored the purchase and freeing of slaves to serve as mission agents (1980:268–69). The C.M.S. station at Freretown in Kenya was based on freed slaves, but ones secured through naval interceptions of slave ships rather than through purchase, which the C.M.S. seemed to assume supported the traffic; Kieran 1971.

15. Oliver 1952:69; even in the year the C.M.S. arrived, natives at Mpwapwa were so sophisticated about trade that they refused to accept all cloth in trade but showed considerable discrimination, Archives, Baxter to Wright, 1 October 1878.

16. See Oliver 1952:205–206; *P.C.M.S.* 1910–11:57; 1913–14:60–61. Anti-Mus-

lim fears also concerned many German missionaries as well, Archives, Axenfeld to Baylis, 21 June 1910; Notes of Rees to Mission Secretary, 29 June 1910; Bolt 1971:112–13; Holway 1972.

17. Of course, after 1870 Alsatians were officially from Germany, but the German government viewed them as ex-Frenchmen. Both Catholic groups, of course, could speak German, Schmidlin 1913:113–26; Bennett 1963:67–69.

18. Archives, Price to Lang, 31 March 1890; Ashe 1971:273; Bolt 1971:112; *C.M.I.* 1880:137–58; 1886:529–45. Oddly, these diatribes repeatedly refer to Jesuits, but none of that order served in the area at that time.

19. Archives, Price to Wright, 14 May 1880.

20. Archives, Wood to Baylis, 25 July 1884.

21. Richter 1934:39–47; Harries 1953:343; cf. Murray 1967:254. Ekechi, in his study of missionaries in southeastern Nigeria, also contrasts Catholic flexibility with C.M.S. intractability and conservatism in response to government needs in education (1971a:183–86, 192–93).

22. Archives, Baxter to Wright, 21 January 1880; Westgate 1918; *C.M.G.* 1913:56; Ekechi describes bitter conflict between the C.M.S. and Catholics in southeastern Nigeria, 1972a: Chapter 9; 1972b.

23. Briggs 1918:44; cf. also Archives, Notes from Westgate to Manley, 1912, ms.

24. Archives, Annual Report for Ussagara Mission, 1911, ms.; cf. *C.M.G.* 1913:12. Such conflicts between rival missions are common worldwide (Berkhofer 1972:92–93); cf. Johnson 1967:182; Delavignette observes that one of the perennial burdens of the colonial administrator was arbitrating between hostile missions (1950:103); cf. also Buell 1965 I:484. When I conferred with British administrators toward the end of the colonial period in Tanganyika, they repeated these complaints.

25. Archives, Manley to Doulton, 5 December 1912.

26. Archives, Westgate to Manley, 27 December 1912.

27. Archives, Axenfeld to Manley, 9 May 1913; Grunder to Manley, 5 December 1912.

28. Von Sicard 1970:204–209, 219–22; 1968; Wright 1971:128. Actually, there appear to be wide differences even among Evangelicals regarding smoking and drinking. Some C.M.S. elsewhere are reported to have allowed some tobacco and alcohol (Anderson 1977:71).

29. Archives, Tucker to Wigram, 20 August 1890; cf. also Cust 1891:58.

30. Archives, Tucker to Wigram, 20 August 1890.

31. Gann and Duignan remark on the German tendency to administer violent punishments (1977:102,184). This must not, however, be seen out of historical context, for Victorian schools and prisons were also well known for harshness and I myself witnessed floggings during the end of the colonial period.

32. Archives, Price to Lang, 2 January 1888; cf. also Wood to Lang, 18 February 1891.

33. Contrast Moffett (1958:381–82) with the more informed and detailed account by Stahl (1964:259–68); cf. also G.F.S. 1893; Archives, Foreign Office to C.M.S., 25 January 1893, 11 February 1893.

34. Archives, Price to Lang, 27 February 1891.

35. *P.C.M.S.* 1903–1904:94; Archives, Executive Conference, 21–22 August 1890; Executive Conference, 18–21 December 1903; Executive Conference, 5–7

June 1901; one account describes an adultery case in which all involved were converts but where the accused got off and returned to flaunt their victory to the mission, Archives, Ussagara-Ugogo Notes II, 1903, ms.

36. *P.C.M.S.* 1906–1907:77; Archives, Executive Conference, 19–25 January 1914.

37. Archives, Executive Conference, 20–22 April 1914; Executive Conference, 18–21 December 1903.

38. Archives, Executive Conference, 18–21 December 1903.

39. *Ibid.* This led the C.M.S. to support the Kaguru claimants to chiefship over the coastal agents promoted by Germans. This was ironic since the chiefship, when finally established by the British, never encouraged Christianity, Beidelman 1978.

40. Archives, Executive Conference, 18–21 December 1903; cf. Gann and Duignan 1977:209.

41. Archives, Wood to Baylis, 4 June 1895.

42. Later, German missionaries proved equally unready to learn English under British rule (Wright 1971:195–97).

43. Archives, Letter from von Götzen to Bishop Tucker, 1 November 1901, in Executive Conference, 16–17 December 1901.

44. Archives, Executive Conference, 12–13 December 1902; cf. Baylis to Biggs, 9 May 1905.

45. *P.C.M.S.* 1912–13:52–53; cf. also Briggs 1918:41; Gann and Duignan 1977:209.

46. Archives, Letter to Missionaries Engaged in Educational Work, Pamphlet, October 1902.

47. *P.C.M.S.* 1903–1904:98; cf. Oliver 1952:198.

48. Archives, Executive Conference, 30 June 1903.

49. As Furnivall observes: "The easiest way to diffuse primary instruction is to make it pay" (1956:399).

50. Mission opposition to Swahili was widespread in East Africa (Gann and Duignan 1977:211).

51. Archives, Executive Conference, 18–21 December 1903.

52. Germans also preferred Muslims since they were not as likely as Christians to criticize the lifestyle of Europeans (Gann and Duignan 1977:98).

53. Archives, Executive Conference, 18–21 December 1903.

7: Missionizing (Sacred and Secular Strategies)

1. Archives, Instructions to A. N. Wood, 8 June 1886; for a discussion of some idealized motives prompting volunteering for mission work, see Anonymous 1893; Cust 1900.

2. Mackay was one of the few C.M.S. missionaries who did write suggesting reformulation of mission theory, Archives, Mackay, July 1889, ms.

3. Archives, Price to Baylis, 2 October 1893; cf. Archives, Instructions to Missionaries, 4 October 1892.

4. Archives, Beverley to Baylis, 31 January 1896.

5. Archives, Deekes to Baylis, 29 September 1893; Price to Lang, 31 March 1893.

6. Archives, Price to Wright, 14 May 1880.
7. Archives, Wood, Itinerating in Ussagara, 1880, ms.
8. This remains a central tenet of all mission work, cf. Martin 1977.
9. Archives, White to Last, 30 June 1881; in view of Last's subsequent conduct, this letter seems ironic.
10. Archives, Instructions Delivered to Dr. E. and Mrs. Baxter, 31 July 1888.
11. Archives, Wood, Itinerating in Ussagara 1880, ms.
12. Archives, Wood, Journal, July 1894, ms.
13. Archives, Baxter to Wright, 21 January 1880
14. Archives, Price to Wright, 21 January 1880.
15. Archives, Rees, Annual Letter from Berega, 1911.
16. Archives, Ussagara-Chigogo Notes, April 1904, ms.
17. Archives, Watt to Lang, 18 June 1886; cf. White 1977:27–33, 46–49, 51–52.
18. Archives, Watt to Lang, 18 June 1886; cf. White 1977:27–33, 46–49, 51–52.
19. For example, *P.C.M.S.* 1903–1904:100.
20. Archives, Doulton's Journal, 9 May 1898; cf. Archives, Doulton to Baylis, 30 September 1896
21. Archives, Cole to Baylis, 11 August 1895; cf. *P.C.M.S.* 1904–1905:85. For other comments on requiring public confession from prospective members, see Doulton 1889; Pruen 1891:272–73.
22. While total immersion was practiced in earlier times, the C.M.S. now baptize with only a token administration of water. Now that there are second and third generation Kaguru Christians, infants are baptized and confession is confined to formal entry into the adult congregation and to revival.
23. Cf. *P.C.M.S.* 1898–99:99–100; *P.C.M.S.* 1886–87:42.
24. Archives, Executive Conference, 16–17 October 1923; Doulton to Manley, 23 October 1923.
25. Archives, Executive Conference, 13–14 November 1909.
26. Revival prompted a wide range of soul-searching comments by both missionaries and sociologists. See Warren 1954; Anderson 1979:118–20, 125–27, 143–44; Langford-Smith 1954; Taylor 1958a:99–104; 1958b:16; Sundkler 1960:72; 1980:15–16, 59, Chapter 5; Barrett 1968:147; Jassy 1973:67–68; Smoker 1971; Warren 1974:200.
27. Contrast the different interpretations of revivals' functions by Sundkler 1960:72; Wilson 1969:136.
28. Barrett notes that revivalists in East Africa were often women and suggests that this relates to their weakened status in the church (1968:147). I know of no female Kaguru revivalists.
29. Archives, Instructions Delivered to Dr. E. and Mrs. Baxter, 31 July 1888.
30. Cf. Sundkler's comments on the tendencies of Swahili thought to conflate illness and sin (1960:241; 1980:95); cf. also Reyburn 1960.
31. Archives, Executive Conference, 2–3 May 1921.
32. Cf. also Archives, Baxter to Wright, 8 May 1879.
33. Useful references to C.M.S. medical work in Ukaguru, other than the books of Paul White, are *Mercy and Truth* 1896;83–84; 1903:357; 1908:299; 1909:132–33, 203–204; 1911:202–205; 1912:201–202; 1915:196–97; 1927:313–14; *Mission Hospital* 1931:176; 1932:176–77; 1933:176–79; *Medical Mission Quarterly* 1896:83–84.
34. For further discussion of the relation between mission work and vaccina-

tion, cf. Archives, Deekes to Baylis, 29 November 1909; *P.C.M.S.* 1891–92:46; 1892–93:46.

35. Since there were four or five times as many Gogo as Kaguru, C.M.S. did translate much into Cigogo and urged workers to learn the language.

36. Cf. Archives, Executive Conference, 5–7 June 1901; Executive Conference, 10–12 January 1906; Baylis to Rees, 2 March 1906, 30 March 1908; Executive Conference, 28–29 July 1905.

37. Archives, Green to Baylis, 24 November 1910.

38. Perhaps this related to the fact that English education had done little for C.M.S. converts at Freretown, cf. Price's influential book (1891:149); Ekechi reports comparable C.M.S. aversion to teaching English in Nigeria (1971:182). One must be careful not to portray all C.M.S. as committed to learning African languages. One of the great C.M.S. heroes, Bishop Tucker, walked 22,000 miles evangelizing in East Africa and never mastered any African tongue (Oliver 1952:222).

39. Standard I is roughly comparable to First Grade in the U.S.A.

40. As late as the 1920s, the C.M.S. taught few skilled trades in most of its schools (Jones 1924:184); cf. Hodge 1971:90; Strayer 1978:20–24. C.M.S. appear to have been more involved in developing practical education in Kenya than in Tanganyika (Strayer 1978:93).

41. Archives, Executive Conference, 29–30 June 1903.

42. Archives, Deekes to Baylis, 29 November 1909.

43. Luchelo and Nguye, ms.

44. Archives, Doulton to Baylis, 1 December 1909. Although a letter, this contains much information on the teaching syllabus and examinations. A briefer account is provided in Archives, Executive Conference, 1 June 1912; Executive Conference, 12–13 December 1902; and in Chambers 1931:27–29.

45. Archives, Lang to Price, 25 February 1886.

46. Archives, Executive Conference, 28–29 July 1905.

47. Archives, Edwards to Lang, received 11 November 1882.

48. Archives, Report of the Ussagara-Ugogo Mission for 1909.

49. Archives, Pickthall to Baylis, 20 November 1909.

50. For an amusing account of this, see Roscoe 1921:32.

51. Archives, Baylis to Doulton, 25 August 1909; 27 January 1910.

52. Archives, Doulton to Baxter, 1 December 1909.

53. Archives, B. Briggs's Journal, 9 March 1909.

54. Archives, Baylis to Doulton, 27 January 1910.

55. Archives, Westgate to Manley, 12 January 1909; Executive Conference, 14 August 1909; Report from Ukaguru, received 12 January 1909; cf. Archives, Manley to Barton, 31 July 1922.

56. Archives, Pickthall to Baylis, 20 November 1909.

57. Archives, Price to Wright, 14 May 1880.

58. Today many missionaries subscribe to secular, scientific explanations for most events and restrict religious explanations to the Bible or intimate aspects of their personal lives (Miller 1973).

59. Cf. Morris 1911.

60. Quoted as representative by Oliver (1952:25). From Cust's perspective, Jesus, a carpenter, would be disqualified; cf. also Mackay 1890:58; Fullani 1919:159–60; for a biography of Cust, see Stock 1909; cf. also Stock 1899:813.

61. Oldham 1924; 1927; for his biography, see Dougall 1970; King 1971:46–52; cf. Archives, Oldham to Manley, 15 December 1924. For criticism, cf. correspondence between Oldham and Leys (Cell 1976).

62. Jones 1924:47. For a C.M.S. evaluation of the Commission, see Wilkie 1921. The Commission financed a tour of the American South by a C.M.S. missionary from Uganda, Grace 1926. King rightly notes the reactionary, implicitly racist views of Jones's reports, though at the time many saw these as liberal; cf. also Berman 1975:6. The views on Black education which Jones promoted derived from those developed in the American South at the Hampton Institute and Tuskegee, namely, that Blacks be given training scholastically inferior to Whites, emphasizing practical skills which would fit them for humbler social occupations. See King 1971, especially 50, 97. In 1937 the Commission on Higher Education in East Africa recommended policies essentially based on Jones, Hailey 1938:1290. Cf. also Leys's denunciation of Jones (Cell 1976:271–72, 276–77, 280–83).

63. Cf. Neill 1966:100–102; cf. Strayer 1978:33, 115 for C.M.S. ambivalence regarding the relation between church and state.

64. Archives, Report of the Tanganyika Mission of the C.M.S. for 1925, ms.

65. Archives, Briggs to Cash, 17 March 1926.

66. By 1937 all evangelistic and catechistal schools were denied government support (Hailey 1938:1242). Even as late as 1942, the C.M.S. continued to resist government control.

67. Archives, Clark to Hinsley, 28 April 1926; cf. also Archives, Briggs to Cash, 2 March 1926; Clark to Briggs, 21 January 1926; Hooper to Briggs, 8 November 1926. Despite these needs for better standards, the C.M.S. spent far less in education (per student) than some competing missions (Thompson 1976:29).

68. Allen 1927? passim; 1927:18–19; 1929:14–21; Allen and Cochrane 1920:2–3, 10–11; Brenner 1979; Sundkler writes that "the whole church programme had been geared to the educational planning of the Governments to such an extent that some of the essential functions of the Church were jeopardized" (1966:95). Luzbetak is right that "it is indeed foolish for any missionary to deny the multifaceted conquences of his seemingly purely spiritual activity" (1970:6). Another well-known mission theorist warns against services impeding evangelism (McGavran 1970:60–62). Markowitz is representative of recent writers in considering it ambiguous for missionaries to reject Western materialism yet impose many of its aspects on aliens (1972:14). Leys suggests that co-optation by government undermines African confidence in missions (Leys 1941:137–38). One of missionaries' most vehement critics, Leys contrasts the parochial, restricted notions of religion held by some missionaries with Christ's view of religion as a way of life embracing all institutions, a view also held by Oldham (1926:232–33).

69. Quoted in Archives, Briggs to Manley, 16 January 1926.

70. Archives, Executive Conference, 10–12 January 1906.

8: Missionizing (The Image of the Native)

1. The gulf between the Kaguru and the C.M.S. paralleled that between the middle class and the poor in England. Norman's characterization of Anglican churchworkers' attitudes toward Victorian slum dwellers applies to attitudes which C.M.S. held toward Kaguru (1976:165, 233–34; cf. Bradley 1976:131).

2. Roman Catholic missionaries in East Africa held similar views. Popular missionary propagandists encouraged these stereotypes in order to raise funds and recruits, cf. Kieren 1969.

3. Archives, Beverley to Baylis, 22 March 1895; cf. *P.C.M.S.* 1896–97:108; Rees, *History,* 1902, ms.

4. Cf. *C.M.G.* 1902:52.

5. Archives, Jeanes to Lang, 5 December 1885. Initially Last thought that Kaguru had no notion of an afterlife (1881:559), yet a year later he reported that the dead were called "sleeping ones" *(wagono)* and that Kaguru had several names for God, thereby assuming that there were indigenous notions comparable to the Trinity (1882:295).

6. Paraphrase from The Wisdom of Solomon 3.1.

7. Watt n.d.:45; divination, magic, and such beliefs fell under the injunctions of Deut. 18.10–12.

8. *P.C.M.S.* 1923–24:15; I encountered similar reactions among C.M.S. when I did fieldwork in 1957–58.

9. Westgate *C.M.G.* 1913:56.

10. Only in 1905 was a course in comparative religion taught prospective C.M.S. missionaries, and then this did not include African beliefs since these were only "superstition" (Hodge 1971:91–92).

11. Archives, Baxter to Wright, 18 April 1879.

12. The writer emphasizes private, personal vice but ignores public abuses prominent during this period in Britain and the colony; cf. Strayer (1976:109) for the class bias Evangelicals showed in the vices they attacked.

13. *Handbook for Workers* 1905:72; such prejudice was common to Catholics as well (Kieren 1969).

14. Archives, Journal of Bertha V. Briggs, 9 March 1909.

15. Archives, Conference at Dar es Salaam on Education, 2 October 1926.

16. Archives, Pruen to Lang, 27 January 1887.

17. Archives, Executive Conference, 9 April 1894.

18. The intention of the author is to praise restraint, yet the case is puzzling since Kaguru traditionally frown on extensive mourning for infants, who are not considered free of the dead and therefore not full humans meriting mourning. Here, restraint seems a heathen virtue. The mission did frown on the loud mourning at funerals of adults.

19. Archives, Resolution of the Executive Conference, 14 August 1909.

20. Archives, Executive Conference, 2–6 June 1904; 28–29 July 1905.

21. Archives, Executive Conference, 10 April 1906.

22. Archives, Executive Conference, 28–29 July 1905. F23. Archives, Executive Conference, 13–15 November 1909.

24. Cf. Strayer 1978:19–20, 88–89.

25. Archives, Journal of Bertha V. Briggs, 9 March 1909, ms.

26. Archives, Journal of Bertha V. Briggs, 9 March 1909, ms.

27. Archives, Executive Conference, 6–8 April 1911; Gal. 5.19–21 were cited to support many such prohibitions.

28. Menstruating women and those in ritual impurity could not sleep with their spouses but lay on the floor.

29. Kaguru thought this indicated a human being's culture as opposed to the unmodified voraciousness of toothy nonhumans.

30. Mixing meat and milk was not allowed. This particular prohibition was also observed by Jews. Food prohibitions related to one's father's kin or to notions of pregnancy or instruction from divination were rejected by missionaries as superstition.

31. Kaguru endorsed labiadectomy, which "softened" women to make them readier for indoctrination.

32. During periods of ritual pollution or when observing prohibitions, hair was left unkempt.

33. This was homeopathic magic to prevent fever and crossed eyes.

34. It was thought that the young came from the land of the dead. Therefore, the dead mourned the newborn and wished them to return, drawing them back through illness. By naming the young after the dead, the ghosts were placated.

35. Urine was considered a cleansing substance.

36. This was related to the pagan rituals performed when a girl was given a labiadectomy.

37. When a Kaguru was in mourning or observing some renunciation following the instructions given at divination, he or she sometimes neither washed nor cut hair.

38. To Kaguru this indicated that the C.M.S. believed in witchcraft. If witchcraft were not a reality, why legislate against it? Certainly Kaguru would agree that witchcraft was bad. This rule also referred to practicing antimagic or countersorcery, which Kaguru saw as self-defense.

39. This was associated with ceremonies such as initiation.

40. One threatened people because one believed they might be sorcerers or witches.

41. If a person were accused of witchcraft or sorcery, he or she might submit to ordeals. One was to drink a poison and survive. Another was to see whether it was painful to have one's ear pierced. Witches were thought to suffer pain while the innocent did not.

42. These were associated with male and female initiation.

43. These were associated with courtship, although it is not clear whether the missionaries made any sexual connection.

44. The missionaries subscribed to sincere emotions and therefore rejected professional mourners.

45. A suspected witch or sorcerer might be informed of suspicions by finding a branch of euphorbia (a poison) in his or her doorway.

46. The Kaguru braided hair and lengthened it by weaving in fiber. This was associated with warriorhood, which involved flirting, dancing, wearing jewelry, and other practices disapproved of by the C.M.S.

47. For the C.M.S., proper marriage involved the consent of a girl's guardians. What bothered missionaries was not only the idea that regular practices were flouted but that human passions were up.

48. This involved notions about pollution that missionaries associated with paganism: the symbolical removing of the associations which the natal kin groups had with the bride.

49. The mission forbade all divination.

50. These were meant to prevent theft and the incursion of malevolent beings.

51. See Beidelman 1963a.

52. Such medicines ensured fertility and prevented malevolence by others who wanted to hinder germination.

53. Kaguru sacrificed to their ancestral dead whenever they thought that their health, fertility, or well-being was jeopardized by the fact that the dead felt forgotten. Propitiation of the dead is the central purpose of most Kaguru ritual.

54. This was to propitiate the dead and cleanse the land with which they were associated.

55. The cloth represents the placenta.

56. Fat was smeared on persons to keep them warm and well groomed. Fat smearing was also a benediction by elders, employing supernatural power which missionaries thought should be reserved for God.

57. In 1963 such practices were still regularly performed throughout Ukaguru even though the mission condemned them. There are few references to these customs in mission correspondence from Ukaguru though rites for women became a famous issue with the C.M.S. in Kenya. One early letter seeks guidance about the proper mission stand on labiadectomy, Archives, Report from Ukaguru, received 12 January 1909.

58. The aim was to exclude pagans who might observe traditional practices. This was impractical since such ceremonies were so expensive that local people pooled their resources, pagan and Christian. Of course, if no feasting, drinking, or dancing was observed, the cost would be less; but kin invited to such celebrations were implicitly obligated to assist those being celebrated. Therefore, it was to the celebrants' interest to attract as many guests as possible.

59. No traditional medicines or protective incantations would be used.

60. This was to prevent beer parties, feasts, and dances.

61. The masks worn by initiates had no deep religious meaning other than to indicate the novices' liminal status. The anointing and washing were associated with the blessing of the dead and the novices' change of status.

62. Circumcisors were paid not only for their skill in cutting but also because they incurred the pollution of spilled blood and provided supernatural protection to ensure a boy's recovery.

63. Archives, Deekes to Baylis, 29 September 1893.

64. Isichei (1970) presents an excellent discussion contrasting African and Christian beliefs and their relation to conversion.

65. Archives, Rees, *History,* 1902, ms; Journal of Wood, August 1894, ms. Perhaps the most interesting record of debate between a missionary and an African remains that between Livingstone and a rainmaker (Livingstone 1857:23–25).

66. Archives, Baxter to Wright, 18 April 1879; *P.C.M.S.* 1883–84:48. Ordinarily, inauspicious infants would have been slain or given to strangers.

67. Archives, Mackay, On Christian Names of Native Converts, 1883, ms.; doubtless many natives might blush at mispronunciations; cf. Strayer 1978:88–89.

68. Archives, Report from Ukaguru, received 12 January 1909.

69. It is not at all clear that this supposedly scriptural ban is well founded (Horan 1976; cf. Harries 1953:332; Ekechi 1976; Newing 1970).

70. Archives, Executive Conference, 21–22 August 1890.

71. Personal communication from a C.M.S. missionary, 1963. The Australian C.M.S. are more conservative than the British; therefore policies in Kenya may have been more flexible (Strayer 1970:131–32).

72. Pickthall laments over this, Archives, Pickthall to Baylis, 9 November 1910. During my fieldwork, I often observed such difficult situations.

73. Archives, Ussagara-Ugogo Notes II, December 1903, ms.; for an extensive discussion of widow-inheritance and Christian missions, see Kirwen 1979.

74. Archives, Executive Conference, 10–12 April 1906; Leenhardt 1930.

75. For example, Archives, Executive Conference, 13–14 November 1909. The confusion in the use of the term *dowry* lies in the fact that dowry goes with a woman into a new household while bridewealth passes into various households of the bride's kin.

76. Archives, Executive Conference Resolution, 14 August 1909.

77. Archives, Executive Conference, 21–22 August 1890; Wood, Journal, July 1894, ms. German Lutherans sought to eradicate circumcision entirely among the Zaramo who neighbored toward the east but do not seem to have been successful (von Sicard 1970:157).

78. Archives, Executive Conference, 28–29 July 1905. To make sense, Kaguru initiation of both sexes had to take place at puberty, not earlier.

79. Cf. Archives, Blackburn to Lang, 8 August 1887.

80. For example, the mission encouraged Kaguru to pray for rain, Archives, Journal of B. Briggs, 9 March 1909.

81. Cf. *Zinyimbo,* hymn 47.

82. Archives, Executive Conference, 28 February 1912.

83. Archives, Baylis to Westgate, 31 May 1912.

84. Archives, Executive Conference, 9–10 November 1910.

85. Archives, Wigram to Hannington, 4 December 1885.

86. Baxter 1879:532; Last 1879:664; Archives, Baxter to Wright, 21 January 1880.

87. Archives, C.M.S. Resolutions on the Subject of Presents to Kings and Chiefs in Africa, 3 July 1888.

88. Archives, Baxter to Lang, 19 July 1886.

89. Archives, Price to Baylis, 25 July 1894; *P.C.M.S.* 1903–1904:97.

90. Archives, Last to Wright, 20 January 1879; 3 March 1879.

91. Archives, Executive Conference, 28 February 1912; Hewitt 1971:182.

92. Archives, Executive Conference, 14–15 July 1902.

93. In the recent past, British Evangelicals were criticized at home for high-handed and authoritarian methods of trying to inflict their morality upon the public (Hewitt 1971:116).

94. Archives, Baxter to Whiting, 29 November 1881.

95. Before the Germans, serious offences such as murder were referred to the Sultan of Zanzibar's agent and sent to the coast, Archives, Baxter to Whiting, 29 November 1881.

96. Archives, Whiting to Baxter, 22 September 1882.

97. Archives, Wood to Baylis, 25 July 1894.

98. Archives, Baylis to Peel, 18 December 1911; cf. also Baylis to Westgate, 24 November 1911; Baylis to Peel, 18 December 1911.

99. Archives, Baylis to Peel, 8 March 1912. What was assumed was that each

settlement could draw up its own rules for secular authority, but where were these to come from except from Kaguru tribal tradition?

100. Archives, Baylis to Peel, 3 April 1912.

9: The Developing Mission

1. The C.M.S. historian Hewitt recognized this in the title of his history of the society, *The Problem of Success* (1971).

2. Archives, Price to Lang, 14 October 1891.

3. *Special Appeal on Behalf of the Victoria Nyanza Mission,* (C.M.S. circular, January 1878); cf. also Baxter to Wright, 18 April 1879.

4. Archives, Baxter to Lang, 6 June 1882.

5. Missionaries also advocated policies for administration and business that led to criticism, cf. Joelson 1920: Chapter 8.

6. Archives, Deekes to Baylis, 16 April 1895.

7. Archives, Wood to Baylis, 24 September 1894; cf. also Wood to Lang, 29 January 1887.

8. Archives, Baylis to Burt and Rees, 23 March 1900.

9. Archives, Lang to Price, 5 March 1892; Beverley to Baylis, 15 February 1897; Baylis to Ussagara-Ugogo Mission, January 1908; 12 November 1908; 25 August 1909; Baylis to Jackson, 25 August 1909; Executive Conference, 10–12 January 1906.

10. Archives, Lang to Price, 28 January 1886.

11. For example, see Archives, Wood to Lang, 2 December 1889.

12. This was obviously quoted in order to encourage contributions for intensifying mission work, *P.C.M.S.* 1912–13:54.

13. Translated from the Swahili by the C.M.S. mission, undated, Archives, received August 1892. The mission secretary's reply appears glib and can hardly have pleased the Kaguru, Archives, Land to Kaguru, 17 October 1892.

14. Archives, Proposed Regulations for Furloughs . . . East African Stations, n.d. 1893?; Baylis to Rees, 24 May 1906.

15. Strayer points out a similar process among the C.M.S. in Kenya (1973b:231).

16. Archives, Pruen to Lang, 24 February 1887; for a eulogy to lady missionaries, see Cust 1895:105–106.

17. Archives, Baxter to Lang, 18 June 1886.

18. Archives, Baylis to Peel, 8 August 1905.

19. Archives, Wood to Baylis, 21 August 1894.

20. Archives, Watt to Lang, 19 July 1886; Price to Lang, 31 March 1890; Tucker to Wigram, 20 August 1890.

21. Archives, Wilson to Wright, 2 October 1876.

22. Archives, Baylis to Parker, 8 January 1904; 14 October 1904; Baylis to Westgate n.d. 1903; 3 February 1905; Resolution on Westgate, 4 April 1905.

23. Archives, Instructions of the Committee, 1879.

24. Archives, Watt to Lang, 26 June 1886.

25. Archives, Price to Lang, 31 March 1890.

26. Archives, Executive Conference, 21 November 1905.

27. Archives, Parker to Baylis, 28 December 1904; 9 May 1906.

28. Archives, Rees to Baylis, 18 January 1906.
29. Archives, Executive Conference, 14–15 July 1902.
30. Archives, Executive Conference, 12–13 December 1902.
31. Archives, Waite to Baylis, 16 April 1895; Baxter to Wright, 13 June 1879; Cole to Lang, 1 January 1887.
32. Archives, Roscoe to Lang, 7 November 1888; cf. also *P.C.M.S.* 1882–83:54; 1883–84:47.
33. For example, Archives, Baxter to Wright, 29 October 1878; Baxter to Wright, 6 December 1878.
34. Archives, Lang to Price, 25 February 1886.
35. Archives, Bishop Tucker to Baylis, 29 October 1894.
36. Archives, Baxter to Lang, 24 January 1882.
37. Marriage arrangements involved much expense for missionaries in the field. By British law a couple had to reside in the same town for one month prior to marriage; and civil marriage had to be performed by a British consulate on the coast, meaning high costs for residence and travel. See Archives, Executive Conference, 9 April 1894; Reeves to Baylis, 18 December 1900.
38. See Neill 1964:259–60; July 1967:193–95; Webster 1964:5–41; Ajayi 1965:241–55; Ayandele 1967:210–16; Ilogu 1974:81–86. For some of the objections which C.M.S. raised to Venn's policy, see Hewitt 1971:420–21.
39. Tucker 1911:112; cf. also Taylor 1958a:86–88.
40. Cust *Notes* 1889:15.
41. Archives, Reeves to Baylis, 16 April 1900; cf. also Stock III 1889:813.
42. Archives, Baylis to Westgate, 24 November 1911.
43. Archives, Manley to Bishop, 26 January 1922.
44. Hewitt 1971:186, 422, 425, 432; cf. Hellberg 1965:130–31.
45. Cf. McGavran 1959:117–18; Kalu 1975; Stock provides the early C.M.S. reaction to such criticism, 1901:241–57; 1912:393–403, 465–81.
46. Stock 1889; Fox 1898; Gollock 1905:81.
47. Warren 1967: Chapter 7; Stock II:336; III:52; Clarke 1915; Lankester 1921.
48. Accounts of local finances are difficult to secure, but see Archives, Estimates of Expenses, 12 October 1900 (German East African mission), ms.
49. Archives, Rees to Baylis, 18 December 1900; cf. Baxter to Lang, 19 July 1885.
50. Archives, Rees to Baylis, 30 November 1900.
51. Archives, Baxter to Wright, 21 January 1880.
52. Archives, Baxter to Wright, 14 July 1879.
53. Archives, Executive Conference, 21–22 August 1890; Executive Conference, 14–15 July 1902; Executive Conference, 9 February 1906; Baxter to Wright, 29 October 1879; Last to Wright, 20 May 1880.
54. Archives, Executive Conference, 10–12 January 1906; 10 April 1906.
55. Archives, Reeves to Baylis, 10 April 1900; Executive Conference, 5–7 June 1901; Baylis to Rees, 17 May 1900; Briggs to Hooper, 15 October 1926.
56. Archives, Rees to Baylis, 16 August 1900.
57. Archives, Educational Conference, Dar es Salaam, 13–15 December 1921.
58. Archives, Parker to Baylis, 9 May 1906; Executive Conference, 5–7 June 1901.

10: The Local Mission

1. When I arrived in Ukaguru, I first resided at the main C.M.S. station at Berega. Later I stayed at Mgugu, two miles distant. Finally, I moved to Idibo about 20 miles northwest; no Europeans worked there, but it had a mission school and church. In travels I encountered many other mission churches, schools, and meeting houses.

2. For a survey of factors determining the location and plan of missions, see Johnson 1967; cf. also King 1974, 1976 on space in colonial situations.

3. I lack figures on the proportion of Ngulu Christians, but this is considerably lower than Kaguru. No Baraguyu and few Kamba adhere to any Christian group. Moffett estimates the African Christian population of Tanganyika as 18 percent (1958:35).

4. The East African Statistic Department in Nairobi gave access to 1957 census forms for these 6 headmanships, the only ones covered in detail of the 44 such areas. These samples provide information on religion and family. The headmanships covered include only one populous area subject to intensive missionizing. Since examples were collected by C.M.S. employees, some interviewees may have presented themselves as Christian even though they were not. Figures list purported Christians with pagan names or as polygynists.

5. Besides including all of Ukaguru (Kilosa), this contains a small portion of Ungulu and extends south of Ukaguru to Kolosa town; but since the C.M.S. has few churches and no schools or medical facilities in these areas, I exclude them.

6. He received no formal secondary education. He was a Muslim Ngulu employed as a dresser by a Native Authority. He converted to Christianity after a revival. His becoming an evangelist led the C.M.S. to train him to become a pastor. He was given special education, including English, after being considered a candidate for bishop.

7. One Kaguru pastor speaks English but was not stationed in Ukaguru; in 1958 he was sent to Australia for further study.

8. In 1957, 7 East African shillings equaled $1.

9. Kaguru often associate Ngulu with superior prowess as traders, curers, and even supposed sorcerers, cf. Beidelman 1964.

10. For example, whether a union should be forbidden because it is prohibited by Kaguru, even though acceptable by European belief (marriage within a clan or to a matrilineal kinsman's wife's sister), and, conversely, whether a union between cross-cousins, endorsed by Kaguru, should be allowed by the church.

11. Berega, Mamboya, Uponela, Magela, Chitange, Mwandi, Talagwe, Iyogwe, Nguyami, Rubeho, Chakwale, Idibo, Chisitwi, Leshata (now closed).

12. Certified teachers are classified in two grades, I and II. Grade II is awarded those with two years' professional training after Standard VII, Grade I those with two years' professional training after Standard X. Both Grade I and Grade II teach primary schools; only Grade I teach at the Middle School (Cf. *Tanganyika Report for the Year 1958*:177). The School Inspector is only Grade II but has so many years service that his salary equals that of the newly hired young Grade I Headmaster.

13. The name was a pun on the Kaguru word *uta,* "bow," implying the union would be a weapon.

14. Some years later I met him in Kenya, employed by government. The Headmaster claimed the mission blocked his transfer to a government school.

15. For a description of life at a station hospital, see White, 1952, 1960.

16. Some parts of White's account deal with Ukaguru and Ugogo, but it is difficult to recognize the area since he overdramatizes its discomforts for the sake of missionary propaganda.

17. In Jean-Jacques Annaud's Academy Award–winning film, *Black and White in Color,* French priests try to convert Africans by claiming that only Christians have the skill to ride bicycles.

18. I refer to men's clothing because very few Kaguru women assume European dress.

In 1957, government schools accepted girls free; later when boys were also admitted free, Kaguru complained that C.M.S. comity forced them to pay for schooling that would be free in secular areas.

19. To an outsider such as myself, mission life seemed dour and overconcerned with what one did not do rather than what one enjoyed. Dunston (1968) presents a striking account of the puritanical, gloomy, constricting influence of Evangelicals upon everyday Australian life.

20. I recall standing with a Catholic priest on the verandah overlooking a large and prosperous mission with many attractive native dwellings. I pointed to a squalid conglomeration of huts beyond the station and was told the miserable hamlet was inhabited by backsliders thrown off mission property.

21. Although it is on the syllabus, teachers are forbidden instruction in cultivating tobacco because it goes against C.M.S. morality.

22. Furnival suggests that, as a colony develops, all such posts become filled and few new ones are available due to a stagnant economy. Teaching becomes a time-serving profession of little prestige and provides few openings for people overeducated for agriculture but undereducated for technical posts. This seems the eventual trend for East Africa (1956:382–83).

23. For example, at Idibo the pastor pled for 15 shillings from each adult, 10 shillings from youths, and 5 shillings from children for constructing a new church. Little was raised. The mission ordinarily requests 6 shillings from all adult members annually.

24. The government was unable to force all Kamba to attend schools and made no effort with Baraguyu.

25. Three reported as Muslim, one a Kaguru.

26. At Berega in 1957 this was 2 shillings.

27. I was not allowed to attend meetings but read reports of its decisions and discussed proceedings with an African member.

28. The head of medical facilities and the Education Supervisor were authorized members. The nurse in charge of shop accounts attended in that capacity. When the committee was empowered to choose another member, it admitted the remaining nurse.

29. Encel remarks on intense anti-Catholicism in Australian life (1970:168–69).

30. Unlike the C.M.S., the Dutch Catholics have no special political sympathy for the British administration.

Bibliography

Achebe, C.

1958 *Things Fall Apart.* London: Heinemann.

Adjei, A.

1944 Imperialism and Spiritual Freedom: an African view. *American Journal of Sociology* 50 (3):189–98.

African Religious Research

1973 African Religious Research III (1). Los Angeles: University of California African Studies Center.

Ajayi, J. F. A.

1965 *Christian Missions in Nigeria 1841–1891.* London: Longmans.

Ajayi, J. F. A., and E. A. Ayandele

1969 Writing African Church History. In *The Church Crossing Frontiers,* edited by P. Beyerhaus and C. F. Hallencreutz, pp. 90–108. Studia Missionalia Upsaliensia XI. Uppsala: Gleerup.

Allen, R.

1919 *Educational Principles and Missionary Methods.* London: Robert Scott.

1927?a *Mission Activities Considered in Relation to the Manifestation of the Spirit.* London: World Dominion Press.

1927b *La Zoute: a Critical Review of 'The Mission in Africa.'* London: World Dominion Press.

1928 *Jerusalem: a Critical Review of 'The World Mission of Christianity.'* London: World Dominion Press.

1950 *Missionary Methods* (1st edition, 1912). London: World Dominion Press.

Allen, R., and T. Cochrane

1920 *Missionary Survey as an Aid to Intelligent Co-operation in Foreign Missions.* London: Longmans, Green.

Altholz, J. L.

1967 *The Churches in the Nineteenth Century.* New York: Bobbs-Merrill.

Anderson, H. G. (ed.)

1948 *The Health of the Whole Man: A Stratagem on C.M.S. Medical Policy.* London: C.M.S.

1956 *The New Phase in Medical Strategy.* London: C.M.S.

Anderson, W.

1977 *The Church in East Africa.* Dodoma: Central Tanganyika Press.

Andersson, E.

1958 *Messianic Popular Movements in the Lower Congo.* London: Studia Ethnographica Upsaliensia XVI.

1968 *Churches at the Grass-roots.* New York: Friendship Press.

Anonymous

1876 *The Victoria Nyanza Mission Instructions.* London: C.M.S.

1883 The Late Mrs. Cole, of Mpwapwa. *Church Missionary Gleaner* 10:123–24.

1885 Mr. Hooper's Party: Another Grave at Mamboia. *Church Missionary Gleaner* 12:133–34.

1893 The Missionary Call and Missionary Candidates. *Church Missionary Gleaner* 108:30–37.

1894a *Zinyimbo ('Hymns for Public Worship' in Kimegi).* London: Society for Promoting Christian Knowledge.

1894b *Nsachilo nswamu kwa Mattayo kwa Nonga ya Kaguru* [The Book of Matthew in Chikaguru]. London: British and Foreign Bible Society.

1902 Superstition in Ussagara. *Church Missionary Gleaner* 29:52–53.

1903 [untitled article]. *Mercy and Truth* 7:357.

1905 Ussagara and Ugogo. In *Handbooks for Workers: Outline Histories of C.M.S. Missions,* I, pp. 67–76. London: C.M.S.

1908 Mamboya. *Mercy and Truth* 12:299.

1909a Ussagara. *Mercy and Truth* 13:132–33.

1909b Mamboya. *Mercy and Truth* 13:203–204.

1910 Mamboya. *Mercy and Truth* 14:204–205.

1911 German East Africa. *Mercy and Truth* 15:202–204.

1912 German East Africa. Mamboya. *Mercy and Truth* 16:201–202.

1913a C.M.S. Medical Missions. A Comparative Survey, 5. German East Africa. *Mercy and Truth* 17:88–91.

1913b German East Africa. Mamboya. *Mercy and Truth* 17:199.

1914a The Main Object of Missionary Work. *Church Missionary Review* 65:654–59.

1914b [untitled article]. *Mercy and Truth* 18:3.

1916 A Visit from a German Patrol. *Church Missionary Gleaner* 43:11.

1917 Prisoners of War. *Church Missionary Gleaner* 44:20–22.

1919 A Survey of the Effect of the War upon Missions. *The International Review of Missions* 8(32):435–90.

1920 The Relation between Medical, Educational and Evangelistic Work in Foreign Missions. *Church Missionary Review* 71:54–62.

1929a Tanganyika Territory. *Mercy and Truth* 33:173.

1929b *East Africa.* Africa and the East Series. London: C.M.S.

1931 Berega. *Mission Hospital* 35:176.

1932 Ukuguru [*sic*]. *Mission Hospital* 36:176–77.

1933 Ukaguru. *Mission Hospital* 37:176–79.

Ashe, R. P.

1890 *Two Kings of Uganda.* London: Sampson Low.

1971 *Chronicles of Uganda* (1st edition, 1894). London: Cass.

Austen, R. A.

1968 *Northwest Tanzania under German and British Rule.* New Haven: Yale University Press.

Axelson, S.

1967 *Culture Confrontation in the Lower Congo.* Falköping: Gummessons. Studia Missionalia Upsaliensia 14.

Ayandele, E. A.
1967 *The Missionary Impact on Modern Nigeria 1842–1914.* New York: Humanities Press.
Baëta, G. G.
1962 *Prophetism in Ghana.* London: SCM Press.
Baëta, C. G. (ed.)
1968 *Christianity in Tropical Africa.* London: International African Institute, Oxford University Press.
Baker, J. G. H.
1958 The Anglican Communion and Its Missionary Task. *The International Review of Missions* 47 (188):445–53.
Balandier, G.
1965 The Colonial Situation: a Theoretical Approach (1st published, 1951). In *Social Change: the Colonial Situation,* edited by I. Wallerstein, pp. 34–61. New York: Wiley.
1970 *The Sociology of Black Africa.* London: André Deutsch.
Bald, D.
1970 *Deutsch-Ostafrika 1900–1914.* Munich: IFO-Institut für Wirtschaftsforschung, Weltforum.
Barrett, D. B.
1968 *Schism and Renewal in Africa.* London: Oxford University Press.
Barrett, S. R.
1977 *The Rise and Fall of an African Utopia.* Development Perspectives 1. Montreal: Centre for Developing Area Studies, McGill University.
Bartels, F. L.
1965 *The Roots of Ghana Methodism.* London: Cambridge University Press.
Bates, M. S.
1953 The Training of Christian Ministers in Non-British Africa. *The International Review of Missions* 43:294–300.
Baudet, Henri
1965 *Paradise on Earth: Some Thoughts on European Images of Non-European Man* (1st edition, 1959). New Haven: Yale University Press.
Bavinck, J. H.
1960 *An Introduction to the Science of Missions.* Philadelphia: Presbyterian and Reform Press.
Baxter, E. J.
1879 Letters. *Church Missionary Intelligencer* 4:532, 534.
1880 Letters from Mpwapwa. *Church Missionary Intelligencer* 5:735.
1883 Letters. *Church Missionary Intelligencer* 8:291.
1896 Letter. *Church Missionary Society Medical Mission Quarterly* 16:83–84.
1898 News from Mpwapwa. *Mercy and Truth* 2:193–94.
1903a Letter. *Church Missionary Intelligencer* 28:687.
1903b Letter. *Mercy and Truth* 7:229–30.
Bayley, David H.
1976 *Forces of Order. Police Behavior in Japan and the United States.* Berkeley: University of California Press.

Beaver, R. P.

1957 Nationalism and Missions. *Church History* 25:22–42.

Beetham, T. A.

1957 The Church in Africa Faces 1957. *The International Review of Missions* 46:17–29.

Beidelman, T. O.

1961a Beer Drinking and Cattle Theft in Ukaguru. *American Anthropologist* 54:534–59.

1961b Umwano und Ukaguru Students' Association: zwei stammespartikularische Bewegungen in einem Häuptlingstum im Tanganyika. *Anthropos* 56:818–45. Republished as: Umwano and Ukaguru Students' Association: Two Tribalistic Movements in a Tanganyika Chiefdom. In *Black Africa,* edited by J. Middleton, pp. 303–25. New York: Macmillan, 1970.

1962 A History of Ukaguru, Kilosa District: 1857–1916. *Tanganyika Notes and Records* 58 and 59:11–39.

1963a Kaguru Omens: an East African People's Concepts of the Unusual, Unnatural and Supernormal. *Anthropological Quarterly* 36:43–59.

1963b A Kaguru Version of the Sons of Noah. *Cahiers d'études africaines* 12:477–90.

1963c Witchcraft in Ukaguru. In *Witchcraft and Sorcery in East Africa,* edited by J. Middleton and E. H. Winter, pp. 57–98. London: Routledge & Kegan Paul.

1964 Intertribal Insult and Opprobrium in an East African Chiefdom (Ukaguru). *Anthropological Quarterly* 37:33–52.

1966a *Utani:* Some Kaguru Notions of Death, Sexuality and Affinity. *Southwestern Journal of Anthropology* 22:354–80.

1966b Intertribal Tensions in Some Local Government Courts in Colonial Tanganyika. Part 1. *Journal of African Law* 10:118–30.

1967a *The Matrilineal Peoples of Eastern Tanzania.* London: International African Institute.

1967b Intertribal Tensions in Some Local Government Courts in Colonial Tanganyika. Part 2. *Journal of African Law* 11:27–45.

1969 Addenda and Corrigenda to the Bibliography of the Matrilineal Peoples of Eastern Tanzania. *Africa* 39:186–88.

1971a Some Kaguru Notions about Incest and other Sexual Prohibitions. In *Rethinking Kinship and Marriage,* edited by R. Needham, pp. 181–201. ASA Monograph 11. London: Tavistock.

1971b The Kaguru: a Matrilineal People of East Africa. New York: Holt, Rinehart & Winston.

1971c Kaguru Descent Groups. *Anthropos* 66:373–96.

1974a Kaguru Names and Naming. *Journal of Anthropological Research* 30:281–92.

1974b Social Theory and the Study of Christian Missions in Africa. *Africa* 44:235–49.

1974c Further Addenda to the Bibliography of the Matrilineal Peoples of Eastern Tanzania. *Africa* 44:295–96.

1978 Chiefship in Ukaguru. *The International Journal of African Historical Studies* 11:227–46.

1981a Third Addenda to the Bibliography of the Matrilineal Peoples of Eastern Tanzania. *Anthropos:* in press.

1981b Contradictions between the Sacred and the Secular Life. *Comparative Studies in Society and History* 23:73–95.

1982 The Organization and Maintenance of Caravans by the Church Missionary Society in Tanzania in the Nineteenth Century. Manuscript. *The International Journal of African Historical Studies:* in press.

Bendix, R.

1945 Bureaucracy and the Protest of Power. *Public Administration Review* 5:194–209.

Bennett, N. R.

1963 *Studies in East African History.* Boston: Boston University Press.

1964 The Church Missionary Society at Mombasa 1873–1894. In *Boston University Papers in African History,* I, edited by J. Butler, pp. 160–94. Boston: Boston University Press.

1971 *Mirambo of Tanganyika 1840?–1884.* New York: Oxford University Press.

Berger, S. D.

1971 The Sects and the Breakthrough into the Modern World: on the Centrality of the Sects in Weber's Protestant Ethic Thesis. *Sociological Quarterly* 12:485–99.

Berkhofer, R. F.

1972 *Salvation and the Savage.* New York: Atheneum.

Berman, E. H.

1974 African Responses to Christian Mission Education. *African Studies Review* 17:529–40.

Berman, E. H. (ed.)

1975 *African Reactions to Missionary Education.* New York: Teachers College Press, Columbia University.

Berque, J.

1967 *French North Africa* (1st edition, 1962). New York: Praeger.

Best, G. F. A.

1967 Popular Protestantism in Victorian Britain. In *Ideas and Institutions of Victorian Britain,* edited by Robert Robson, pp. 115–42. London: Bell.

Beti, Mongo

1971a *The Poor Christ of Bomba* (*Le Pauvre Christ de Bomba,* 1956). London: Heinemann.

1971b *King Lazarus* (*Le Roi miracule,* 1958). New York: Collier.

Beyerhaus, P., and C. F. Hallencreutz (eds.)

1969 *The Church Crossing Frontiers.* Studia Missionalia Upsaliensia XI. Uppsala: Gleerup.

Bhebe, N.

1979 *Christianity and Traditional Belief in Western Zimbabwe 1859–1923.* London: Longmans.

Bolt, Christine

1971 *Victorian Attitudes to Race.* London: Routledge & Kegan Paul.

Bond, G., W. Johnson, and S. Walker (eds.)

1979 *African Christianity.* New York: Academic Press.

Bonilla, V. D.
1972 *Servants of God or Masters of Men? The Story of a Capuchin Mission in Amazonia.* Harmondsworth: Penguin.
Bradley, Ian
1976 *The Call to Seriousness: the Evangelical Impact on the Victorians.* New York: Macmillan.
Branner, John
1977 Roland Allen: Pioneer in a Spirit-Centered Theology of Missions. *Missiology* 5:175–84.
Breed, C. E.
1930 Relations between Missionaries and other Europeans Abroad. *Church Missionary Outlook* 3:9–29.
Briggs, J. H.
1918 *In the East African War Zone.* London: C.M.S.
Brooke, Clarke
1967 Types of Food Shortages in Tanzania. *The Geographic Review* 57:333–57.
Brookfield, H. C.
1972 *Colonialism, Development and Independence.* Cambridge: Cambridge University Press.
Brown, G. Gordon
1944 Missions and Cultural Diffusion. *American Journal of Sociology* 50:214–19.
1957 Some Problems of Culture Contact with Illustration from East Africa and Samoa. *Human Organization* 16:11–14.
Buell, R. L.
1965 *The Native Problem in Africa* (1st edition, 1928). London: Cass.
Bulme, H.
1921 The Quantitative and Qualitative Aspects of Medical Missionary Enterprise. *Church Missionary Review* 72:22–32.
Burnett, John
1969 *A History of the Cost of Living.* Harmondsworth: Penguin.
Carleton, A.
1967 Comment on 'Prefatory Findings in the Sociology of Missions.' *Journal for the Scientific Study of Religions* 6:59–60.
C. C. F.
1888 Mohammedism in Africa. *Church Missionary Intelligencer* 13:65–83.
Cell, J. W. (ed.)
1976 *By Kenya Possessed: the Correspondence of Norman Leys and J. H. Oldham 1918–1926.* Chicago: University of Chicago Press.
Chadwick, Owen
1966 *The Victorian Church,* Part 1. New York: Oxford University Press.
Chambers, G. A.
1931 *Tanganyika's New Day.* London: C.M.S.
1946 The Church in Central Tanganyika. *East and West Review* 12:75–78.

Christie, J.
1876 *Cholera Epidemics in East Africa.* London: Macmillan.

***Church Missionary Intelligencer* (ed.)**
1890 C.M.S. Missionaries as Evangelical Churchmen. *Church Missionary Intelligencer* 15:283–89.
1894 The C.M.S. and the Board of Missions. *Church Missionary Intelligencer* 19:88–95.

Church Missionary Society
Church Missionary Annual Report. London: C.M.S.
Proceedings of the Church Missionary Society. London: C.M.S.
1876 *The Victoria Nyanza Mission Instructions.* London: C.M.S.
1878 *Special Appeal on Behalf of the Victoria Nyanza Mission.* London: C.M.S.
1902 *The Centenary Volume of the C.M.S. 1799–1899.* London: C.M.S.
1905 *Handbooks for Workers: Outline Histories of C.M.S. Missionaries* I. London: C.M.S.

Clarke, C. W. A.
1915 Some Thoughts on the Present Financial Position of the Church Missionary Society. *Church Missionary Intelligencer* 40:812–19.

Cohen, W. B.
1971 *Rulers of Empire: the French Colonial Service in Africa.* Stanford: Hoover Institution Press, Stanford University.
1980 *The French Encounter with Africans.* Bloomington: Indiana University Press.

Cole, A. H.
1961 The Relation of Missionary Activity to Economic Development. *Economic Development and Cultural Change* 9:120–27.

Cole, Henry
1892 At Kisokwe. *Church Missionary Gleaner* 22:76.
1902 Notes on the Wagogo of German East Africa. *Journal of the Anthropological Institute* 32:305–38.

Coser, L. A.
1974 *Greedy Institutions.* New York: Free Press.

Coupland, Reginald
1938 *East Africa and Its Invaders.* Oxford: Clarendon Press.
1939 *The Exploitation of East Africa 1856–1890.* London: Faber & Faber.

Cressy, D. (ed.)
1961 *The Prison: Studies in Institutional Organization and Change.* New York: Holt, Rinehart & Winston.

Crowder, Michael
1964 Indirect Rule—French and British Style. *Africa* 34:197–205.
1970 The White Chiefs of Tropical Africa. In *Colonialism in Africa 1870–1960* II, edited by L. Gann and P. Duignan, pp. 320–50. Cambridge: Cambridge University Press.

Crozier, M.
1964 *The Bureaucratic Phenomenon.* Chicago: University of Chicago Press.
1973 *The World of the Office Worker.* New York: Schocken Books.

Crummy, D.
1972 *Priests and Politicians.* Oxford: Clarendon Press.

Curtin, Philip
1964 *The Image of Africa.* Madison: University of Wisconsin Press.

Cust, R.
1885 The Female Evangelist. *Church Missionary Intelligencer* 10:687–710.
1886 *A Cry for Missions and a Missionary Spirit.* Hertford: S. Austin.
1889 *Notes on Missionary Subjects.* London: Elliot Stock.
1891 *Africa Rediviva or, the Occupation of Africa by Christian Missionaries of Europe and North America.* London: Elliot Stock.
1892 *The Hero Missionary and the Heroic Missionary Society.* C.M.S. Pamphlet. Hertford: S. Austin.
1895 Dr. Cust on Missions and Missionaries. *Church Missionary Intelligencer* 20:105–10.
1900 The Committee of the C.M.S.—a Retrospect. *Church Missionary Intelligencer* 25:729–36.

Dachs, A. J.
1972 Missionary Imperialism—the Case of Bechuanaland. *Journal of African History* 4:647–58.

Dahrendorf, R.
1969 *Society and Democracy in Germany.* New York: Anchor.

Daneel, M. L.
1970a *The God of the Matopo Hills.* Africa Study Centre Communications. The Hague: Mouton.
1970b *Zionism and Faith-Healing in Rhodesia.* Africa Study Centre Communications. The Hague: Mouton.
1971, 1974 *Old and New in Southern Shona Independent Churches* I, II. The Hague: Mouton.

Davidson, J.
1948 Protestant Missions and Marriage in the Belgian Congo. *Africa* 18:120–28.

Davies, Horton
1961 *Worship and Theology in England, From Watts and Wesley to Maurice 1690–1850.* Princeton: Princeton University Press.

Davis, R. H.
1973 Interpreting the Colonial Period in African History. *African Affairs* 72:383–400.

De Craemer, W.
1977 *The Jamaa and the Church.* Oxford: Clarendon Press.

Deekes, D.
1900 Missionary and Builder. *Awake* 10:125.

Delavignette, R. C.
1964 *Christianity and Colonialism* (1st edition, 1960). New York: Hawthorn.
1968 *Freedom and Authority in French West Africa* (1st edition, 1950). London: Cass.

Deng, F. M.
1971 *Tradition and Modernization.* New Haven: Yale University Press.

DeWolf, Jan
1977 *Differentiation and Integration in Western Kenya.* The Hague: Mouton.

Dickson, Kwesi, and P. Ellingworth (eds.)
1969 *Biblical Revelation and African Beliefs.* London: Lutterworth.

Dillon-Malone, C. M.
1978 *The Korsten Basketmakers.* Manchester: Manchester University Press.

Dodds, E. R.
1970 *Pagan and Christian in an Age of Anxiety.* New York: Norton.

Doornbos, M.
1976 Ethnicity, Christianity, and the Development of Social Stratification in Colonial Ankole, Uganda. *International Journal of African Historical Studies* 9:555–75.

Dore, R.
1973 *British Factory, Japanese Factory.* London: Allen & Unwin.

Dougall, J. W. C.
1936 *Missionary Education in Kenya and Uganda.* Edinburgh: Edinburgh House.
1937 The Relationship of Church and School in Africa. *The International Review of Missions* 26:204–14.
1946 The Reason for Medical Missions. *The International Review of Missions* 35:251–55.
1970 J. H. Oldham. *International Review of Mission* 59:9–22.

Doulton, E. W.
1906 Work amongst the Wagogo. *Church Missionary Gleaner* 33:54–55.

Doulton, Mrs.
1889 Brightness and Gloom in Ussagara. *Church Missionary Gleaner* 25:102.

Dubb, A. A., and A. G. Schutte (eds.)
1974 Black Religion in South Africa. Special Number, *African Studies* 33 (2):79–129.

Duignan, P., and L. H. Gann (eds.)
1973 *Colonialism in Africa 1870–1960 V. A Bibliographical Guide to Colonialism in Sub-Saharan Africa.* Cambridge: Cambridge University Press.

Dunstan, Keith
1968 *Wowsers.* North Melbourne: Cassell Australia Press.

Echewa, T. O.
1976 *The Land's Lord.* London: Heinemann.

Ekechi, F. K.
1971a *Missionary Enterprise and Rivalry in Igboland 1857–1914.* London: Cass.
1971b Colonialism and Christianity in West Africa: the Igbo Case, 1900–1915. *Journal of African History* 12:103–16.
1972 The Holy Ghost Fathers in Eastern Nigeria, 1885–1920: Observations on Missionary Strategy. *African Studies Review* 15:217–39.
1976 African Polygamy and Western Christian Ethnocentrism. *Journal of African Studies* 3:329–49.

Elliott-Binns, L. E.
1936 *Religion in the Victorian Era.* London: Lutterworth.
Ellison, J., and G. H. S. Walpole (eds.)
1907 *Church and Empire (Introduction). London: Longmans, Green.*
Encel, S.
1970 *Equality and Authority, a Study of Class, Structure and Power in Australia.* Melbourne: Cheshire Press.
Engmann, A. W.
1943 A Teacher in Africa. *The International Review of Missions* 36:324–28.
Etherington, N.
1976 Mission Station Melting Pots as a Factor in the Rise of South African Black Nationalism. *International Journal of African Historical Studies* 9:592–605.
Exley, R. and H.
1973 *The Missionary Myth.* London: Lutterworth.
Fabian, J.
1971 *Jamaa: a Charismatic Movement in Katanga.* Evanston: Northwestern University Press.
Fasholé-Luke, E., R. Gray, A. Hastings, and G. Tasie (eds.)
1978 *Christianity in Independent Africa.* Bloomington: Indiana University Press.
Fisher, H. J.
1973 Conversion Reconsidered: Some Historical Aspects of Religious Conversion in Black Africa. *Africa* 43:27–40.
Flint, John
1963 The Wider Background to Partition and Colonial Occupation. In *History of East Africa* I, edited by R. Oliver and G. Mathews, pp. 352–90. Oxford: Clarendon Press.
Flynn, J. S.
1904 Notes on an Analysis of the C.M.S. Contribution Lists. *Church Missionary Intelligencer* 29:321–34.
Fountain, O. C.
1966 Religion and Economy in Mission Station-Village Relationships. *Practical Anthropology* 13:49–58.
1971 Some Roles of Mission Stations. *Practical Anthropology* 18:198–207.
Francis, E. K.
1950 Toward a Typology of Religious Orders. *American Journal of Sociology* 55:437–49.
Fullani bin Fullani
1919 Religious and Common life, a Problem in East African Missions. *The International Review of Missions* 30:155–72.
Furnivall, J. S.
1956 *Colonial Policy and Practice* (1st edition, 1948). New York: New York University Press.
Gann, L. H., and P. Duignan
1967 *Burden of Empire.* New York: Praeger.
1977 *The Rulers of German Africa 1884–1914.* Stanford: Stanford University Press.

G. F. S.

1893 The Closing of the Chagga Mission. *Church Missionary Intelligencer* 18:246–55.

Gaume, F. (ed.)

1872 *Voyage à la côte oriental d'afrique pendant l'année 1866 par le R. P. Horner.* Paris: Gaume.

Giallombardo, Rose

1896 *Society of Women.* New York: Wiley.

Gollock, M. C.

1905 The Redemption of Money in C.M.S. Minds. *Church Missionary Review* 56:80–87.

Gottneid, Allan J. (ed.)

1976 *Church and Education in Tanzania.* Nairobi: East African Publishing House.

Grace, E. M. D.

1926 Negro Education in America. *Church Missionary Review* 77:251–60.

Gray, Richard

1968 Problems of Historical Perspective: the Planting of Christianity in Africa in the Nineteenth and Twentieth Centuries. In *Christianity in Tropical Africa,* edited by G. G. Baëta, pp. 18–30. London: International African Institute, Oxford University Press.

1969 The Origins and Organization of the Nineteenth-Century Missionary Movement. *Tarikh* 3:14–22.

Greaves, L. B.

1957 The Educational Advisership in East Africa. *The International Review of Missions* 36:329–37.

Greschat, H. J.

1974 *Westafrikanischen Propheten.* Marburger Studien zur Afrika und Asienkunde. Marburg: Dietrich Reimer.

Groves, C. P.

1948–58 *The Planting of Christianity in Africa,* I–IV. London: Lutterworth.

Guenther, M. D.

1977 The Mission Station as 'Sample Community': a Contemporary Case from Botswana. *Missiology* 5:457–65.

Guillebaud, Lindsay

n.d. *A Grain of Mustard Seed: the Growth of the Ruanda Mission, C.M.S* Oxford: Church Army Press.

Hailey (Lord)

1938 *An African Survey.* London: Oxford University Press.

Halliburton, G. M.

1971 *The Prophet Harris.* London: Longmans.

Hardin, D. C.

1971 The Missionary and the Concept of Scope. *Practical Anthropology* 18:222–26.

Harding, H. G.

1920? *The Story of C.M.S. Medical Missions.* London: C.M.S.

Harries, L.

1953 Christian Marriage in African Society. In *Survey of African Family Life,* edited by A. Phillips, pp. 325–460. London: International African Institute, Oxford University Press.

Hartford-Battersby, C. F.

1898 *Pilkington of Uganda.* London: Marshall.

Hastings, A.

1979 *A History of African Christianity.* Cambridge: Cambridge University Press.

Haule, C.

1969 *Bantu 'Witchcraft' and Christian Morality.* Schöneck-Beckenried: Nouvelle Revue de Science Missionare.

Hayward, V. E. W. (ed.)

1963 *African Independent Church Movements.* Edinburgh: Edinburgh House Press.

Headland, Emily

1890 Victoria Nyanza Mission. In *Brief Sketches of C.M.S. Missions, Designed to Provide Material for Missionary Addresses,* Part 1, pp. 74–91. London: Nisbet.

Hecht, J.

1956 *The Domestic Servant Class in 18th Century England.* London: Routledge & Kegan Paul.

Heise, D. R.

1967 Prefatory Findings in the Sociology of Missions. *Journal for the Scientific Study of Religions* 6:39–63.

Hellberg, Carl J.

1965 *Missions on a Colonial Frontier West of Lake Victoria.* Studia Missionalia Upsaliensia VI. Uppsala: Gleerup.

Herskovits, Melville

1962 *The Human Factor in Changing Africa.* New York: Knopf.

Hetherwick, A.

1932 *The Gospel and the African.* Edinburgh: Clark.

Heussler, Robert

1963 *Yesterday's Rulers.* Syracuse: Syracuse University Press.

1968 *The British in Northern Nigeria.* London: Oxford University Press.

1971 *British Tanganyika. An Essay and Documents on District Administration.* Durham: Duke University Press.

Hewitt, Gordon

1971 *The Problem of Success. A History of the Church Missionary Society 1910–1942,* I. London: SCM Press.

Hind, J.

1906 The Minister's Responsibility in Regard to Foreign Missions. *Church Missionary Intelligencer* 31:102–107.

Hobbs, Violet. H.

1927 Medical Work in Kongwa, Tanganyika Territory. *The Mission Hospital* 31:313–16.

Hodge, Alison

1971 The Training of Missionaries for Africa: the Church Missionary Society's Training College at Islington, 1900–1915. *Journal of Religion in Africa* 4:81–96.

Hodgshon, E. G.

1928 Settling on Kongwa. *Eastward Ho!* 38:40–42.

Holmes, Brian (ed.)

1967 *Educational Policy and the Mission Schools.* London: Routledge & Kegan Paul.

Holway, James

1972 C.M.S. Contact with Islam in East Africa. *Journal of Religion in Africa* 4:200–12.

Hooper, W.

1911 Missionary Policy. *Church Missionary Review* 62:72–82.

Horan, H.

1976 Polygamy Comes Home to Roost. *Missiology* 4:443–53.

Horn, P.

1975 *The Rise and Fall of the Victorian Servant.* London: St. Martin's Press.

Horton, Robin

1970 One Hundred Years of Kalabari Religion. In *Black Africa,* edited by John Middleton, pp. 192–221. New York: Macmillan.

1971 African Conversions. *Africa* 41:85–108.

1975 On the Rationality of Conversion. *Africa* 45:219–35, 373–99.

Hutchinson, Edward

1876 *The Victoria Nyanza: A Field for Missionary Enterprise.* London: J. Murray.

Ifeka-Moller, Caroline

1974 White Power: Social Structural Factors in Conversion to Christianity, Eastern Nigeria, 1921–1966. *Canadian Journal of African Studies* 8:55–72.

Iliffe, John.

1969 *Tanganyika under German Rule 1905–1912.* Cambridge: Cambridge University Press.

1979 *A Modern History of Tanganyika.* Cambridge: Cambridge University Press.

Ilogu, E.

1974 *Christianity and Ibo Culture.* Leiden: Brill.

Ingham, Kenneth

1958 *The Making of Modern Uganda.* London: Allen & Unwin.

Isichei, Elizabeth

1970 Seven Varieties of Ambiguity: Some Patterns of Igbo Responses to Christian Missions. *Journal of Religion in Africa* 3:209–27.

Jahoda, G.

1961 *White Man: a Study of the Attitudes of Africans to Europeans in Ghana before Independence.* London: Oxford University Press.

Jarrett-Kerr, M.

1972 *Patterns of Christian Acceptance.* London: Oxford University Press.

Jassy, Marie-France Perrin
1973 *Basic Community in the African Churches.* Maryknoll, N.Y.: Orbis Books.

Jeffreys, W.
1956 Some Rules of Directed Culture Change under Roman Catholicism. *American Anthropologist* 58:721–31.

Joelson, F. S.
1920 *The Tanganyika Territory.* London: Fisher, Unwin.

Johnson, H. B.
1967 The Location of Christian Missions in Africa. *The Geographical Review* 58:168–202.

Johnson, Walton R.
1977 *Worship and Freedom.* London: International African Institute.

Jones, Thomas Jesse
1924 *Education in East Africa,* Phelps-Stokes Fund. London: Edinburgh House Press.

Jules-Rosette, B.
1975 *African Apostles.* Ithaca: Cornell University Press.

July, R. W.
1967 *The Origins of Modern African Thought.* New York: Praeger.

K.
1880 On Jesuit Aggression. *Church Missionary Intelligencer* 5:137–58.
1885 On Missions in Mohammedan Lands. *Church Missionary Intelligencer* 10:761–73.
1886 On the Character of Jesuit Missionary Teachings. *Church Missionary Intelligencer* 11:529–45.
1888 The Arab in Central Africa. *Church Missionary Intelligencer* 13:493–508.

Kalu, O. U.
1975 The Peter Pan Syndrome: Aid and Selfhood of the Church in Africa. *Missiology* 3:15–29.

Kieren, J. A.
1969 Some Roman Catholic Missionary Attitudes in Nineteenth Century East Africa. *Race* 10:341–59.
1970 Abushiri and the Germans. In *Hadithi* 2, pp. 157–201. Nairobi: East African Publishing House.
1971 Christian Villages in North-eastern Tanzania. *Transafrican Journal of History* 1:24–38.

King, Anthony D.
1974 The Language of Colonial Urbanization. *Sociology* 8:81–110.
1976 *Colonial Urban Development.* London: Routledge & Kegan Paul.

King, K. J.
1971 *Pan-Africanism and Education.* Oxford: Clarendon Press.

King, S. J.
1921 The Power behind the Sickness. *Awake* 31:76–77.
1922 Chilonda's Struggle. *Eastward Ho!* 32:70–71.
1924 'Common Things' in Tanganyika. *Church Missionary Outlook* 51:114–16.
1927 A week-end at an Out-Station. *Eastward Ho!* 37:116–69.

Kinglsey, Mary
1897 *Travels in West Africa.* New York: Macmillan.

Kirwen, M. C.
1979 *African Widows.* Maryknoll, N.Y.: Orbis Books.

Kitson Clark, D.
1962 *The Making of Victorian England.* Cambridge: Harvard University Press.
1973 *Churchmen and the Condition of England 1832–1885.* London: Methuen.

Kuper, Hilda
1947 *The Uniform of Colour.* Johannesburg: Witwatersrand University Press.
1971 Colour, Categories and Colonialsim. In *Colonialism in Africa 1870–1960,* edited by V. Turner, pp. 286–309. Cambridge: Cambridge University Press.

Landford-Smith, N.
1954 Revival in East Africa. *The International Review of Missions* 43:77–81.

Lankester, H.
1897 Medical Missions. *Mercy and Truth* 1:245–50.
1921 The Financial Position of the C.M.S. *Church Missionary Review* 72:347–48.

Lankester, H., and A. H. Broume
1897 Some General Observations on General Medical Mission Policy. *Mercy and Truth* 1:219–23, 255–57.

Last, J. T.
1878 Letter. *Church Missionary Intelligencer* 3:645–46.
1879 The Tribes on the Road to Mpwapwa. *Church Missionary Intelligencer* 4:659–65.
1880 Letter. *Church Missionary Intelligencer* 5:742–44.
1891 The Ussagara Mission: Mamboia. *Church Missionary Intelligencer* 4:554–61.
1882 A Journey into the Nguru Country from Mamboia, East Africa. *Proceedings of the Royal Geographical Society* 4:517–43.
1883a Letter. *Church Missionary Intelligencer* 8:293–94.
1883b A Visit to the Masai People Living beyond the Borders of the Nguru Country. *Proceedings of the Royal Geographical Society* 5:517–43.
1883c A Visit to the Wa-itumba Iron-workers and the Mangaheri near Mamboia, in East Central Africa. *Proceedings of the Royal Geographical Society* 5:581–92.
1885 *Polyglotta Africana Orientalis.* London: Society for Promoting Christian Knowledge.
1886 *Grammar of the Kagúru Language.* London: Society for Promoting Christian Knowledge.

Latourette, K. S.
1945a *A History of Christianity in the Nineteenth and Twentieth Centuries* V. New York: Harper.
1945b Advance through the Storm. A. D. 1914 and After, VII. In *A History of the Expansion of Christianity.* New York: Harper.

Lee, Annabelle [pseud.]
1968 African Nuns: An anthropologist's Impression. *New Blackfriars* 49:401–409.

Leenhardt, M.
1930 Dowry Systems among Primitive Peoples. *The International Review of Missions* 19:220–30.

LeRoy, R. P.
1884 Lettre du R. P. LeRoy. *Annales de la Propagation de la Foi* 56:42–59.

Leys, Norman
1926 *Kenya* (3rd edition). London: Hogarth Press.
1941 *The Colour Bar in East Africa.* London: Hogarth Press.

Linden, Ian
1974 *Catholics, Peasants and Chewa Resistance in Nyasaland 1889–1939.* London: Heinemann.
1977 *Church and Revolution in Rwanda.* Manchester: Manchester University Press.

Livingston, David
1957 *Missionary Travels and Researches in South Africa.* London: J. Murray.

Loewen, Jacob A. and Anne
1967 The Missionary Role. *Practical Anthropology* 14:193–208.

Long, Norman
1968 *Social Change and the Individual.* Manchester: Manchester University Press.

Loram, C. T.
1923 Education in Africa. *Church Missionary Review* 74:156–60.

Loth, H.
1963 *Die christliche Mission in Südwestafrika.* [East] Berlin: Akademie-Verlag.

Low, D. A.
1971 *Buganda in Modern History.* London: Weidenfeld & Nicolson.
n.d. *Religion and Society in Buganda 1875–1900.* East African Studies 8. Kampala: East African Institute of Social Research.

Luchelo, M., and M. Mguye
n.d. Untitled manuscript [translation from Swahili of oral history of C.M.S. station at Uponela, Ukaguru]. Ukaguru.

Luck, Anne
1972 *Charles Stokes in Africa.* Nairobi: East African Publishing House.

Luzbetak, L. J.
1961 Toward an Applied Missionary Anthropology. *Anthropological Quarterly* 34:165–76.
1970 *The Church and Cultures.* Techny, Ill.: Divine Word Publications.
1976 Unity in Diversity: Ethno-theological Sensitivity in Cross-Cultural Evangelists. *Missiology* 4:207–16.

Lynch, H. R.
1964 The Native Pastorate Controversy and Cultural Ethno-Centrism in Sierra Leone 1871–1874. *Journal of African History* 5:395–413.

McCracken, J.

1977 *Politics and Christianity in Malawi:* 1875–1940. Cambridge: Cambridge University Press.

McGavran, D. A.

1933 Missionaries and Indigenous Standards of Living. *The International Review of Missions* 22:33–49.

1955 *The Bridges of God: a Study in the Strategy of Missions.* London: World Dominion Press.

1959 *How Churches Grow.* London: World Dominion Press.

1970 *Understanding Church Growth.* Grand Rapids: W. B. Eerdmans.

Mackay, A. M.

1889 Muscat, Zanzibar and Central Africa. *Church Missionary Intelligencer* 14:19–24.

Mackay, J. W.

1890 *A. M. Mackay by His Sister.* London: Hodder & Stoughton.

Malinowski, Bronislaw

1936 Native Education and Culture Contact. *The International Review of Missions* 25:480–515.

Manley, G. T.

1908 The Church and Modern Thought. *Church Missionary Review* 59:129–238.

1913 Africa's Choice: Islam or Christ. *Church Missionary Review* 63:594–602.

Markowitz, M. D.

1970 The Missions and Political Development in the Congo. *Africa* 40:234–47.

1973 *Cross and Sword: the Political Role of Christian Missions in the Belgian Congo, 1908–1960.* Stanford: Hoover Institute, Stanford University Press.

Martin, Malcolm

1977 The Missionary and the Holy Spirit. *Missiology* 5:223–39.

Martin, Marie-Louise

1975 *Kimbangu. An African Prophet and His Church.* Oxford: Blackwell.

Maunier, Rene

1949 *The Sociology of Colonies.* London: Routledge & Kegan Paul.

Mbiti, John S.

1969 *African Religions and Philosophy.* London: Heinemann.

Meyer, H.

1909 *Das Deutsches Kolonialreich* I. Vienna: Bibliog. Institut.

Miller, Elmer S.

1973 The Christian Missionary: Agent of Secularization. *Missiology* 1:99–107.

Mitchell, J. C.

1966 Theoretical Orientations in African Urban Studies. In *The Social Anthropology of Complex Societies,* edited by M. Banton, pp. 37–68. ASA Monograph 4. London: Tavistock.

Mobley, H. W.

1970 *The Ghanaian's Image of the Missionary.* Leiden: Brill.

Moffett, J. P. (ed.)
1958 *Handbook of Tanganyika.* Dar es Salaam: Government Printer.
Moorhouse, Geoffrey
1973 *The Missionaries.* London: Eyre Methuen.
Mohr, H.
1965 *Katholische Orden und deutscher Imperialismus.* [East] Berlin: Akademie-Verlag.
Monticello, R. V.
1976 Contradictions and Challenges: Some Reflections on the Church's Service Ministry. *Missiology* 4:161–70.
Morris, H.
1911 The Relation of Missions to Government. *Church Missionary Review* 62:129–36.
Muldrow, W. F.
1971 Identification and the Role of the Missionary. *Practical Anthropology* 18:208–21.
Mullens, Joseph
1877 A New Route and a New Mode of Travelling into Central Africa, adopted by the Rev. Roger Price. *Proceedings of the Royal Geographical Society* 21:233–44.
Murphree, M. W.
1969 *Christianity and the Shona.* London: Athlone Press.
Murray, A. Victor
1967 *The School in the Bush* (1st edition, 1929). London: Cass.
Mylne, Louis George
1908 *Missions to Hindus, a Contribution to the Study of Missionary Methods.* London: Longmans, Green.
Nakane, C.
1970 *Japanese Society.* Berkeley: University of California Press.
Neill, Stephen
1964 *A History of Christian Missions.* Harmondsworth: Penguin.
1965 *Anglicanism* (3rd edition). Harmondsworth: Penguin.
1966 *Colonialism and Christian Missions.* New York: McGraw-Hill
Newing, E. G.
1970 The Baptism of Polygamous Families: Theories and Practice in an East African Church. *Journal of Religion in Africa* 3:130–41.
Nida, Eugene A.
1954 *Customs and Culture: Anthropology for Christian Missions.* New York: Harper and Row.
1957 The Roman Catholic, Communist, and Protestant Approach to Social Structure. *Practical Anthropology* 4:209–19.
Nock, A. D.
1961 *Conversion* (1st edition, 1933). New York: Oxford University Press.
Nolan, F. P.
1971 The Changing Role of Catechist in Tabora 1879–1967. In *African Initiatives in Religion,* edited by D. B. Barnett, pp. 50–60. Nairobi: East African Publishing House.

Norman, E. R.

1968 *Anti-Catholicism in Victorian England.* New York: Barnes and Noble.

1976 *Church and Society in England 1770–1970.* Oxford: Clarendon Press.

Nzekwu, O.

1962 *Blade among the Boys.* London: Hutchinson.

O'Brien, R. C.

1972 *White Society in Black Africa: the French of Senegal.* Evanston: Northwestern University Press.

Oldham, J. H.

1918 Christian Missions and the Education of the Negro. *The International Review of Missions* 7:242–47.

1924 Christian Education in Africa. *Church Missionary Review* 75:305–14.

1927 The Christian Mission in Africa as Seen at the International Conference at La Zoute (September 1926). *The International Review of Missions* 16:24–35.

Oliver, Roland

1952 *The Missionary Factor in East Africa.* London: Longmans.

O'Neill, T.

1878 *Sketches of African Scenery from Zanzibar to the Victoria Nyansa.* London: C.M.S.

Park, Robert Ezra

1944 Mission and the Modern World. *American Journal of Sociology* 1:177–83.

Parker, Bishop Henry

1887 Letter. *Church Missionary Intelligencer* 12:692–94.

Parker, Bishop Henry, and J. Blackburn

1888 The Country between Mombasa and Momboia. *Proceedings of the Royal Geographical Society* 10:92–93

Parrinder, G.

1953 *Religion in an African City.* London: Oxford University Press.

1969 *Religion in Africa.* Harmondsworth: Penguin.

Pauw, B. A.

1960 *Religion in a Tswana Chiefdom.* London: International African Institute, Oxford University Press.

1975 *Christianity and Xhosa Tradition.* London: Oxford University Press.

Peel, Bishop William George

1904 Usagara and Ugogo Revisited 1902–1903. *Church Missionary Intelligencer* 19:109–19.

1906 Troubles in German East Africa. *Church Missionary Intelligencer* 31:108–12.

Peel, J. D. Y.

1967 Religious Change in Yorubaland. *Africa* 37:292–306.

1968 *Aladura.* London: International African Institute, Oxford University Press.

1977 Conversion and Tradition in Two African Societies. *Past and Present* 77:108–41.

Phillips, D. H.

1975 The American Missionary in Morocco. *Muslim World* 64:1–20.

Pickthall, Miss

1912 An Interesting People. *Church Missionary Gleaner* 39:165.

Pipes, Mrs.

1895 Dangers and Difficulties of Missionaries. *Church Missionary Intelligencer* 20:43–46.

Pirouet, M. L.

1978 *Black Evangelists.* London: Rex Collins.

Price, R.

1876 *Report of the Rev. R. Price of His Visit to Zanzibar and the Coast of Eastern Africa.* London: London Missionary Society.

Price, W. S.

1891 *My Third Campaign in East Africa, a Story of Missionary Life in Troublous Times* (2nd edition). London: William Hunt.

Pruen, C. M.

1887 Some Features of Mpwapwa. *Church Missionary Intelligencer* 12:752–54.

1889 Through German East Africa. *Church Missionary Intelligencer* 14:97–107.

Pruen, S. T.

1887 From London to Mpwapwa. *Church Missionary Gleaner* 14:40–41.

1888 A Visit to Mamboia. *Church Missionary Gleaner* 15:70–71.

1891 *The Arab and the African.* London: Seeley.

Ranger, Terence

1965 African Attempts to Control Education in East and Central Africa 1900–1939. Past and Present 32:57–85.

Ranger, Terence, and J. Weller (eds.)

1975 *Themes in Christian History in Central Africa.* London: Heinemann.

Rapoport, R. N.

1954 *Changing Navajo Religious Values: a Study of Christian Missions to the Rimrock Navajos.* Papers of the Peabody Museum II, No. 2. Cambridge: Harvard University Press.

Raum, O.

1927 Christianity and African Puberty Rites. *The International Review of Missions* 16:581–91.

1937 Dr. Gutmann's Work on Kilimanjaro: Critical Studies of His Theories of Missionary Methods. *The International Review of Missions* 26:500–13.

1965 German East Africa: Changes in African Tribal Life under German Administration, 1892–1914. In *History of East Africa* II, ed. by V. Harlow and E. M. Oliver, pp. 163–208. Oxford: Clarendon Press.

Reardon, Ruth Slade

1968 Catholics and Protestants in the Congo. In *Christianity in Tropical Africa,* edited by G. G. Baëta, pp. 83–100. London: International African Institute, Oxford University Press.

Rees, D. J.

1902a History of the C.M.S. in German East Africa. Manuscript. London: C.M.S. Archives.

1902b [unsigned] Superstition in Usagara. *Church Missionary Gleaner* 29:52–53.

1913a In the Berega Country. *Church Missionary Gleaner* 40:154–155.

1913b Brave African Teachers. *Awake* 23:53.

1914 Learning to Pray. *Awake* 24:103–104.

Rees, D. J., and E. Baxter

1912 German East Africa. *Church Missionary Review* 63:156–61. *Registrar of Missionaries and Native Clergy From 1804 to 1904.* London: C.M.S.

Reid, E.

1934 *Tanganyika Without Prejudice.* London: East Africa Press.

Reyburn, W. D.

1960 Sickness, Sin and the Curse: Old Testament and the African Church. *Practical Anthropology* 7:215–22.

Richter, D. J.

1934 *Tanganyika and Its Future.* London: World Dominion Press.

Rivers, W. H. R.

1920 Anthropology and the Missionary. *Church Missionary Review* 71:208–15.

Rohlen, Thomas

1974 *For Harmony and Strength.* Berkeley: University of California Press.

Rosberg, C., and J. Nottingham

1966 *The Myth of 'Mau Mau.'* New York: Praeger.

Roscoe, J.

1889 Letter. *Church Missionary Intelligencer* 14:170–71.

1921 *Twenty-Five Years in East Africa.* Cambridge: Cambridge University Press.

Rotberg, Robert I.

1964 *Missionaries as Chiefs and Entrepreneurs: Northern Rhodesia 1882–1924.* In *Boston University Papers in African History,* edited by J. Butler. Boston: Boston University Press.

1965 *Christian Missionaries and the Creation of Northern Rhodesia.* Princeton: Princeton University Press.

Rowbotham, A. H.

1942 *Missionary and Mandarin. The Jesuits at the Court of China.* Berkeley: University of California Press.

Rubingh, E.

1969 *Sons of Tiv, a Study of the Rise of the Church among the Tiv of Central Nigeria.* Grand Rapids: Baker Book House.

Rutherford, Noel

1971 *Shirley Baker and the King of Tonga.* Melbourne: Oxford University Press.

Salamone, F. A.

1972 Structural Factors in Dukawa Conversion. *Practical Anthropology* 19:219–25.

1975 Continuity of Igbo Values after Conversion: a Study in Purity and Prestige. *Missiology* 3:33–44.

1976 Learning to Be a Christian: a Comparative Study. *Missiology* 4:53–64.

Sangree, W. H.

1966 *Age, Prayer and Politics in Tiriki, Kenya.* London: Oxford University Press.

Schapera, I.

1958 Christianity and the Tswana. *Journal of the Royal Anthropological Institute* 88:1–10.

Schlosser, K.

1949 *Propheten in Afrika.* Braunschweig: A. Limbach.

Schmidlin, J.

1913 *Die katholischen Missionen in den deutschen Schützgebieten.* Münster: Aschendorffsche.

Scott, W. H.

1968 Some Contrasts in Missionary Patterns. *Practical Anthropology* 15:269–76.

Shenk, W. R.

1977 Henry Venn's Instruction to Missionaries. *Missiology* 5:467–85.

Shepperson, G., and T. Price

1958 *Independent African.* Edinburgh: University Press.

Shorter, Aylward

1974 *African Culture and the Christian Church.* Maryknoll, N.Y.: Orbis Books.

1975 *Prayer in the Religious Traditions of Africa.* London: Oxford University Press.

Shorter, Aylward, and E. Kataza (eds.)

1972 *Missionaries to Yourselves: African Catechists Today.* Maryknoll, N.Y.: Orbis Books.

Sibtain, N. deS.

1968 *Dare to Look Up: A Memoir of Bishop George A. Chambers.* Sydney: Angus & Robertson.

Sicard, S. von

1968 The First Ecumenical Conference in Tanzania, 1911. *The Bulletin of the Society for African Church History* 2:323–33.

1970 *The Lutheran Church on the Coast of Tanzania 1884–1914 with special reference to the Evangelical Lutheran Church in Tanzania, Synod of Uzaramo-Uluguru.* Studia Missionalia Upsaliensia XII. Lund: Gleerup.

Sithole, N.

1972 *The Polygamist.* New York: The Third Press.

Sixdorf, Herr

1894 [article.] Zanzibar: *The Gazette,* 20 June.

Slade, Ruth M.

1959 English-Speaking Missions in the Congo Independent State (1878–1908). Brussels: Académie royale des sciences coloniales, Mem. 8 (n.s.) XVI, 2 (Histoire).

Smalley, W. A.

1958a Cultural Implications of an Indigenous Church. *Practical Anthropology* 5:51–65.

1958b Respect and Ethnocentrism. *Practical Anthropology* 5:191–94.

Smalley, W. A. (ed.)

1967 *Readings in Missionary Anthropology.* Tarrytown, N.Y.: Practical Anthropology.

Smith, Anthony

1963 The Missionary Contribution to Education (Tanganyika) to 1914. *Tanganyika Notes and Records* 60:91–110.

Smith, Edwin

1930 *The Golden Stool.* London: Edinburgh House Press.

1956 The Earliest Ox-Wagons in Tanganyika. *Tanganyika Notes and Records* 40:1–14; 41:1–15.

Smith, Edwin (ed.)

1936 *African Beliefs and Christian Faith.* London: United Society for Christian Literature.

Smith, G. Shergold

1877 Letter. *Church Missionary Intelligencer* 2:147.

Smith, N.

1966 *The Presbyterian Church of Ghana 1835–1960.* Accra: Ghana University Press.

Smoker, D. E. W.

1971 Decision-Making in East Africa Revival Movement Groups. In *African Initiatives in Religion,* edited by D. B. Barrett, pp. 96–108. Nairobi: East African Publishing House.

Spanton, E. F.

1928 Missions and Governments in African Education. *The Church Overseas* 1:99–108.

Spriggs, E. R.

1910 The Day of Small Things. *Awake* 20:32–33.

1915 'Beloved Persis' and Others. *Awake* 25:46–47.

Stahl, Kathleen M.

1964 *History of the Chagga People of Kilimanjaro.* The Hague: Mouton.

Stanley, H. M

1899 *Through the Dark Continent,* I and II. (1st edition, 1877). London: Newnes.

Stanton, H. V. W.

1923 A Study of African Missions. *Church Missionary Review* 74:225–34.

Stock, Eugene

1882 The Missionary Career of Dr. Krapf. *Church Missionary Intelligencer* 7:65–80, 133–46.

1898 The 'Policy of Faith' Forty Five Years Ago. *Church Missionary Intelligencer* 23:481–83.

1899 *The History of the Church Missionary Society, Its Environment, Its Men and Its Work,* I, II, III (1899), IV (1916). London: C.M.S.

1901 Future Independent Churches in the Mission-field. *Church Missionary Intelligencer* 26:241–57.

1903 The Position of the Society. *Church Missionary Intelligencer* 28:881–88.

1907 *A Historical Survey of Women's Work in the C.M.S.* London: C.M.S.

1909 The Late Dr. Cust. *Church Missionary Review* 59:716–23.

1912 Mr. Roland Allen on Missionary Methods. *Church Missionary Review* 63:393–403, 465–81.

1914 The C.M.S. and Native Church Organization. *The International Review of Missions* 3:266–83.

1919 Bishop Peel. *Church Missionary Review* 70:329–35, 443–54.

Stewart, D. D.

1891 The Greatness of God Shown in the Slow Christianizing of the Earth. *Church Missionary Intelligencer* 16:473–77.

Stones, R. Y.

1923 A Safari in Tanganyika Territory. *The Mission Hospital* 27:90–92

Strayer, R. W.

1973a Missions and African Protest: a Case Study from Kenya 1875–1935. In *Protest Movements in Colonial East Africa: Aspects of Early African Responses to European Rule,* pp. 1–37. Eastern African Studies XII. Syracuse: Syracuse University Press.

1973b The Dynamics of Mission Expansion: a Case Study from Kenya, 1875–1915. *International Journal of African Historical Studies* 6:229–48.

1975 Mission History in Africa: New Perspectives on an Encounter. *African Studies Review* 18:1–15.

1978 *The Making of Mission Communities in East Africa.* London: Heinemann.

Stuntz, Hugh

1944 Christian Missions and Social Cohesion. *American Journal of Sociology* 50:184–88.

Sundkler, Bengt

1948 *Bantu Prophets in South Africa.* London: Lutterworth.

1960 *The Christian Ministry in Africa.* Uppsala: Swedish Institute of Mission Research.

1976 *Zulu Zion.* London: Oxford University Press.

1980 *Bara Bukoba.* London: Hurst.

Sykes, G.

1958 *Society of Captives.* Princeton: Princeton University Press.

Symonds, R.

1966 *The British and Their Successors.* Evanston: Northwestern University Press.

Tanganyika Report to the League of Nations for 1921.
London: H.M.S.O.

Tasie, G. O. M

1978 *Christian Missionary Enterprise in the Niger Delta 1864–1918.* Leiden: Brill.

Taylor, J. V.

1957 *Christianity and Politics in Africa.* London: Penguin.

1958a *The Growth of the Church in Buganda.* London: SCM Press.

1958b *Process of Growth in an African Church.* International Missionary Council Research Pamphlet 6. London: SCM Press.

Taylor, J. V., and D. A. Lehman

1961 *Christians of the Copperbelt.* London: SCM Press.

Tempels, P.

1959 *Bantu Philosophy* (*La philosophie Bantoue,* 1945). Paris: Présence Africaine.

Temple, C. L.

1918 *Native Races and Their Rulers.* Capetown: Argus.

Temu, A. J.

1972 *British Protestant Missions.* London: Longmans.

Thompson, A. R.

1976 Historical Survey of the Role of the Churches in Education from Pre-colonial Days to Post-Independence. In *Church and Education in Tanzania,* edited by A. J. Gottneid, pp. 3–130. Nairobi: East African Publishing House.

Tippett, A. R.

1969 *Solomon Islands Christianity, a Study in Growth and Obstruction.* World Studies of Churches in Mission. London: Lutterworth.

1977 Conversion as a Dynamic Process. *Missiology* 5:203–21.

Tisdall, W. St. C.

1907 Islam and Christian Missions. *Church Missionary Review* 57:206–10.

Tucker, A. R.

1898 Bishop Tucker's Charge. *Church Missionary Intelligencer* 23:89–102.

1911 *Eighteen Years in Uganda and East Africa.* London: Arnold.

Turner, H. W.

1967 *African Independent Church* I and II. Oxford: Clarendon Press.

1977 *Bibliography of New Religious Movements in Primal Societies.* Vol. I: *Black Africa.* Boston: Hall.

Uganda, Bishop of

1931 Marriage: Pagan and Christian. *Church Missionary Outlook* 4:238–47.

Veblen, T.

1939 *Imperial Germany and the Industrial Revolution* (1st edition 1915). New York: Viking Press.

1943 The Opportunity of Japan (1915). In *Essays in our Changing Order,* edited by Leon Ardzrooni, pp. 248–66. New York: Viking Press.

Vicar in the Diocese

1899 Annual Subscribers to Foreign Missions in an English Diocese. *Church Missionary Intelligencer* 24:732–38.

Wagner, Günther

1937 An Anthropologist's Criticism. *The International Review Of Missions* 26:508–13.

Walker, R. R.

1914 Alfred Robert Tucker. *Church Missionary Review* 65:489–92.

Waller, E. H. M

1922 The Diocenization of the Work of the C.M.S. *Church Missionary Review* 73:204–10.

Walpole, Rev. Canon

1907 The Vocation of the Anglo-Saxon Race and England's Responsibility. In *Church and Empire,* edited by J. Ellison and G. H. S. Walpole, pp. 21–41. London: Longmans, Green.

Warren, Max A. C.

1943 The Idea of the Missionary Society. *East and West Review* 9:69–76.

1951 *The Christian Mission.* London: SCM Press.

1954 *Revival: an Enquiry.* London: SCM Press.

1960 *Challenge and Responses: Six Studies in Missionary Opportunity.* New York: Society for Promoting Christian Mission, McGraw-Hill.

1964 *The Missionary Movement from Britain in Modern History.* London: SCM Press.

1967 *Social History and Christian Mission.* London: SCM Press.

1974 *Crowded Canvas.* London: Hodder & Stoughton.

Watt, Mrs. S. [Rachel]

n.d. *In the Heart of Savagedom.* London: Marshall.

Weber, Max

1948 The Protestant Sects and the Spirit of Capitalism (1920). In *From Max Weber,* edited by H. H. Gerth and C. W. Mills, pp. 302–22. London: Routledge & Kegan Paul.

1965 *The Sociology of Religion* (1922). London: Methuen.

Webster, J. B.

1964 *The African Churches among the Yoruba 1888–1922.* Oxford: Clarendon Press.

Welbourn, F. B.

1961 *East African Rebels.* London: SCM Press.

1971 Missionary Stimulus and African Responses. In *Colonialism in Africa 1870–1960* III, edited by V. Turner, pp. 310–45. Cambridge: Cambridge University Press.

Welbourn, F. B., and B. A. Ogot

1966 *A Place to Feel at Home.* London: Oxford University Press.

West, F. J.

1966 The Study of Colonial History (1961). In *Social Change: the Colonial Situation,* edited by E. Wallerstein, pp. 643–57. New York: Wiley.

West, M.

1975 *Bishops and Prophets in a Black City.* Capetown: David Philip.

Westermann, D.

1937 *Africa and Christianity.* London: Oxford University Press.

Westgate, T. B. R.

1904 Stony Ground in Eastern Equatorial Africa. *Church Missionary Gleaner* 21:20–22.

1909 The Home of the Wagogo. *Church Missionary Gleaner* 36:119–20.

1913a A New Era. *Church Missionary Gleaner* 40:56.
1913b Sacred Rainstones. *Church Missionary Gleaner* 40:154–55.
1918 The German Protectorate: the Flashlight of Figures. *Church Missionary Review* 69:164–68.
1919 The Huron Training College at Kongwa. *The Canadian Churchman* (15 May):313, 321–22.

White, Paul
1952 *Doctor of Tanganyika* (1st edition, 1942). London: Paternoster.
1960 *Jungle Doctor Panorama.* London: Paternoster.
1977 *Alias Jungle Doctor: an Autobiography.* London: Paternoster.

Whyte, W. F.
1959 *Street Corner Society* (1st edition, 1943). Chicago: University of Chicago Press.

Wilkie, A. W.
1921 The African Educational Commission. *Church Missionary Review* 72:215–25.

Williams, C. M.
1920 *Nationalism: Its Relation to Missions.* London: C.M.S.

Willoughby, W. C.
1928 *The Soul of the Bantu.* New York: Doubleday, Doran.

Wilson, Bryan
1969 *Religion in a Secular Society* (1st edition, 1966). Harmondsworth: Penguin.

Wilson, Monica
1959 *Communal Rituals of the Nyakyusa.* London: International African Institute, Oxford University Press.

Winter, E. H., and T. O. Beidelman
1967 Tanganyika. In *Contemporary Change in Traditional Societies* I, edited by J. Steward, pp. 57–204. Urbana: University of Illinois Press.

Winter, J. C.
1979 *Bruno Gutmann 1876–1966.* Oxford: Clarendon Press.

Wipper, Audrey
1977 *Rural Rebels.* London: Oxford University Press.

Wishlade, R. L.
1965 *Sectarianism in Southern Nyasaland.* London: International African Institute, Oxford University Press.

Wood, A. N.
1888 Making Medicine in East Africa. *Church Missionary Gleaner* 26:86–87.
1889 Itinerating in Usagara, 1888. *Church Missionary Intelligencer* 14:24–32.
1890 Journal of the Rev. A. N. Wood. *Church Missionary Intelligencer* 15:183–85.
1901 The Little Travelling Medicine Woman. *Awake* 11:37–38.
1903 An Idol Pulled Down. *Awake* 13:121–22.
1905a Africa's Sunny Fountains. *Church Missionary Gleaner* 32:172–73.
1905b How the Work Grew at Itumba. *Church Missionary Gleaner* 32:186–87.

1905c Writing Down a Language. *Awake* 15:125–28.
1907a The Daily Life of the Wassagara. *Awake* 17:51–53.
1907b The Daily Life of the Missionary In Ussagara. *Awake* 17:68–69.
1907c The Daily Life of the Native Christian. *Awake* 17:80–81.

Wright, Marcia
1971 *German Missions in Tanganyika 1891–1941.* Oxford: Clarendon Press.

Wrigley, C. C.
1959 The Christian Revolution in Buganda. *Comparative Studies in Society and History* 2:33–48.

Wyllie, R. W.
1974 Pastors and Prophets in Winneba. *Africa* 44:186–93.
1976 Some Contradictions in Missionizing. *Africa* 46:196–204.

Index